THE
SHARP END
A CANADIAN SOLDIER'S STORY

James R. Davis

THE SHARP END

A CANADIAN SOLDIER'S STORY

Douglas & McIntyre
VANCOUVER/TORONTO

Douglas & McIntyre Ltd.
1615 Venables Street
Vancouver, British Columbia
V5L 2H1

Canadian Cataloguing in Publication Data

Davis, James R., 1962–
    The sharp end

    ISBN 1-55054-663-5

    1. Davis, James R., 1962–   2. Canada. Canadian Armed Forces—Biography.
3. Soldiers—Canada—Biography.   4. Canada, Canadian Armed Forces—
Military life. I. Title.
U55.D38A3 1997   355'.0092   C97-910387-8

Editing by Brian Scrivener
Cover design by Peter Cocking
Front cover photograph by Elyard Harris
Back cover photograph by Rob Sweet
Text design by Val Speidel
Printed and bound in Canada by Friesens
Printed on acid-free paper ∞

The publisher gratefully acknowledges the support of the Canada Council for the Arts and of the British Columbia Ministry of Tourism, Small Business and Culture. The publisher also acknowledges the financial support of the government of Canada through the Book Publishing Industry Development Program.

to K & B

for always being there

CONTENTS

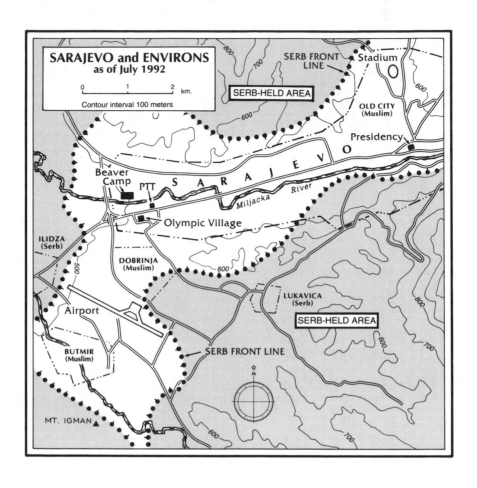

SARAJEVO and ENVIRONS
as of July 1992

0   1   2   km.

Contour interval 100 meters

SERB FRONT LINE — Stadium

SERB-HELD AREA

OLD CITY
(Muslim)

Presidency

S A R A J E V O

Beaver
Camp   PTT

Miljacka   River

Olympic Village

ILIDZA
(Serb)

DOBRINJA
(Muslim)

LUKAVICA
(Serb)

SERB-HELD AREA

Airport

BUTMIR
(Muslim)

SERB FRONT LINE

MT. IGMAN

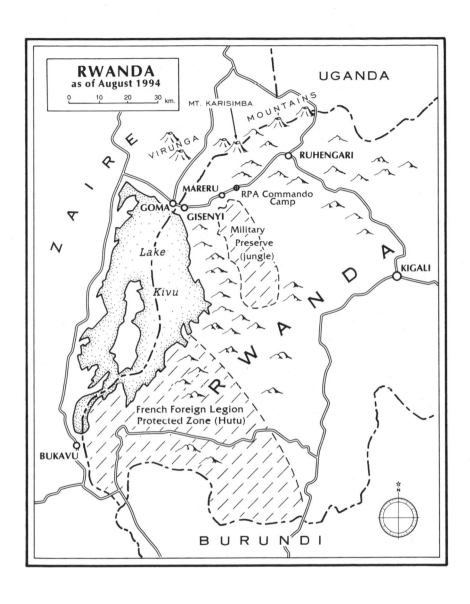

RWANDA
as of August 1994

0   10   20   30 km.

UGANDA

MT. KARISIMBA

V I R U N G A   M O U N T A I N S

RUHENGARI

Z A I R E

MARERU

GOMA

GISENYI

RPA Commando
Camp

Military
Preserve
(jungle)

Lake

Kivu

R W A N D A

KIGALI

French Foreign Legion
Protected Zone (Hutu)

BUKAVU

B U R U N D I

N

GLOSSARY

AK 47. Rugged, fully automatic assault rifle exported widely by the former Soviet Union.

AKS. Version of the AK 47 featuring a folding stock. Highly sought after for its "cool" factor.

APC. Armoured Personnel Carrier.

Beaver Camp. Abandoned JNA base located in the west end of Sarajevo. Home to November company of the battlegroup.

Bloggins. Generic term used in the Forces to designate "the average soldier."

C5. Canadian designation for a now-retired Browning medium machine gun.

C7. Basically an improved version of the famous U.S. 5.56 mm M16 rifle, it is the standard personal weapon of the Canadian Forces.

Callsigns. Term used to describe both radio nicknames and identify small units or individuals.

Carrier. Slang reference to an M113 APC.

Chetniks. Serbian extremist group.

CO. Commanding Officer. This title is given only to the commander of a full unit, such as a battalion or squadron.

Combats. Simple way of referring to the issue olive-drab combat uniforms.

Dragonov. Russian-made semi-automatic 7.62 mm sniper rifle used by former Soviet satellites around the world.

Deathslide. Typical obstacle course item featuring a long rope fixed at the top of a hill on the high end and to a distant base at the lower end. The soldier slides down it hanging on to a handle. Can be dangerous if you let go.

Devil's Brigade. Nickname given to the First Special Service Force by German commanders during World War II.

.50 Calibre. Large machine gun normally mounted on vehicles and aircraft. Each Canadian MII3 mounted one on the top of the vehicle.

FSSF. First Special Service Force was a joint Canadian–American commando unit formed during World War II. Commonly referred to as "The Devil's Brigade," this unit was the forerunner of the U.S. Green Berets and the Canadian Airborne Regiment.

FNG. "Fucking New Guy"

Gurkha/Goorkha. Name of the hill people of Nepal. Since the early 1800s, they have been recruited as mercenaries for the British, Indian and Brunei governments due to their love of fighting.

"Go to ground." Army slang meaning "Going to sleep."

GPMG. "General Purpose Machine Gun." A weapon normally light enough to be carried by one man and used to provide extra firepower at the platoon level.

Hootchie. Term used to describe a soldier's sleeping arrangement. Usually a pad and a sleeping bag protected by a waterproof sheet.

Jeep/Ilitis. German-made, four-cylinder light truck used by the Canadian Forces as their standard-pattern four-wheel-drive vehicle.

JNA. "Jugoslav National Army." Serb controlled both before and during the war.

Kukri. Large curved knife used by Nepal's Gurkha mercenaries.

Lynx. Cut-down version of an MII3 APC used by infantry and tank units for armoured recce. Now out of service.

M16. Easily recognizable rifle of the U.S. Army.

M72. Fibreglass tube housing a 66 mm rocket.

M84. Yugoslav-built variant of a Soviet main battle tank known as the T72.

MII3. 1960-vintage, aluminum, armoured personnel carrier. The standard "Battle Taxi" of the Canadian Forces.

MLVW. Medium Logistics Vehicle, Wheeled. The military's primary supply truck.

Muslim. General reference to any non-Serb Bosnian, regardless of religion.

NCO. Non-Commisioned Officer.

OC. Officer Commanding. The proper title for a sub-unit commander. A sub-unit describes any smaller organization within a unit such as a rifle company or a recce platoon.

Patricias. Nickname for the "Princess Patricia's Canadian Light Infantry." This western-based, Anglo regiment is one of three full-time regular infantry regiments in the Canadian Forces.

Pivo. Serbo-Croat word for beer.

PTT. Acronym for name (in Serbo-Croat) for the telephone exchange offices for the city of Sarajevo.

RCR. Royal Canadian Regiment. Consists of three regular battalions and one reserve.

R22R. Royal 22nd Regiment or "Van Doos." Canada's French-language regular infantry regiment.

REMF. "Rear Echelon Mother Fucker." A derogatory phrase coined by Americans, it refers to any non-combat military personnel in an operational theatre.

Ring Knocker. Nickname for all officers who have graduated from a military college. An "old boy" network within the Forces that is considered an essential to reach the senior ranks.

RPA. Rwandan Peoples Army. A Tutsi-led rebel force that defeated the Rwandan Hutu national army in 1994.

RPG–18. Rocket Propelled Grenade. Refers to a Russian shoulder-fired missile weapon used by infantry forces as an anti-tank weapon. Comes in several variants such as the RPG–16 and RPG–18.

RSM. Regimental Sergeant-Major.

SAS. Special Air Service. A British special forces unit tracing its lineage back to the North African deserts of World War II. Presently considered the top military unit in the world.

SOP. Standard Operating Procedures.

SSF. Special Service Force. A 1970s descendent of Canada's First Special Service Force. This quick-reaction brigade included the Canadian Airborne Regiment. It was deactivated in 1995.

Sunray. Radio nickname for the commander of any unit.

T55. 1950-vintage Russian tank common in former Soviet satellite states.

TDF. Territorial Defence Force. The Bosnian-Muslim version of a national army. This was a loose organization that was under the doubtful control of the Bosnian government.

Track. Slang reference to the M113 Armoured Personnel Carrier.

Top roping. Climbing safety system used in practice where climbers are secured to a rope attached to the mountain above them and controlled by another climber.

TOW. Terminally operated, Optically tracked, Wire-guided missile. A standard NATO anti-tank system, it could be mounted on a variety of vehicles and even broken down and hand-carried.

2IC. Officer 2nd In Command.

UNPROFOR. United Nations PROtection FORce. The name of the mission to Yugoslavia.

Van Doos. See R22R.

Webb gear. Webb gear or "webbing" describes the pouch-covered belt worn by infantry soldiers in most armies. Attached to a sturdy belt are ammunition pouches, water bottles, grenade pouches, bayonets, survival gear and other assorted items. The entire rig is usually supported by shoulder straps and can weigh up to twelve kilograms.

White Eagles. Radical, extremist, para-military Serbian group operating in Yugoslavia.

FOREWORD

THE FOLLOWING TALE is a recounting of my transformation from a rebellious, wayward youth into a wizened old soldier. The events recorded herein are true to the best of my knowledge. Many portions are based on diaries that I kept while serving abroad. To ensure the accuracy of these accounts, I have had each segment reviewed by other soldiers who took part in them with me. Im sure there are a few errors here and there and I take sole responsibility for them. I have purposely changed some names to protect the reputations of serving and retired members.

I would like to thank the many people who helped me in getting this book out to you, the reader. To Scott McIntyre and all his staff at Douglas & McIntyre for their belief in the story. To Brian Scrivener for taking my ramblings and turning them into something understandable. To my family for all their years of support. The vast majority of the credit must go to all the great men and women I had the honour of serving with for the last eleven years. As Field Marshall Bernard Montgomery once put it, "Each man an emperor!"

I hope you will have as much fun reading it as I did living it. Enjoy.

Chapter   1

BEGINNINGS

W E WERE ON THE ROOF *of the* PTT *building in downtown Sarajevo. The sun had set and night was falling on the city. The four of us peered over the parapet and out into the streets. Fighting raged about us in all directions. Artillery fire lit the sky in brilliant flashes, and tank fire off to the south echoed through the dark streets. Machine guns, surrounding our position, rattled off in long bursts, their tracers like angry green and red insects tearing out across the night sky.*

From our vantage point, it was easy to see that the main battle was taking place eight hundred metres to the south, centred on a small ridge separating us from the suburb of Dobrinja. We had been expecting a Bosnian–Croat push in this area for some time. The fighting had quickly spread about the city as every-where the Muslim fighters tried to hold on to their embattled perimeter.

After observing the fighting for nearly two hours, we began to receive air burst artillery close to our building. As these bursts grew closer, showering the sky with fragments, we were forced to leave our rooftop position. The explosions were hitting very close to the building now, and the order was given for all personnel to evacuate to the bomb shelter in the basement.

Without any protection on the roof, life was getting a

little too exciting, even for us. While waiting for the
worst to pass, we received some ominous news. It seemed
the battle was threatening to overrun some UN *observers*
up on the mountains surrounding the city. They were
positioned to observe Serbian artillery and mortar
emplacements, reporting who fired, when, and at whom.
Now the Bosnian–Croat assaults were in danger of
reaching these observers. In the darkness, they were quite
likely going to be mistaken for combatants and killed. We
got the job.

The UN *officer in charge of operations that night was*
Colonel Petrounev. A Russian Airborne officer and
veteran of Afghanistan, he was thought by us to be a very
hard man. As a practical soldier, he responded as a soldier
would; if an outpost is in trouble, send relief.

For us, the implications were clear. A move, by night,
through the city and up into the hills was pretty much
suicide. Every Bosnian, Croat and Serb out there, hearing
the approach of our heavy tracked vehicles in the dark,
would think us the enemy and spare us no mercy. To pass
through Muslim lines, cross no-man's-land, enter Serb
lines and locate our observers in the dark was nearly
impossible. To get them out the same way, all during the
biggest battle the city had seen in a long time, was not a
good way to grow old and grey peacefully.

While we readied our weapons and equipment, I could
not help but consider that two years ago the Russians
were our sworn enemies. Now a Russian Airborne officer
was ordering me on a suicide mission.

I will admit, now, that I was honestly ready to give it a go. To
this day, I don't know why. My journal entry for that night read,
"*. . . personally, I was quite willing to give the mission a try.*
Death before boredom. . . ."

"Alright, gentlemen, I want those hat badges shining like a new
minted nickel in an eagle's ass in a power dive!"

The Company Sergeant-Major's moustache twitched as he
sized up his company parade. He stood before a collection of
roughly sixty soldiers on the parade square at Kapyoung Barracks

in Winnipeg, Manitoba. Dressed in our olive drab combat uniforms, under the morning sun, we awaited whatever other colourful instructions were to be forthcoming.

The Third Battalion of the Royal Canadian Regiment had, only days before, returned to Canada from a six-month UN tour of Cyprus. Following a short leave period it was back to the work of sorting out the unit for resuming its domestic roles. During a tour of duty, the battalion will be manned up to almost full strength and every position within the unit is filled with its allotment of troops. On return to Canada, the unit is largely reorganized to allow for promotions, postings of soldiers to other bases, attendance at courses and to allow new soldiers arriving at the unit to join their new companies. Turnover, in the summer months, at infantry units can be up to thirty percent. With an average strength of anywhere from six hundred to a thousand men and women, there can be a lot of confusion.

Standing on that parade square, amongst the other elements of the battalion, was November company. The company consisted, on this particular morning, of roughly fifty Cyprus veterans, tanned and possessing that practised nonchalance of the seasoned soldier, and about fifteen "New Guys." Also referred to as "TQ threes," for Trade Qualification Three, these individuals had just completed their basic training and Infantry Battleschool. This made them, officially, "Privates Untrained." Even worse, this crew of raw recruits was in the Forces under the Federal Government's Youth Training Employment Program (YTEP). In this scheme unemployed young men and women from eighteen to twenty-five were put through military basic training as a job creation program. YTEPs were only contracted for one year and were under no obligation to re-sign. It was generally held that their training was below the normal standard for regular recruits. All said, it meant that these characters were not held in the highest esteem.

Standing in the third rank, staring generally straight to his front was Private Davis, J. R. I remember thinking to myself that morning, "What have I gotten myself into?"

In front of us was Company Sergeant-Major Hodgins. Five-and-a-half-feet tall, with bright red hair cropped close and a huge handlebar moustache. His blue eyes stared right through you. Every time he spoke he let out such a stream of the most colourful sayings that you wanted to laugh. I did, but to myself only. Scattered about me in the ranks of the company, were my fellow "New Guys." Mostly Newfoundlanders and Cape Bretoners, they had been my companions in our transformation from irresponsible youth to young infanteers of the oldest regular regiment in Canada. It was now the summer of 1986. It had taken almost a year to reach that parade square. It was an experience I wouldn't readily repeat.

By the summer of 1985, I was bored. I had graduated from high school in 1980 and had immediately headed out from my home in Barrie, Ontario, for the mountains of Banff National Park. A cousin of mine was working in Lake Louise and invited me to join him. With the ski season approaching there would be lots of work. So with my father's old army duffle bag over my shoulder, I climbed into the cab of a tractor trailer headed for Calgary. My mother had used her influence to get me a free lift in a company truck from the business where she worked. Actually, the ride wasn't totally free; I had to unload shipments at several stores en route.

I spent a great winter skiing, partying and generally avoiding responsibility. Living in a small room in a trailer that consisted of a bed, a locker and a chair, I had to cook, clean and care for myself. Unknown to me, this would be good preparation for my early days in the Forces.

On my return to Ontario after the season ended, I took my savings and bought a 1969 Mustang. It was in rough shape, but I had always loved old Mustangs. My summer was spent working at the garage pumping gas and tinkering with my car. Having no real budget for repairs the Mustang became an improvised automotive device utilizing cast-off tires from the local dump and headlights operated by stereo speaker wire. After losing my keys swimming one day, I was forced to hot wire the car. With no spare keys for the Mustang, I rigged up an array of toggle switches on the roof and buttons under the dash that had to be flipped in sequence to start the engine. It was quite the beast, and a fire hazard.

As fall approached, I prepared to head back out to Lake Louise for another season of fun. I was joined on this trip by a high school friend who had already secured himself a position on the ski patrol. Except for one night spent in a ditch outside Thunder Bay, the trip was a thirty-six-hour marathon covering some three thousand kilometres. The Mustang, despite its unorthodox components, held up well.

Unfortunately, this year, I couldn't find a decent job. As my money ran out, I decided to head back to Ontario. With only enough money for gas, I spent five days on the road sleeping in parking lots and having nothing to eat. Not much fun, but a lesson learned. I could survive a lot of discomfort if I had to.

Over the next few years, I held a wide variety of jobs including drummer in a rock and roll band, disc jockey, factory worker and gas station attendant. My most interesting spell of employment started with me applying to be a carpenter at a large ranch that was a home for troubled youth. I was turned down as a carpenter, having no experience, but the personnel manager noted in the "hobby" portion of my application that I enjoyed sports. She asked me if I thought I could teach football to a bunch of kids.

"Paid to play sports," I thought, "Good job," and responded with a positive, "No problem!"

So began a most interesting year in which I taught physical education at the on-site school and ran recreational programs in the evening. The kids were all boys ranging in age from seven to eighteen. Some were criminals, others had been abused, and some were genetically out of control. The farm was well organized to deal with them all, and I was to give them that requirement for all kids—simple play. For some, it was an outlet for aggression and for others a chance to gain self-confidence.

While I worked at the ranch, I was always coming up with new ideas for adventure. I thought about joining the French Foreign Legion or going after a cruise ship job. Unfortunately, my life was a continuing round of monotony. I could never manage the finances required to head for either France or the Caribbean.

Meanwhile, the Mustang had breathed its last breath, so I bought a Triumph TR–7. After several expensive months, I wedged it between two oak trees at 115 kilometres an hour. I crawled away with two sprained ankles and a face turned into a mask of blood with big flaps of flesh hanging off. I walked five kilometres home and nearly scared the life out of my mother. After recovering from her shock, she rushed me off to the hospital.

The police had been notified but were unable to find the car as it had sort of disintegrated after squeezing between the trees. Apparently, it had also broken through a telephone pole prior to reaching the trees. Consequently, there was not much left. For myself, I was unaware of any of this. I was doped up awaiting neuro-surgery in the local hospital.

The police officer came to see me in the emergency ward for better directions to the wreck. I must have managed a clear description because he returned some time later a ghostly white colour. He could not believe anyone had survived that crash, let alone walked away. I assured him the car had been mine and that it was a TR-7. I also lied and said that I had been wearing my seat belt. No sense getting a ticket. He left and I went to see the surgeon.

Apparently, I was fine, and after twenty-four hours was sent home with a patch over one eye. I had torn the skin away from near my right eye and would have an inch-long scar. Fortunately, the scar runs right beneath my right eyebrow, so it is invisible. My ankles were a bit swollen and I wasn't going to be running for a few weeks, but otherwise I was fine.

Very quickly boredom set in again. When an old friend suggested we quit our jobs and head west, I was all too happy to move on. I quit my job at the ranch and, in a peculiar looking VW Rabbit that I had nicknamed the "Millennium Duck," we headed for Edmonton. Unfortunately, we got drunk in Nipigon, Ontario, and spent all of our travel money. We were forced to turn around and head back to Barrie.

My travel companion, Jeff McCartney, managed to get a job in Brampton, Ontario, and while I was helping him move in with some friends who had a townhouse in the area, I decided to stay. They had a spare bedroom and I moved in. I got a job pumping gas and once again began dreaming of adventure.

This is where I found myself in August 1985. I was about ready for anything. I was still working at the gas station and going nowhere. I happened to be reading a borrowed newspaper when I saw a recruiting advertisement for the Canadian Armed Forces. As I was only days away from my twenty-third birthday and ready for a change, I decided to give them a call. I was invited down for an interview and some tests a couple of days later.

I showed up at the Toronto recruiting centre not knowing what to expect. I was interviewed by a sergeant who asked me a few vague questions. While sitting there, I looked over at a stack of magazines on a desk in the corner. On top of the pile was a copy of *The Maroon Beret: Journal of the Canadian Airborne Regiment*. On the cover was a paratrooper leaping from an aircraft. I looked at the recruiter and said, "That's what I want to do!"

The recruiter looked at me with a hard, exploring stare. I

could not tell if he was sizing me up as a possible paratrooper or a complete fool for wanting to jump out of planes.

"We'll see," was all he said.

Next, I was ushered into a big room with about twenty others and given a general knowledge test. It covered math, history, some mechanical and electrical questions like, "What does AC/DC stand for?"

I recall that I was the first one finished the test. I took it to the front and then sat back down. Over the next few minutes others began taking their papers up. It hadn't been difficult at all, and I wondered what was taking everyone so long. While we were waiting for the last candidates to finish, a recruiting officer walked in and asked if anyone wanted a job right away. There were openings in the infantry and the artillery, he said. All I knew was that the Airborne was infantry and threw up my hand. A couple of other candidates responded as well. The recruiter laughed and told us to follow him.

We were led to a series of cubicles where we watched films about our trade choices. From there we went back to the waiting area. After about ten minutes, I was called in to see our merry recruiter. He looked at me and said he thought that I had made a mistake. I did not know what he was talking about, so I just sat there looking dim. He held up a chart that listed all the trades in the Forces. Down the left side were numbers that corresponded with the test scores. He explained that as your scores increased you could apply for better jobs. I had scored in the highest category and, as such, had my choice of any trade that I wanted. Up at the top of the chart was Intelligence Operator and Aero-engine Technician or something like it. On the bottom of the chart, for those with an IQ slightly above a disability, were the trades of Cook and Infantry.

The recruiter explained that I could do anything on the chart. Infantry was a terrible job. I did not even look at the chart. All I said was "Infantry."

The recruiter sighed and, because he had to fill a quota, led me out in the hallway.

"Which Regiment do you want, the Patricias or the RCRS?" Not having a clue what he was talking about I gave him my dim look again.

It had obviously worked because he went on. "The Princess

Patricia's Canadian Light Infantry are stationed in western Canada," he said, pointing at a map on the wall. "The Royal Canadian Regiment is in the east, except for the Third Battalion in Winnipeg."

All I could think of was, "The Princess what?"

Thinking I was just giving him my dim look again he went on in a conspiratorial tone, "I can tell you that 3RCR is going to Germany in a year and a half and that is probably where you will go."

That did it. Germany was not exactly the jungles of New Guinea, but it was better than Brampton, Ontario.

"I'll take the Royal Canadian Regiment," I said boldly.

The recruiter looked at me as if he still thought I was out of my mind, but he shrugged and led me back to his office. I signed my paperwork and was sworn in the next day.

On 13 September 1985, five days after walking into the recruiter's, I was on board a Forces Boeing 707 headed for the Cornwallis Recruit Training Centre in Nova Scotia.

BASIC TRAINING

I TOLD MY DRIVER *to take it easy as we approached the Rwandan Peoples Army (RPA) checkpoint. Behind me was a motley column of civilian and military vehicles. As commander, I was riding in the right front seat of a twenty-passenger bus. Behind me were three large two-and-a-half-ton trucks, a white UN Bedford truck and a military pick-up. Perched on top of the tarpaulin-covered trucks and spread throughout the vehicles were fourteen other Paratroopers from 3 Commando of the Airborne Regiment. We also had ten Combat Engineers with us, the majority of whom were riding in the bus.*

The RPA troops at the roadblock were waving us to halt. I looked at my driver and told him to move up nice and slow. As we had planned, the trucks behind me held back about one hundred metres in case things went bad. This was our first encounter with the RPA and we had no idea what type of reception we would receive. My rifle was beside me, on the engine cover but out of sight to the RPA at the moment.

As we pulled up and stopped, we were confronted with five RPA soldiers armed with AK 47 rifles and RPG grenade launchers. The man I took to be the Commander approached our vehicle. Fortunately, my driver spoke

some French and would do our translating. To my
eternal regret and embarrassment I had not, to date, ever
mastered our second language.

"Bonjour," said our driver easily.

The RPA soldier just stared at me. Unlike the other
military units arriving in the country at that time, we were
not working for the United Nations. I wore my Maroon
Beret and my C–7 was now clearly visible beside me.

I nodded to the driver and he launched into our
planned speech about moving up to the Zaire border to
establish a hospital. The RPA soldier looked at me and
then back down the column to the other Airborne troops
casually observing the countryside from their positions on
top of the trucks. I think that it was pretty obvious that
we were not doctors.

"You are UNHCR?" he asked us cautiously, referring to
the United Nations High Commission for Refugees. This
was the organization coordinating most of the efforts in
Rwanda.

"Yes," I lied. It was easier than explaining who we
really were.

With one more suspicious look that for me lasted an
eternity, he stepped back and ordered his men to let us
pass. I smiled and waved as we pulled out.

That soldier never knew how close he had just come to
a violent death. In the whole of our heavily laden convoy
was not one item of medical equipment. We were loaded
to the teeth with enough ammunition and explosives to
start a small war. The tarpaulins covered our deadly
cargo, and the Commandos riding on them had their
weapons ready at their feet in case the situation went bad.
If the RPA had wanted to look in those trucks. . . .

———

Cornwallis, as the Canadian Forces Recruit Centre is universally known in the military, was a grey and unappealing place to a young man who had seen much of Canada. The whitewashed wood buildings and austere atmosphere were depressing and, in their own way, foreboding. Very quickly the staff instructors rushed me and roughly one hundred other unprepared young men through our in-clearance procedures. I recall, clearly, all of the men in my training platoon lined up in our quarters. Before us was a large wash basin. The instructor was explaining that he was going to leave the room for five minutes. Anyone possessing knives, knuckle dusters, drugs or any other "contraband" was to place these items in the bucket. This was to be a "freebie." After this, anyone found with these items would be kicked out. After the instructor left, out came the pocket knives, jack knives, aspirin and cough medicine. We were not allowed any medicines not issued by the Forces. No sharp edged items were permitted, including scissors.

The rough-looking character beside me leaned over and whispered that he had thought of bringing his .38 calibre pistol but could see now he was lucky he did not. This guy looked like a biker. When the instructor asked us if we had any questions, the biker put up his hand and began explaining that he was a Karate black belt and wanted to know if there would be time each day for him to practise his art.

A flat "No" was all he got in response.

The next day our hair was buzzed "down to the wood." We were issued baggy coveralls and sent back to our quarters. I had made a couple of friends already, but after our haircuts we could not even recognize each other. For some of our fellow recruits it was traumatic. There were many blank expressions that day. Zombie-like young men were wandering aimlessly about the building wondering what they had done.

The vast majority of my fellow recruits were only eighteen or nineteen years old. Most had just graduated from high school. For many, it was their first time away from home. In these days before politically correct social reformers settled on the army, the recruiting standards were eighteen- to twenty-four-year-olds only. At twenty-three, I think I was the oldest recruit there. I felt like an old man for the first time in my life.

Our Basic Training course lasted eleven weeks. It was really a processing plant for young rebellious youth. It cranked out, in batches of forty to eighty, disciplined and responsible young men and women. The program is designed in a calculated way to take most any personality type, from almost any background, and strip him of his identity. Certainly our early days, wandering around bald and in our coveralls, were identity destroying. Once his identity is gone, the recruit is convinced he is an unworthy pile of human refuse. Incapable of any action without his mommy there to help him, the recruit loses his self-esteem completely.

It is at this point that the staff watches you closely. Many recruits are so unprepared for this dehumanization that they become suicidal. Some turn mean and attack each other. The program counters this condition by keeping recruits so busy that they are perpetually exhausted and have no energy for fighting. During this point in the course many quit. Others are informed that they have failed some critical requirement and are sent home.

I won't say that I had an easy time of it, but a lot of this treatment didn't have too much effect on me. As the "old man," I had left my rebellious days behind me and was quite confident in my personality. We each took rotating turns being the "course senior." I was doing an almost constant rotation as either course senior or section senior. All of this meant only that, on top of everything else we were doing, I had more to do. I think that my biggest contribution was the night that I prevented the course from giving a "blanket party" to one of our less motivated members. In a blanket party, a group of recruits holds a blanket tightly down over a victim who is then beaten ruthlessly about the legs and abdomen.

I was also plagued by one character, who was the laziest, most obnoxious member of our recruit platoon. He went on to have quite an interesting, if short, military career. He was a bully, basically, always resenting whatever authority was imposed on him. While the rest of us scrubbed wax off floors with steel wool, he would lie down under his bunk and go to sleep. No matter what I said, acting as section or course senior and responsible for organizing work, he argued. I overcame this finally by putting him in charge of the work parties. I do not think that he had ever been the leader of anything before and, as a result, he took to it with a vengeance. The other recruits moaned whenever I did this because he did not take any crap. He had spent too much time dishing it out and knew all the lines.

As the weeks went by, the course was designed to slowly rebuild your confidence. You were re-born in the military mold. Each week, at the mandatory barber visits, you were allowed a little more hair. Eventually, you got the weekends off as a reward and could go into town. Here we drank away our meagre recruit pay and all came home with immense hangovers.

It was during these days that I made some good friends. Friends that I have kept ever since. There is no comparison to any other line of work in the world than the military for male bonding. The majority of these close friends are Newfoundlanders. As a group, they are the most honest, big-hearted and trustworthy folk that I have ever met. The Army's Combat Arms would fall apart without their presence. All hard workers, if there is a tough job to be done, they would always be in there putting in their all to get the task done. It was a great day for Canada when Newfoundland joined the confederation. Unfortunately, Canada has never chosen to treat the Island with the respect that it deserves.

Strangely, I do have some fond memories from this period. I remember clearly standing rigidly at attention in a field while our instructor told us his best jokes. Anyone caught laughing or even cracking a smile had to drop and start doing push-ups. The instructor would be nose to nose with you crossing his eyes and telling his best one-liners. Combined with uncontrolled fits of belly laughter happening on the ground beside you, it was impossible to resist. Some were laughing so hard that they ended up collapsed on the ground, unable to control themselves.

In our locker layout we were supposed to have a picture laid out of someone we loved. Most of us had no picture and we were always picked on by the staff inspecting us. One guy kept showing us these two hundred snapshots of his girlfriend. She wanted to be a model and had given this guy a multitude of pictures of her in a variety of poses. We did not like this guy much because he was a whiner. When we found him one day crying in his bed with a letter torn up beside him, we knew that she had dumped him. Later we found all her photos at the bottom of the trash can. We waited a couple of days and then, on inspection one morning, we all had pictures of the same girl in our lockers. It took the staff inspecting us a little while to figure it out. When they did, we got a blast, but it had been worth it for a bit of fun. Unfortunately, it was too much for the whiner and he quit shortly thereafter.

––––––––

When Basic Training ended in early November, we were hustled aboard a plane bound for Petawawa, Ontario, and the Royal Canadian Regiment Battleschool. Basic covers topics like drill, weapon stripping and bed making. Now we were to learn our trade: Infanteers. For anyone who had thought Cornwallis was tough, they obviously had never heard of Battleschool. Our instructors were now long-service infantry NCOs. Cornwallis

staff had been drawn from across the forces and included Air
Force and Navy types. A rough-looking lot in their Special Service Force smocks, our new trainers presented a whole new view
of the Forces. The Battleschool was located across the road from
the Canadian Airborne Regiment's lines and everywhere were
camouflage-smock-covered soldiers going about their business.
This was the army we had been imagining.

The Battleschool program still involved kit and quarters routine but concentrated mostly on teaching the skills required of
combat soldiers. Physical toughness was emphasized and controlled aggression encouraged. We carried our weapons with us
everywhere and were pushed hard. Training covered basic tactics,
patrolling, ambushes, camouflage and the myriad of subjects
involved on the modern battlefield.

We almost immediately began losing candidates. Whether from
injury, failing to pass tests or voluntary releases, our numbers
began to dwindle. Our training in 1985 took place after human
rights measures prevented our instructors from abusing us physically, but they were not prevented from punishing us verbally or
institutionally. If you did not measure up, you were called down
as useless or an "abortion." If the staff really thought you could
not cut it, you would be given so much extra work you eventually
quit or failed something. This treatment could at times be harsh
but, in the end, produced a soldier hardened by his experiences
and consequently far more reliable under pressure later on during
the tours to war zones abroad. Within a few years the Human
Rights and Safety Nazi crowd forced the lowering of standards to
the point that the quality of our young soldiers became horrendous. Candidates were so pampered that when they finally
arrived at their units and discovered what army life is really like,
they almost all quit. I have never seen statistics, but in the units I
served in the retention rate at the end of the first engagement was
less than fifty per cent. Only recently have training standards
begun improving again.

Our instructors at the school made a tremendous impression on
me. They were all uncompromising men who could tear into you
like a grizzly or laugh outrageously with equal ease. Some drank
too much, many had several failed marriages. Most were prema-
turely gray with rugged features brought on by years of hard living. All of them carried a long list of injuries, and we could see their

discomfort after nights spent out training under the stars. Yet each one of them, in their late twenties or thirties, could run a group of cocky youngsters into the ground or shoulder twice the weight of any of us. Their physical toughness, matched with unbreakable self-confidence, was an example of what a man could achieve if he set his sights high enough. To have been counted amongst them, as a peer, is probably my greatest accomplishment.

I was quartered in a room with three others who had come with me from Cornwallis. Gary Ezekiel, or "Zeke" as he is still called by his friends from those days, was a Newfoundlander and a "Towny." P. W. Clarke slept across from me and, also an Islander, he was a "Bayman." These nicknames referred to whether they had come from the cities or the fishing communities. The fourth member of our room was a Sikh named Gosel. His full name was much longer, but to us he was Gosel. Others came and went from our room, but it was the four of us who saw training all the way through.

Our experiences in Battleschool were probably identical to most of the courses that went through the school in those days. Out of those days several tales are worth the telling.

One of our instructors, a Master Corporal (Mcpl) George Laidlaw, was a character. At least six-foot-three, he had size four-teen feet, reddish orange hair and a ready smile. He would tell us one day that he had really wanted to be a stand-up comedian. One morning, during inspection, he was eyeballing one of the candidates when he suddenly grabbed a soldier and threw him across the room. He took his pace stick, a metre-long wooden baton that all instructors carried, and began attacking a bed. He beat it furiously with his pace stick as every man in the room stared at him in shock. Finally, he stopped and cautiously reached forward, picking up a large dust bunny, a ball of dust, and held it up for all to see.

"You should thank me, I just saved your life. This sucker was going for your throat," he declared in a solemn tone and marched out of the room. We never quite knew if George was insane or just had a weird sense of humour. Although we did not dare laugh while he was present, we all had a good howl later when the story was told. I have now known George for over a decade and I am still not sure about him. He remains one of those men who has always made soldiering fun.

Polishing boots is a skill that some just never perfect. I never did. The one of us who had the most trouble was Gosel. No matter what he did he just could not get his boots to gleam. On the morning of a big room inspection, we had all been up since five a.m. waxing floors, mopping hallways and adjusting our locker layouts. Gosel spent the morning furiously attacking his boots trying to get a shine out of them. With only twenty minutes to go until the inspection we returned to the room from doing our "station jobs." These included assigned tasks like scrubbing toilets or cleaning the laundry room. As we walked into the room we found Gosel spreadeagled naked on the bed. The window was open and out on the snowy ground lay Gosel's boots, his boot polishing kit and his clothes. He was having a complete nervous breakdown over his inability to polish his boots properly. We all freaked! If the instructors found him like that we would lose our weekend off-base privileges. Teamwork was essential, and if your kit was incorrect, your buddy was blamed for not sorting you out. We grabbed Gosel, who was a blathering fool at this point, and forced him back into his clothes. At one point, he broke away and tried to throw more kit out the window. After we threatened to beat the hell out of him, he came to his senses and let us dress him. Perry and I ran outside and got his kit. We all worked furiously to try to get him dressed and his kit squared away. In the end, our instructor showed up hung over from an all-night binge and had no interest in inspecting us. We all thanked our personal gods for our good fortune.

In the days before the western world seized on the idiotic quest for political correctness, the army was a haven for men who lived hard and often died young. Our instructors swore continuously, drank regularly and did not give a damn about social norms from the civilian world. If you could do your job, your personal life was your own business. We admired our instructors all the more for their unrefined ways. For me, the professional soldier can never be a model of civilian mores. The men who make a life out of pushing limits will always be, in their hearts, the swaggering and rough-around-the-edges lot from days gone by.

An example of how much our instructors influenced us could be clearly seen in Gosel. As our graduation neared, some press-hungry officers decided Gosel should wear a turban for graduation. Gosel had never worn one while he was in the Forces and refused to wear anything but his green beret for our ceremony.

He had been with us since day one in Basic and he had become his own man, not a Sikh or anything but a soldier. The co had Gosel issued an army olive drab green turban so that he could show the multi-cultural content of the schools. Gosel held his ground and refused to wear it. Our platoon instructors agreed with Gosel, and finally our course second-in-command, Warrant Officer Earl Gapp, a hard character qualified as a U.S. Army Ranger, told Gosel he could wear his beret.

Our graduation party was held in the base yacht club, and my two brothers, my old friend and traveling companion, Jeff, and a girlfriend from my civilian days, Marilee, had driven up for the graduation. We all had a good time, with Zeke and Perry taking Jeff and my brothers, Rob and Jordy, across the Ottawa River and into an after-hours nightclub.

A couple of days later we packed up our kit and said goodbye to Petawawa. Off we headed on another aircraft for Winnipeg and The Third Battalion of the Royal Canadian Regiment.

Chapter 3

GARRISON LIFE

MY FIRST OFFER *of employment as a mercenary was tempting. A sum of $10,000 U.S. a month on four-month renewable contracts was not something to be laughed at. The paycheques were banked in Switzerland, he explained. The Dutch mercenary smiled and waited for my reply.*

"Jump ship," he said. "We could use some good men."

I smiled back and looked at the scene around me. The village, or what was left of it, was a complete ruin. As I watched, other bedraggled mercenaries crawled out of collapsed cellars and gutted houses to see the newcomers. About a platoon of mercenaries, mostly Europeans, lounged around our patrol vehicles. They were dressed in a variety of camouflage uniforms, which, along with their weaponry, hinted at their nationalities. All looked like they had been having a tough go of it.

As I talked with them I discovered Belgians, Germans, a French Legionnaire and a fellow I believe to have been Australian. Some shied away from us. Others were eager for a bit of news.

"It's not so bad," my recruiter continued. "I'm on my second contract."

I had to admit, $40,000 U.S. tax free was more than I

could make in two years with the Canadian Forces. All
you had to do was live to spend it. . . .

It was a sunny but cold afternoon as we rushed out of our new quarters and fell into three ranks, facing the building. We stood before our new home, a large, two-storey, concrete building consisting of about eighty rooms. It was in the standard military "C"-block format and fronted onto the base parade square. Inside, we were accommodated two to a room, which after Battleschool was downright cozy. I shared a room with P. W. Zeke was next door. All of my buddies from our training days were there.

It was April 1986, and we were finally there: our first posting as soldiers. We had trained since September 1985 with only a break at Christmas. Despite the hectic pace, none of us were tired. We had survived. Many had quit along the way or failed and were held back for another training cycle. We had passed the test. Now we could relax. We were soldiers.

Or so we thought.

As one of our new NCOs lectured us, I got the distinct impression we were still, in his eyes, not much higher on the food chain. Still, if they hadn't made us quit up to now, there is no way I was packing it in here. Whatever was coming, we would survive it.

"No doubt you will all end up in the Grant," he said, referring to a local bar frequented by soldiers, "but remember that the dollies here have all been around a bit. Keep your helmets on. These ladies want nothing more than to land themselves some young buck with a regular paycheque. Just because you're away from mommy for the first time and have some money in your pockets, don't go marrying the first dolly you wake up with. Don't let your dick do your thinking for you. Any questions?"

With that warning ringing in our ears it was off for our first weekend in Winnipeg. As with all young men, the advice went largely unheeded. By the time we left for Germany, more than a few Grant girls were accompanying my fellow soldiers. Quite a few other troops made regular Monday morning trips to the medics for a shot. There are many great and bawdy tales that come down from those days, but I shall not tell them here.

At this time the battalion was in Cyprus. "M" company, known by its phonetic as "Mike," was the only remaining sub-unit. Mike company looked after the base and any rear-party duties. In May of 1986, Mike was off to CFB Shilo for some battle training. It loaded up its M113 APCs and was off.

All of the new recruits had been assigned to the absent November company. Twenty of us, under the leadership of Sergeant Bobby Girard, followed them in our own APCs. Our task was to act as an enemy force. This was to be a tremendous beginning to our military careers. Essentially, we were to act as guerrillas and provide Mike company with a challenging and unpredictable opponent. Very quickly, Sergeant Girard allowed our enthusiasm to flow. He encouraged our use of initiative and, with a lot of supervision, let us set some cunning traps for Mike company.

The general flow of the battle began with Sergeant Girard taking us to a preplanned position where we would have several hours to prepare our defenses. Our favourite trick was to dig a pit just large enough for a single man to crouch in. This would be covered with sod until it was undistinguishable from the ground around it. Inside was an individual with his weapon and grenade simulators. In each position would be several of these in addition to the regular defenses. As Mike company fought its way through the position they would miss these "spiderholes" completely. After they had passed by, the occupant would pop up and wreak havoc in the company's rear.

Eventually, we would just lay out a piece of sod on the ground and the advancing troops would spend several minutes clearing these fake spiderholes. With their attention focused on the ground, we would open up on them from perches in the trees above them.

Never knowing when and where we would appear, Mike company was having a difficult time fixing and destroying us in a stand-up fight. On one occasion I crawled into a clump of brambles with a C5 machine gun and my fellow guerrillas covered me in grass and sticks. Totally invisible, I waited for my prey. Soon Mike company attacked and swept through our position. Our forces, retreating before their firepower, were drawing Mike company on. Many troops swept passed my bush, but I waited; I wanted bigger prey. Finally, my patience was rewarded. The company commander, his signaler and the Company Sergeant-Major knelt down, not one metre from my barrel. Here was a prize worth netting. Unfortunately, the muzzle blast from the C5 firing blanks made it too dangerous to open fire at such close range.

Instead I jumped to my feet screaming and was immediately cut down by the signaler's quick reactions. As I lay there feigning death, I could see the company commander was visibly shaken by what would have been his certain death in combat.

Sergeant Girard would later be commended for the spirited performance of his little band of cutthroats. He would also be berated for letting a certain young soldier walk around his bivouac with a combat scarf wrapped around his head like a PLO operative. Personally, I was quite proud of my new headgear fashion and, afterwards, only removed it when the OC was about.

We harassed Mike company night and day, allowing them no rest. On one occasion, I was walking down a trail alone with the C5 machine gun slung over my shoulder. It was after midnight on a moonless night and visibility was only a few metres. I had been waiting in ambush for a patrol, but it had not appeared. Acting as cut-off, I had to walk back up the trail several hundred metres to link up with the others in my party. As I walked, I became aware of a curious bunch of black lumps on the trail ahead of me. Against the light sand colour of the trail I could make out quite a few of them.

I was only about a metre away when one of the lumps said, "Halt!"

I had stumbled onto a platoon-sized patrol halted in the middle of the trail. Without hesitation, I squeezed the trigger on the C5. It roared into life, shattering the stillness of the night.

Now, because of the darkness, all of our eyes were accustomed to almost no light. When that C5 opened up, the flame from its barrel lit up the scene like a spotlight. Before me, twenty soldiers from Mike company, totally blinded, crashed out into the brush in total confusion trying to escape the ambush. I will always remember the "deer caught in a headlight" look of that rear sentry who had challenged me. Amid the total chaos before me, I began to realize that I was seriously outnumbered. As if to emphasize the point, my C5 suddenly stopped firing. Predictably, I had a malfunction. Now, in the deafening silence, I knew it was only a moment before someone realized I was alone. Screaming something unintelligible, that I hoped sounded Russian, I sprinted back down the trail leaving my totally bewildered opponents wondering what the hell had just happened.

Many other enjoyable little skirmishes later, we returned to Winnipeg, sated. In the mess soon after, Zeke, P. W. and I, with all the rest of our little band, re-lived our exploits over jugs of draft. We finally had a taste of what the army lifestyle was all about. Later, the boys headed down to the Grant Hotel and beyond to impress the ladies with tales of high adventure. I headed back to my room. As I fell asleep that night, I felt like I was finally home.

The next two months passed quickly. We all went through a driving course which taught us to drive wheeled military vehicles. Except for one individual who had never driven before, all went well.

Private "Smith" was a farm boy from Napanee, Ontario, and had never driven before signing up. During the next month he hit two buildings, drove over a cliff, ran a dump truck off the highway and had one minor collision, the last being a moment of confusion between reverse and first gear in a jeep. Popping the clutch, he roared backwards into a parked pick-up truck. Fortunately, little damage was done and Smith passed the course with the rest of us.

During this time we had heard a few stories of the battalion's fortunes in Cyprus. The most memorable incident was when the CO, Lieutenant Colonel Cox, had fallen from the death slide on the obstacle course. With a broken pelvis and numerous other injuries, he had returned to Canada. None of us had ever met the CO but we heard he was a pretty tough character. Four weeks after the accident, we were all in the base church for church parade when the doors opened and in comes the CO walking on two canes. He passed up the middle aisle so we all could see him and took a seat in the front row. Among the troops and especially the senior members was a flurry of whispers at his appearance.

I thought to myself, "He's one tough bastard."

That was to be our first introduction to an almost legendary officer in the Royal Canadian Regiment. As anyone who ever served with him will tell you, he is one hard man. It wasn't to become clear to us how hard until later on that year when the battalion returned from Cyprus.

It was a humbling time for our crew. With no other troops around we had gotten a little cocky about our new line of work. Now, split up and mixed into the other platoons of the returning company, we found out how much the remainder of the battalion thought of us. As the New Guys, we mopped the floors, did the duties, picked up the garbage and did all those normal jobs relegated to those on the bottom of the pecking order. There was never any hostility, no hazing, just the confident laughs of all the senior troops who finally had someone with less "TI."

TI, or "Time In," was for the Canadian Army what "short" was to Vietnam vets a generation before us. Whoever has more TI is almost always higher on the food chain than you. We had to "do our time" before we could be treated as well as those ahead of us. Frankly, it was no big deal. We had swabbed many a floor in Battleschool, so if we had to do it again, there was no problem. We hadn't gone to Cyprus and couldn't tell Cyprus war stories. We didn't measure up. Our little enemy force stories did not compare to the tales from abroad. Instead of depressing us, though, it only made us hungrier to prove ourselves.

Military life consists normally of three types of work. Garrison life has you working Monday to Friday, usually seven o'clock until about four. Then there are courses, where you are involved in an intense school atmosphere combining classroom and field training. Finally there are the exercises. These can be anywhere from twenty-four hours to several weeks. The atmosphere of military life changes with each different environment. In garrison, life is spit and polish. Courses are pressure cookers and test time. Exercises are more relaxed, discipline-wise, but are twenty-four hours a day with little sleep and bland food.

Of the three, the absolute worst for me had to be garrison time. Despite having nights and weekends off, the daily drudgery was terrible. I always longed for the challenge of the exercises. Ranging abroad in the woods and fields of the prairies could not be compared to life on base. Certainly field life was at times misery and discomfort, but those times just made the exercise more of a challenge.

A typical day in garrison began at about 0700 hours with morning parade. You never missed morning parade. Not if you didn't want extra duties or a charge to be laid against you. Normally, you were dressed in sweat-suits or some combination of webb gear or rucksacks. The company would form up in three ranks as platoons. The platoon second-in-command, or 2IC, would take attendance. From there the Sergeant-Major would arrive and the platoon 2ICs would report. Here the Sergeant-Major would pass on whatever points or tasks for the day were necessary. Then the officers would arrive. After several "attentions" and "stand at eases," the Sergeant-Major would report the status of the company to the Company Commander. Known as the "OC" for Officer Commanding, he would then have the company spread out and begin stretching in unison for PT. Physical Training, or "PT," is the term for the daily exercise program all combat arms take part in. Other non-combat trades occasionally do PT, but it is at the CO's discretion and usually consists of badminton or volleyball. For us, it could be anything from a ten-kilometre run to a rucksack march.

PT ends at around 0830 hours and at this point the troops are dismissed. Everyone now has until 0930 hours to shower, change into the dress of the day and have coffee. Dress of the day could be either combats, our olive drab field uniform or a pressed and polished "Work Dress" uniform. At 0930 was another parade under the Sergeant-Major who would detail work for the day. Platoon 21ICs would then dispatch their troops to service vehicles, clean weapons or maintain our equipment.

We would normally break for lunch at about 1130 hours. Single soldiers living in "the shacks," as our quarters were known, would head to the mess hall for lunch. Married men or guys living off-base would head home for lunch. Many troops would head for the Junior Ranks Mess, a club for the young men where they would have a beer and watch strippers provided by the Mess Entertainment Committee. This was, of course, in the days before we all realized that it was morally wrong to condone and support such activities.

At 1300 hours it was back to work with another parade. The afternoon's work would be detailed and off we would go until about 1530 or 1600 hours. At the end of the day, the Sergeant-Major would come down and have a dismissal parade. Here we would be told what was happening the next day or who the unit hockey team was playing that night. When nothing else was left to be done, we would be sent on our way for the rest of the day.

This routine continues Monday to Friday, the year round. The only exception to our routine would be Friday. In most units Friday is the Commanding Officer's Day, designed to allow the CO to get out and have a look at his troops. In Winnipeg, under Lt Colonel Cox, this invariably began with a battalion parade. One week we would be on the parade square, at minus twenty degrees centigrade, dressed in berets and combat jackets. These summer clothes meant that we would be frozen in minutes. The next week the parade would be inside the drill hall with the heat pumping, dressed for the Arctic. In minutes we would all be suffering from heat prostration. Regardless of our dress and location, Lt Colonel Cox would always make us wait at least forty minutes before he would arrive to take over the parade. We would see him peek out of the mess hall, coffee in hand, as we stood motionless. It was a test of our steadiness. In the summer we would sweat and swoon under the heat and in winter suffer frostbite and endless colds.

On the first morning parade after returning from Cyprus, Lt Colonel Cox intended to make his training philosophy quite clear to us by beating a dummy viciously with a hockey stick before a shocked battalion. Speed, Aggression, Violence were the principles of successful soldiering, according to the CO. Every parade was an experience.

One morning in particular, we stood for over one-and-a-half hours in the cold, waiting. When the CO finally appeared and we were called to attention, many found that they were unable to move their feet. Their boots had melted the ice covering the parade square with body heat. As we grew colder the water surrounding our feet froze once again, locking our boots to the pavement. We looked like one thousand epileptics having a seizure while trying to break free of the ice.

Once the CO took over the parade we would be faced with another problem. Both Lt Colonel Cox and our Regimental Sergeant-Major stuttered. We never thought any less of them for it, but it did present certain difficulties when responding to drill commands. The whole battalion would sometimes be leaning forward waiting for the instant the CO would overcome a particularly difficult consonant. To make matters worse, the CO and RSM had different methods of overcoming their stuttering. The CO, not giving a damn, just stuttered away until he got it. The RSM covered up his stuttering by replacing any lapse in pronunciation with the word "and." A typical command would be something like, "Stand at and, ah, and, ah ... ease!" Each time he said "and ah," we would anticipate the completion of the command and begin moving our legs. Then hearing another "and ah," we would straighten back up. With all the jerking legs we looked like a bunch of Elvis impersonators in uniform.

Once we got over the initial drill movements the CO would

choose a Company to inspect. His choices were Mike, November, Oscar, Romeo and Quebec. Because he would stutter over Mike and November, we never got inspected. Oscar was easy for him so they got nailed almost every Friday.

"I will inspect R-R-R-R . . . Oscar company." Romeo company would let out a collective sigh. Spared once again.

No one wanted to be inspected by the CO. He was a terror. His biggest pet peeve was our socks. Military issue socks are grey wool and used to have coloured bands across the toe. If the CO caught you with two different colours on your socks you were charged. If you didn't have your name in your underwear, you were charged. Following behind him was the OC, the RSM taking notes, the Company Sergeant-Major and your Platoon Commander. If you were picked up for anything, or the CO even commented on something, you had to endure a long queue of superiors waiting to have a go at you. Such pressure would strike dread into the hearts of soldiers.

On one occasion the CO stopped before Corporal Ron Hickey. The CO asked him a question and, unfortunately, Corporal Hickey stuttered.

"Are you m-m-m-mocking me, C-C-Corporal Hickey?" demanded the CO.

"N-N-N-No sir," responded Hickey.

"R-R-RSM, charge this man!" said the CO.

Luckily for Hickey, it was made clear to the CO that Hickey did in fact stutter on occasion and the charges were dropped.

––––––––––

If life in garrison seemed difficult, we were soon to discover that field training under the CO could be even more difficult. Our first exercises with Lt Colonel Cox were called Star Track I and II. In both we were dismounted, meaning no vehicles, and each man carrying weights of up to forty-five kilos. Each day we would march up to twenty kilometres and, at the end, dig full trenches with overhead protection. Then we would spend the night in our two-man trenches taking turns sleeping. All night long there would be "stand-to's" where every man would be at his battle position in response to a probe by the enemy force. In this way we averaged about four hours, or less, sleep a night. To compound our difficulties, the CO would impose logistic problems on the unit resulting in reduced rations and water. On average we would have one meal per day, split between two men. There would be one jerry-can of water issued to each thirty-man platoon. Considering the physical energy we were exerting each day, these amounts were seriously low.

For any of us who thought Battleschool had been tough, we were quickly disabused of that notion. Each day we got weaker. The pain from our injuries would be unbearable and marching a torture. Under the weights we carried, our backs and shoulders would be rubbed raw. Some lost large sections of skin. We would trudge on and on in a haze, never quite reaching that point where the pain would cause the circuit breakers in our brains to trip and cause numbness.

We didn't worry about our shoulders much because our feet were always far worse. Our socks would be soaked with blood after every march. Many had feet that were large oozing sores. Some stopped taking their boots off because, as soon as they did, their feet would swell up to the point that they couldn't get their boots back on.

Generally, your packs get lighter as you go because you eat your rations and consume some stores. The CO got around this by issuing large steel anti-tank mines that were inactive and filled with cement. Others carried steel pickets, shovels, axes and picks. We also carried machine guns, anti-tank weapons, mortars, claymores, grenades and enough ammunition to fight a long battle.

Every exercise was a test of our strength. Only pride and a determination to succeed kept us going. When each exercise was over, we would return to Winnipeg and heal. By the time our bodies had recovered, we would be getting ready for another exercise. The training was always designed to be progressive. After we had been tested in grueling dismounted training, we would deploy with our M113 APCS.

These mounted exercises would be a little easier on the body because you traveled, for the most part, in your vehicles. Your kit was stored in the vehicle and you never strayed far from it. The vehicle, thirteen tons of aluminum, was your home. Inside would be up to ten men. During the day the troops would sleep, bouncing along in the back of the vehicle, while your section commander had the driver follow the platoon officer around on endless manoeuvres. Occasionally, we would put in an attack and it would be pandemonium in the back as we all got ourselves squared away. Then we would wait for the words to come across the radio from the OC, "Dismount, dismount, dismount!"

At this command the driver would lock up the tracks and the vehicle would pitch forward, throwing all of us in the back into a heap by the engine compartment. Then the whole rear of the vehicle would fall open and we would be tumbling out helter-skelter to take up our positions for the attack. From there we would advance forward, skirmishing our way across the enemy position. When it was over we would mount up, fall asleep and do it all over again.

As night fell, it would be time to halt, dig in and send out patrols. In one memorable patrol I followed my section 2IC out on a reconnaissance patrol. There were three of us, armed with sub-machine guns and, faces blacked out, we crept out of our defensive works and headed into the night.

I had always loved patrolling. In a small group or alone in the dark, you are on your own. Your success or failure depends only on your nerve, cunning and luck. Since your mission is usually to scout the enemy, you know that somewhere ahead of you is danger. It makes the senses come alive and the blood race. Some soldiers take naturally to this type of work while others never find its appeal. For me, there was never any greater job in the Forces than to be out in the night, creeping like a ghost into the enemy's camp and watching him, unseen.

On this night our task was to scout Mike company. They were our enemy for this exercise. Several patrols were out trying to fix their position. My patrol commander was a Master Corporal McCleod. Easily two metres tall, he had a full beard and was thickly built. He had spent the majority of his career in the battalion's Pioneer platoon, a group of engineers tasked with explosive work or construction of bunkers. He did not take too well to patrolling. His plan on this night was to get us close to a ridge we were to check out and then let his two troops spread out and search the feature. All went well until we reached our release point, roughly one kilometre from our objective. The problem was that between us and the ridge was a huge, wide-open field. He said he would wait in the treeline while I crossed the field to scout the ridge ahead of us. The other soldier, whose name I cannot recall, was to swing around the field following the tree line and look for signs of enemy activity in the woods.

I am guessing that he thought this was insane and he wasn't going to get caught. He would send us and let us get caught instead. Being young guys with no TI, it would be a good experience for us. When the enemy ran out to capture us, he would observe the activity and return to confirm that the enemy was on the ridge or in the woods.

Compounding the problem for me was the bright, moonless night that would give me away the moment I left the treeline. I probably could have crawled through the grass all the way, but that would take hours and I was only allowed thirty minutes.

I considered my dilemma for a moment and then made my plan. Without a word to McCleod, I stood up, threw my rifle across my shoulder and walked out into the field. I began walking towards the ridge at a casual walking pace. I might have been walking in a park in Winnipeg for all the concern I showed.

My plan was based on shyness. Soldiers always want a bit of privacy when they have a bowel movement. The normal routine is to grab a shovel and a roll of toilet paper and find some nice, quiet place to conduct your business. With my rifle perched on my shoulder, impersonating a shovel, my plan was to stroll up to the ridge like I was returning from a good bowel movement. I hoped my casual appearance would reassure any sentries that I belonged there and would not bother with me. My biggest concern was trip flares. Small pyrotechnics connected to a trip wire, they lit up the night when set off. I could never bluff my way through that, so I just sauntered on, trying to avoid any shrubs or tree stumps that might hold these booby traps.

When I had reached a distance of about two hundred metres from the ridge, I was startled by a burst of machine gun fire. Suddenly, firing erupted across the whole ridge. I dropped to the ground and waited for the troops to sprint out to bag and tag me. As I lay there, I watched troops scurrying up the hill away from me. A parachute flare was fired from someplace on the ridge, lighting up the night like day. Before my eyes, as clear as can be, was the whole company's rear area. MI13s were lined up with hatches open. The Company Quartermaster's truck was there, as well as the OC's jeep. There was a modular tent set up and, beside it, the command track bristling with antennae.

Up on the ridge the whole company opened up. More paraflares were launched and I was able to pick out the machine gun emplacements and most of the trenches. I realized that one of our other patrols had probably bumped the front of the position on the crest of the ridge. I was behind them. When my unfortunate compatriots on the other side of the ridge had been discovered, a "Stand to" had been called and virtually every man in Mike company would be up on the ridge behind his weapon. This left the rear area unattended. So, using the motto of a famous British Regiment, "Who dares wins," I got to my feet and walked into their camp.

I quickly discovered the individual sleeping hootchies and by counting them tied up in neat rows, got a fair idea of the numbers dug in here. Then I crawled into several APCs and confirmed their radio frequencies. I then stood in the middle of the vehicle park wondering what to do next. I thought to prove I had been there I would record their licence plate numbers. Here I discovered my biggest mistake; I had no pen or paper. I began rooting around in the vehicles but had no luck. Instead I went over to the OC's and the CQ's truck and memorized the plate numbers.

I had been on the position roughly ten minutes and knew I had at least another ten before anyone returned. The firing had mostly stopped now and I knew they would remain at stand to for at least an hour. The officers and senior NCOs would likely begin returning soon to send reports and bring up ammunition. I thought I would check out the command track and the tent before leaving.

I approached the command track and, expecting to hear the duty radio operators inside, I took it slowly. Upon reaching the vehicle, I still had not heard any noise so I peeked inside the rear hatch. It was ajar and dark within. Slowly I pulled the hatch open and was surprised to find no one inside. I climbed in, hoping to find a map or trace. I did, but in a moment of clear thinking, realized I still had a kilometre of open ground to cover when I left and someone would surely notice the map missing shortly. I resigned myself to confirming their command frequency and climbed back out of the vehicle.

I made my way to the tent. Inside was a light, probably a Coleman lantern, burning brightly. Going round to the rear of the tent I pulled apart the seams and peered inside. Once again, there was no one there. Even the CQ (Company Quartermaster) must be up on the ridge. I pulled up the flap and crawled inside.

Inside the tent was ammunition, water, rations, kit bags and all the other items a quartermaster lugs around. On a table along one side of the tent was a coffee pot and some small tins of pudding. Selecting a chocolate pudding, I pulled off the lid and, borrowing the sugar spoon, dug in. We had been on the move for days and didn't get any treats like this. I finished off two pudding tins, had a final glance around and crept out the back of the tent.

My thirty minutes were almost up, so I swung my rifle up on my shoulder and strolled back out into the field.

Back in November company's defensive position several hours later, I was hauled up in front of our OC, Major Lorne O'Brien. I produced a sketch of the position showing Mike company's complete layout, numbers and the licence plate numbers as best I could recall them. With such a windfall of information, he couldn't wait and immediately called his driver to take him up to Battalion HQ so he could gloat over his company's excellent patrolling skills.

The epilogue to this story was that Mike company's OC had been so taken aback by the report that he accused Major O'Brien of cheating somehow. As for me, I was rewarded with only one shift on sentry that night.

Life in the Third Battalion continued on in much the same fashion. We worked very hard and Lt Colonel Cox let us out from under his thumb occasionally for some fun. Work hard, play hard. For us New Guys, we eventually won some respect among our more experienced fellows. Surviving any of the CO's exercises was proof enough of your manhood.

I had been around long now enough to realize that all my superiors were not the infallible supermen we were led to believe. As in any line of work, there are success stories and failures. Generally, our training process weeded out those unfit for the lifestyle. Sometimes though, the occasional lemon made it through. Leadership and loyalty for our NCOs and officers quickly became a matter of our respect for them and was no longer based solely on their rank.

We developed a great deal of loyalty to those of our leaders whom we saw as professionals. It was not necessary to like them, only to respect their leadership qualities. Often the NCOs and officers we grew to have the greatest feelings of loyalty towards were those who displayed one important attribute: they placed the interests of their soldiers above their own career concerns.

The leader who stopped and said, "Wait a minute, the troops really don't need to do this," was the leader who won our respect. The effect was especially reinforced when we witnessed a leader stand by his decision in the face of criticism or concern from his superiors. This is not necessarily to imply that a good leader should not follow orders. It refers to a situation where initiative can be used due to a uninformed decision by a superior.

An example of this took place during the handover of our equipment to the Patricias prior to departing for Germany. The Patricias had sent a Warrant Officer over in advance to ensure all our kit was clean and in good order before he would assume responsibility for it. This Senior NCO had our CO's authority to ensure that our kit was up to scratch. For two weeks this NCO would show up in the morning and inspect our stores. Each day he would say it was still dirty and order us to clean it all again. Our Senior NCOs could not argue his authority and we would clean it again. Finally, our Sergeant-Major had enough. Regardless of what the CO and RSM wanted, this was a waste of our time. The next time this Warrant Officer came strolling up the stairs declaring our kit still unacceptable to anyone listening, he ran straight into Sergeant Major Hodgins.

"Sergeant-Major, it is still not good enough," he declared.

Several of us were standing within sight of these two. Even from our distance we saw the Sergeant-Major's moustache twitching. This always was a prelude to an outburst of some kind. The Sergeant-Major took his pace stick and jammed it into the Warrant Officer's chest. We couldn't hear the exchange, but that Warrant Officer was scared. He turned white and never spoke a word. The Sergeant-Major had him on his tip-toes against the wall and let him have an earful.

The Sergeant-Major wasn't the biggest man in the world, nor was he overly muscular. Yet before that withering stare you were never in doubt that he was the toughest, meanest soldier you could have the misfortune of crossing.

When it was over, that Warrant Officer didn't show himself again until after we had left for Germany. That was only one of many occasions when the Sergeant-Major defied the system when he saw his charges being abused. To us he was the best example of what a soldier, and a leader, should be.

On the opposite side of the coin were the leaders who saw their position as simply a stepping stone to bigger and better things. An officer whom I was to work for clearly fit this bill. "Major Lord," as I will call him, was a well-to-do young officer who was always well turned out and impeccably dressed. He almost appeared to find his military duties as an inconvenience. He was easy to identify, even at a distance, because he always affected a Napoleonic pose, strutting about with one hand permanently in his pocket. With the other arm swinging merrily, he would swagger about, giving the unintended impression of a rooster.

In garrison he was invisible. Rumoured to live in a penthouse downtown, he spent his time composing impressive articles for military journals or building his considerable bank accounts. We, the troops, never saw him. Occasionally, he would take us on morning PT, but this seemed an inconvenience as well. He would speed off like a bat out of hell, leaving a long trail of gasping troops behind, as if the sooner it was over, the sooner he could get back to more important business.

In the field he was just as rarely visible. When the Battalion deployed on manoeuvres the OC would not move without his personal jeep trailing close behind. As soon as play ended for the day, he would issue his orders for the company to dig in and climb into his jeep for a trip onto the base. There he would work out in the base gym to maintain his well-defined physique. After showering and enjoying a good meal, he would snuggle up in a nice bed in the officers' quarters with orders for his driver to collect him in the morning.

Meanwhile, out in the boonies, the rest of us dogs of war would spend most of the night digging elaborate trenches and bunkers. None of us had bathed in more than a week and having only one change of clothes we would stink like old socks. Finally, at midnight, the trenches would be complete and we would settle down to a night of sentry duties, patrolling and manning observation posts. The young lieutenant platoon commanders would be out doing their best to lead their troops and set a good example. Together, all of us would be bleary-eyed as dawn broke.

After a good breakfast, the OC would appear in his jeep reading the morning paper. We weren't allowed to interrupt his morning paper reading. The stock report was always far more important than our rooting in the dirt.

Occasionally, Lt Colonel Cox would visit. In his refined

manner, the OC would switch to his "Superior Warrior" persona and lead the CO through our battle position. Explaining our well-planned dispositions to the CO, provided conveniently by his now-exhausted platoon commanders, he would elucidate his tactical plan. Pausing at a huge machine gun bunker that had taken twenty men until dawn to complete, he would make it clear that it had been quite hard digging, but we had all worked hard and managed it. The CO would in turn compliment the OC on the good performance of his company and usually left it to the OC to pass on his impressions to the troops.

Instead we were usually treated to a list of the mistakes we had made in our emplacements, pointing out gaps in the fire plan.

In one memorable incident, that was not uncommon, the OC walked up to inspect another large machine gun trench under construction. The troops inside, myself included, had been working all night on other trenches and had spent the last four hours digging this one. The OC looked at the trench and then the countryside around us. He turned to our platoon commander, doggedly following him about the position, and ordered, "I want this trench moved five metres over that way and facing to the south." He then turned on his heel and sauntered off to the next trench with the platoon commander, scribbling furiously, in tow.

For us, it meant we had to fill in this trench and start all over again a couple of metres away. For one soldier this was too much. He swung his shovel over his head and lunged towards the OC's turned back. Braining the OC wouldn't solve anything, but it might make an impression on Major Lord. Fortunately for the OC, our ever-impressive Sergeant-Major was there. He stepped in the way of the charging soldier. Not saying a word, he just smiled and twitched that handlebar moustache. You could see the understanding in his eyes, and the individual dropped his shovel. The Sergeant-Major turned and followed the OC, who had walked off, totally unaware of the incident behind him, lecturing our platoon commander on the finer points of defensive warfare.

Shortly afterwards our section commander came up and explained that he had just heard about the OC's instructions.

"Leave it where it is," he said.

Sure enough the OC got back into his jeep after finishing his inspection and didn't return for two days. When he did, he never noticed that we had left the now impressively finished bunker where it was. In deference to his wishes we did change its firing direction to the south.

This OC had no apparent concern for his troops. He didn't make any attempt to share our hardships. His only field time was accomplished because of direct instruction by the CO. If he could avoid getting dirty, he would.

For us, we had no loyalty to him. We would follow his orders because we legally had to, but not one man among us would take an extra step to make a good impression. Fortunately, and in spite of him, the company had pretty good morale due mostly to the good senior NCOs we had. As long as someone was looking out for our interests we were satisfied.

Another officer who failed to inspire was our platoon commander of the time. "Lieutenant Brown" was a graduate of a military college where he had hoped to get a good education and some pocket money. Intending to become a logistics officer while working on his accountant's certification, he was a man with a plan. After spending a couple of years handling accounts for the military and building up an impressive resume, he would leave the Forces, a young entrepreneur, with money in the bank.

Unfortunately for Lieutenant Brown, and those who had to serve under him, the year he graduated there were no openings for logistics officers. Now faced with a large debt to repay the military if he left the Forces, he had to choose a second trade. Considering the "cooks and rifleman" requirement, he chose the Infantry. More likely, it was chosen for him. Regardless of how he got there, he was now a combat leader of men who didn't give a damn about stock options and a diversified investment portfolio.

In retrospect, he probably should have got along well with our OC, Major Lord. If they did so privately, it was never visible publicly. More likely, Major Lord saw a liability in our hapless platoon commander. The potential for his making mistakes that could embarrass the company's well-managed image meant Lieutenant Brown was eternally chastised by our OC.

In the OC's defence, I will say that, nine times out of ten, Brown deserved whatever he got. The lieutenant's career was memorable only for its short duration and his monumental ability to never get anything right.

Some reading this will probably, at this point, say that I am making more out of this than was true. Everyone makes a few mistakes now and again. This guy seems more like a TV sitcom character than a real individual. Not only do I swear that every instance is true, I can produce a dozen witnesses to back up these stories. Read on.

Lieutenant Brown was not a pretty sight to begin with. His six-foot-three-inch frame was gangly and awkward in appearance. He had a slim face, thin brown hair and a large nose that supported a pair of wire glasses. He was slightly knock-kneed and would have made a great Ichabod Crane.

It was Monday morning, the Battalion was preparing to depart for CFB Shilo and some field training. Brown arrived late. As the rest of us packed our kit into our APCs for the long drive, no one had any time to supervise the Platoon Commander. Left without supervision, the lieutenant mounted up in his carrier and, as our turn came, headed out for two weeks of exercise. No one noticed, including Brown, that he had forgotten his rifle.

Lieutenant Brown had difficulty walking across rough ground. He rarely made it a few yards without stumbling. Our senior NCOS, noticing this, worked out a simple betting system; whenever the lieutenant began to walk anywhere, there would be a standing bet of two dollars. They would call out how far they thought he would get, and when Brown inevitably stumbled, whoever was closest won the bet.

Upon noticing the platoon commander climbing out of his trench or leaving his APC, the betting would begin.

"Five," would call out Sergeant Sheppard.

"Ten," would be the response from Sergeant Thompson.

All eyes in the platoon would then watch the lieutenant take three steps, hook one foot on another and fall flat on his face. For us, the soldiers, we would shake our heads and get on about our business.

Lieutenant Brown didn't just have problems on terra firma. As a mechanized outfit we spent a lot of time with APCs. The top deck of an APC was a tangle of protrusions, antennae and camouflage nets. Most of us quickly became accustomed to it and had no difficulties. The Platoon Commander was not so fortunate.

On regular occasions he would climb up out of his hatch, catch a foot and lose his balance. Up until this point it was something all of us did. The lesson the lieutenant never learned was not to grab an antenna for balance. The antennae were mounted on springs and were designed to be extremely flexible. With his arms flailing, off he would tumble while trying to hold on to an antenna, falling the two metres to the ground. On many occasions he would be saved by his troops who tried to keep an eye on him. Every so often though, when you left him unattended for only a few seconds while you took care of some little task, off he would go.

On a cold and wet night in the early spring we were allowed out of the field for a quick shower. We threw our spare clothes in kit bags on top of the vehicles and drove into the Base area. Stopping in a large, slush-covered yard, we grabbed our kit and headed off to the base gym for a scrub and a change of clothes. We left Lieutenant Brown on top of the carrier searching for his kit. We should have known better. When we returned nearly an hour later we found a completely soaked lieutenant huddled in a nearby doorway, shivering. He had done another header off the APC and landed in ten centimetres of water. Afterwards, he decided to just change into dry clothes instead of showering. After furiously searching for his kit bag, he couldn't find it and, nearly frozen, decided to just get in the carrier and wait. Unfortunately, our rules say that unattended carriers must be locked to safeguard the weapons and equipment inside. So, an hour later, we found a bitter and hypothermic officer. He immediately accused the soldiers of stealing his kit bag of dry clothes. Zeke climbed up on his APC and there, at the top of the pile, was the Platoon Commander's kit bag.

Another incredible accomplishment occurred when Lieutenant Brown was tasked to take his platoon and make a dusk assault on an enemy position. One that, unfortunately, was near the base. Immensely intent on finally proving his competence once and for all, we made a lightning strike on the Base golf course.

Having smashed through the wire fencing in the falling darkness, we roared around the greens and fairways in our tracked, thirteen-ton APCs, lining up what Brown was sure was the enemy strongpoint. On order, we dismounted and made a speedy assault. Certainly, that golf course would be safe from the Fantasian hordes for some time to come.

There are many more interesting stories of Lieutenant Brown's military antics, but I believe the point has been made. He was to linger on for several more years until, finally, he left the Forces for a more tempered career in the civilian world. I wish him well.

Before leaving the platoon, he was to share with us in one more disastrous adventure. It was an exercise known as "Trench Hotel" and was to be one of the darkest periods in the life of 3RCR. Even the name was an attempt at humour by the CO who was obsessed by defensive warfare.

I like to refer to the whole incident as "The Remembrance Day Massacre."

It began with the Battalion deploying to CFB Shilo in early November of 1987. The weather was cold, but there was no snow on the ground yet. We were all hoping to spend our two weeks out and get back before winter set in. Just in case, we all brought along our arctic clothing packed in kit bags carried by the CQ.

The exercise started off with the usual marches, patrols and, above all, trench digging. Unlike winter exercising at any other unit, we slept in our trenches. The norm today was to take a lesson from the Finns of World War Two, who would sleep all cozy in tents to the rear of their battle positions, only venturing forth to man the trenches. Lt Colonel Cox wouldn't allow it and our tents remained packed up. Von Clausewitz, a military philosopher, would certainly have considered us ". . . troops toughened by hard physical training." How hard was to become evident very soon.

Several days into the exercise, I found myself in my undershirt, sweating, on the side of a hill as I worked to complete a machine gun trench. Private Ron Wright and I fought a losing battle with sandy soil to fashion a functional defensive position. Every time we got down to a reasonable depth, the loose, sandy walls would cave in. The temperature, in the sun, must have been around twenty degrees. Or it felt like it to us as we sweated away. We had finally got the basic trench dug out when we spotted the CO and the RSM approaching up the hill. They had been inspecting the work and were headed for our trench.

A machine gun trench, at that time, was a "U"-shaped affair with a roof added later. We had a C5 machine gun sitting on the firing platform in the centre of the "U." The idea was that the gun sat in the middle and we could move up either side of the "U" to load ammunition or change a hot barrel. The open end of the "U" faced the enemy.

As the CO reached us he asked a few questions about our task, what our arcs of fire were and where our withdrawal route was. We answered as best we could. Then the CO stepped over one of the sides of the "U" to stand with a leg on either side of the barrel of the gun. Ron and I looked at each other. The trench walls were sure to give way any second. Should we warn him?

While I thought about how best to diplomatically ask the CO to move, the situation resolved itself. The sandy wall under the machine gun gave way and the CO tumbled down into the bottom of the trench. The machine gun fell in on top of him and both were covered in a landslide of sand. With the CO totally buried in sand, we looked up to the RSM. He shook his head and told us to dig him out. Carefully, we took our shovels and freed the rather chastised Commanding Officer. Pulling the machine gun off him, he jumped to his feet, trying to recover some military bearing.

The CO clambered out of our now-ruined trench and said, "Well, I owe you a case of beer for that one," and hurried off before anything else happened. We never saw our case of beer and had to spend another hour digging out our trench.

As evening drew on the temperature began to drop. A light snow fell on our shoulders as Ron and I laboured to get the roof built over our trench. We were still dressed in fairly light clothes and our uninsulated combat boots. Gore-Tex had not yet entered the military lexicon and very quickly we became soaked as we put the final touches on our trench.

Full dark had descended on us when we finally sat down to cook up some rations for supper. The snow was falling heavily now and already half-a-metre of snow had accumulated outside. I had to keep going out and clearing away the snow from our firing slit. The temperature continued to drop and we began shivering in our little hole in the ground.

At first we tried wedging ourselves together for body heat. It worked for a while but eventually, as the temperature hit about minus twenty-five Celsius, we began to suffer the effects of hypothermia. Knowing if we both drifted off to sleep we might die, we took turns sitting up over a small candle watching the other rest.

Our trench was about two hundred metres from the remainder of the platoon. We were out on a flank with the job of firing across our platoon's front when attacked. Consequently, we were quite alone. At about ten o'clock I headed out into the blizzard and staggered down to the nearest trench. I shouted inside and

was told quite clearly to bugger off as it was much too crowded
in there already. I headed back to our own trench but became
lost in the white-out. I wandered around for nearly an hour
before finding my way back. Inside Ron was out cold. Literally. I
shook him awake and made him take a turn at the candle. I
explained that it seemed the company was just going to wait out
the storm.

By this time my feet were two blocks of ice. Our uninsulated
combat boots were no match for the cold. We had no sleeping
bags at the moment because our rucksacks were in our APCs
parked more than a kilometre away in the vehicle hide. Knowing
that sooner or later we would be rotated back to get our gear, we
waited. Neither of us wanted to try to walk back to the APC in
the storm. I had gotten lost traveling two hundred metres.

Sometime around midnight, our lieutenant stuck his head into
our trench and told us to put out our candle.

"It will give away our position to the enemy," he stated. Then
the head disappeared and, once again, we were alone. We put out
our candle for the moment but realized quickly that no enemy
would be out in that storm and re-lit our only heat source.

At around 0400 hours the platoon 2IC showed up with our
back-up kit. We weren't being allowed any sleeping gear, but we
were permitted to get into our warm arctic clothes. By dawn, we
were crawling out of our trenches, haggard and exhausted from a
sleepless and frigid night. The morning sun is always a morale-
building sight, and we quickly forgot our ordeal and got on with
the next phase in training.

The training plan called for us to fill in our trenches and move
by APC to an assembly area close to the base. The CO had devised
a section-sized competition for the unit to take part in.

An Infantry section is normally an eight-to-ten-man group
commanded by an NCO. It is the basic combat element of an
infantry rifle platoon. Each rifle platoon consists of three rifle
sections and an HQ element. The section carries two light
machine guns and occasionally a support weapon such as an
anti-tank launcher or a light mortar. The CO's contest would test
the basic skills and fitness of his soldiers.

The battalion's support platoons, such as Recce and Mortars,
were to break down into section-sized groups and compete as
well. With three rifle companies in the battalion consisting of

three platoons each, this made for twenty-seven section teams. Adding in the support company entries, there would be a total of about thirty-five competing teams.

The competition was to begin the next morning. Until then, the companies were to dig in at a new position close to the base and the start of the contest. In another treeline, on another hill, we began to dig again. The day was grey and snow continued to fall. The temperatures still held in the minus twenties.

Back in Winnipeg, the snow had continued to fall, burying the city under drifts several metres high. Road crews were unable to keep up with the amount of snow and essential services began to shut down. Fire crews and ambulances were unable to move. Many people, especially senior citizens, could not get out to get groceries. Meals-on-Wheels, responsible for feeding home care patients across the city, were unable to make their deliveries.

The city council apparently turned to the military hoping we could handle emergency duties until the roads could be cleared. Unfortunately, all but a couple of broken APCs were in CFB Shilo, several hundred kilometres to the west. The base mechanics got a couple of these APCs running and, crewed with our rear party, they worked non-stop rescuing people and delivering essential services.

We spent the night under the stars again that night. We were allowed our sleeping gear this time, so it wasn't totally wretched. In the morning we awoke covered in a layer of snow. The temperature had not improved, but the snow was tapering off. Under grey, heavy skies we climbed aboard our APCs and headed for the competition.

The contest was to cover two days. The first day consisted of a series of stands where we had to display a certain skill or knowledge. Mine laying, judging distance and communication troubleshooting were typical of our tests. At the end of the day it was back to our trenches and another night under the open skies.

On this night we took the unprecedented precaution of setting up one ten-man tent per platoon. The forecast called for the temperature to drop to nearly minus thirty degrees that night. If anyone became hypothermic the tent could be heated by a gas stove and the casualty could be treated there. The CO demanded that no one was to sleep in the tents except in an emergency.

Day two of the competition was a race. Sections would depart at five-minute intervals to negotiate first an obstacle course and then a fifteen-kilometre road run. It was a timed event and the route would be watched by umpires to prevent cheating.

The day broke cold and clear. Despite the bright sunshine, the temperature was minus thirty-four degrees Celsius. Instead of bundling up, my section, under the direction of our section commander Sergeant Roger Sheppard, peeled off our warm clothes and put on our uninsulated combat boots. Dressed only in combat jackets designed for summer use, combats and long underwear we headed off to our competition.

Hidden in our APC, with the heater roaring, we awaited our start time. Finally, as the time drew near we were forced to abandon our little traveling oven and jog over to the start line. Within minutes we were frozen and my feet, once again, turned to blocks of ice.

With the start of the race, we sprinted off through the obstacle course. Unfortunately, our section 2IC was injured on one of the obstacles and had to retire to the medical van. On completion of the obstacle course we were off onto the fifteen-kilometre run.

Trying to work some heat into our extremities we kept up a rapid pace. Within the first few kilometres we began overtaking other teams. Most had dressed in Arctic clothing with parkas and mukluks against the cold. Providing a comfortable body temperature at rest, these heavy clothes were causing the competitors to begin overheating very quickly. Combined with the fact that we were already dehydrated, owing to the frozen status of all of our water supplies, many competitors began to fall out. We began to pass lone stragglers, stumbling along and obviously in difficulty.

It wasn't long before we came upon an individual collapsed in the middle of the trail. He was only semi-conscious so we got him up off the ground and tried to get his temperature down. Zeke sprinted ahead to find an ambulance while we sat our comrade in the snow bank. He was still somewhat groggy, but feeling better. The ambulance appeared momentarily, already on its way to the base hospital with one soldier who had gone into cardiac arrest. Handing off our charge to the medics we continued our run, passing more and more struggling teams and individuals.

By now several ambulances were making continuous circuits of the route collecting unconscious and delirious soldiers. I remember the ambulance passing us with one of our company NCOs in the passenger seat. He was obviously only semi-conscious with his eyes rolling about and his tongue hanging out of his mouth.

For ourselves, we felt pretty good. Our light clothing was having the desired effect and keeping our temperatures down to a normal level. Our problem was dehydration. With no liquid to drink we were beginning to stop sweating, a sure sign of problems near at hand. It was now a race to see if we could reach the finish before dehydration stopped us.

In the race, our only competition was a team from Recce platoon. They had dressed in wool combat sweaters and mukluks. We followed them for a long time, closing the gap steadily. Finally, with only a couple of kilometres to go, we passed them as some of their members were beginning to fall back. A team's time was counted only when the last team member crossed the finish line. Recce was forced to slow to collect their struggling teammates.

In the last kilometre we began to have our own problems. Ron was beginning to slip. He was slowing down and becoming withdrawn. Soon he began to lose his grip and he slipped into a semiconscious state. Losing bodily control now, he wasn't sure where he was or what was happening. Help lay at the finish line, so, with Zeke and me supporting his limp form, we staggered towards the finish.

The rest of us were beginning to have difficulties as well. I was cramping badly from the lack of liquids and the others were obviously fading. We could see Recce rallying behind us and, determined to hold them off, we made the big push to the finish line.

After crossing the finish line we dragged Ron over to the medical van where he quickly began to recover as he was forced full of juice and oranges.

We were all ordered over to a nearby building to report and, entering the lobby of the building, were assaulted by a sight I will remember for a long time. Spread over every square centimetre of space were soldiers in varying states of consciousness, some collapsed in heaps, others on stretchers with medics feeding them water.

An obviously overworked medic ran up to us and held up three fingers in front of my face.

"How many?" he demanded.

"Three," I replied.

He quickly moved on to the others in my section and led away the obviously borderline Ron. We found a corporal we knew and asked him what the hell was going on. No one knew, he said, but it was a mess. Everywhere delirious soldiers called for their mothers or carried on conversations with invisible friends.

The race had been a disaster. We were to find out soon after that the medics had filled the base hospital with casualties. One soldier's heart had stopped several times and the doctors were working hard to keep him alive. Once the hospital was filled, the casualties were taken to a nearby mess hall where they covered the tables and floors. Still more came and a third building was filled to the brim with heat and dehydration casualties.

The Base Chief Medical Officer had called in all his off-duty staff and alerted the local community hospital. Soon the more serious patients were being shipped off to the civilian hospital as the ranks of casualties increased. The community hospital apparently called in all its emergency staff as well.

Finally, overwhelmed by the massive numbers of casualties, the Medical Officer is said to have called NDHQ in Ottawa and the military Surgeon-General. Astonished by the situation underway in CFB Shilo, he immediately launched an investigation.

Back in Shilo, we were unaware of all of this. Zeke and I had volunteered to go back out and help with the stragglers. I was on the way to my APC to get into some warmer clothes when I walked passed Lt Colonel Cox and RSM Riley. Normally, we don't salute in the field, but I guess we were technically on base. Either way, I didn't salute and I didn't care. Obviously, the RSM did, and he immediately called me over and had me up to the chow, asking if I still saluted the Commanding Officer.

Slowly, I hauled my rifle off my shoulder, where it had been slung, and began to swing it into position for a rifle salute. I must have looked a complete mess, because the CO interrupted.

"Don't bother," he said, quietly turning away.

I shrugged and, not caring much either way, wandered off to my APC. Later, with a clearer head, I realized that the CO had been in a bit of shock himself considering the developing situation. His battalion, aggressive and tough, had competed with such determination that it had run itself to near death. His finely honed machine was collapsing around him.

It must be said that none of us had any hard feelings for the CO over the whole affair. He was a hard man and trained his soldiers that way. In this case, he set us a challenge and we threw ourselves into it. We were never told that we had to meet some critical time or achieve some impossible goal. It was just a competition. Anyone of us could have held back if we wanted to.

In the years following, all of us would brag that we trained under Cox. He really was the last of his kind in the Forces as battalion commanders go. In fact, before we left for Germany, the battalion had a t-shirt made up. It read, "I Survived the Colonel Cox World Tour 86–88!"

Later we, the survivors, were transported back to our trenches. The OC, having no idea what had occurred since he had probably spent the day sipping cocktails in the officers' mess, insisted that we still sleep in our trenches. The tents were out of bounds until the CO directed otherwise. Out of our twenty-five man platoon only five of us remained. Too tired to care, we crawled into our sleeping bags and fell into a deep sleep. The OC naturally returned to his cozy bed on base.

The next morning was Remembrance Day. The Battalion Padre had planned a service in a field near the base. After breakfast, we were ordered to mount up and attend the service. Climbing aboard two APCs, the seventeen men remaining in November company, normally eighty strong, headed off to the ceremony.

I will never forget that service. It was sad, really. The battalion consisted of no more than seventy troops still standing. Out of more than eight hundred that had deployed, these were the survivors. The padre made a valiant effort of trying not to emphasize our present state, but every time he referred to the "battalion," we all paused a bit and glanced about at our decimated ranks. When it was over, we mounted back up in our vehicles and headed back to our trenches. In the next couple of days, our comrades would slowly return to the field to rejoin the companies. The pace of training never passed more than a state of going through the motions. We all just wanted to go home and rest.

As I bounced along in the back of the carrier, I decided I would call this event "The Remembrance Day Massacre," and so it became.

———

In these early days, I can generally conclude that I was impressed with our quality of NCOs and rather concerned about our officers. Of course, there were good officers and poor NCOs, but by and large these conclusions were true from my perspective.

It wasn't until several years later that I was to learn the real balance required between the two groups. Officers command; NCOs run the army. Over time I was to be very fortunate, serving under some of the best officers this country has ever produced. Equally, I met and worked with some tremendous NCOs, some of whom I have already mentioned.

My early preoccupation with leadership skills was to pay off when, after two years in the Forces, I was selected to attend an "Infantry Section Commanders' Course," or "ISCC." This leadership course would qualify me up to the rank of Master Corporal.

The promotion system in the non-commissioned ranks began with "Private-Untrained." After two years a soldier, having completed certain training requirements, was given his first hook and promoted to "Private-Trained." The soldier then had to complete another two years and some on-the-job training to be promoted to "Corporal." Here the soldier would remain until he completed the Infantry's ISCC leadership course. Once the candidate was successfully through the course he could be promoted to "Master Corporal," the first level of command. This was, and remains, an intermediate leadership rank designed to test the young NCO and prove his leadership capabilities.

I graduated from the ISCC in March of 1988. I was hauled in front of Lt Colonel Cox several weeks later under the impression I was in trouble for something. The RSM marched me in front of the CO, who, with a great grin, presented me with my Master Corporal stripes.

I was now an NCO and a leader of men. Sort of. I was on the bottom of the leadership ladder with many superiors watching my every move and assessing my every decision. Not one to shy away from a challenge, I dug in with enthusiasm.

Almost immediately, the battalion deployed for four weeks to Edmonton to conduct our final exercise prior to departing for Europe. As a new Master Corporal, I blundered my way along. These were exciting exercises because they were conducted in an era when the average soldier fired more than the couple of hundred bullets a year he is allowed today. With our Cold War budgets, we had more ammunition than we could expend. In one scenario, we attacked a simulated Soviet position repeatedly for several days. For each attack, F–18 fighters strafed and bombed it, M109 artillery units flattened it, tanks dissected it, and we stormed across, happily tossing grenades and emptying more than a few magazines.

When it was all over, we boarded the buses that would take us back to Winnipeg for our final weeks. We cleaned up, turned in our gear and prepared to move.

So ended my time in Winnipeg. One month later I was on a plane for Germany.

Chapter 4

GERMANY

WE WERE BEING *hunted.*
*I knew he was there, somewhere below me. I
could feel him. He was close. Keeping my rifle
pointed at the floor, I edged towards the corner of the
room. A rule I had learned a long time ago: if you're in
trouble inside a building, find a corner and get your back
into it. That way, any danger is always in front of you.*

*As I backed into the corner I looked over at Brian. He
was looking out a hole blasted in the wall. From the
shadows, he was planning our next move. With his total
concentration on the courtyard outside, I knew he wasn't
aware of the danger inside the building with us. I couldn't
call out and I didn't dare take my hands from my weapon
to wave. Instead I turned my attention back to the floor.
There were at least three large holes. He would be near
one of them, watching, waiting for a glimpse of one of us.*

*We were on a "special mission." It was one of the
types of work I often received. If an unconventional job
came along I would inevitably get the nod. Maybe
because I worked well alone, or possibly because I could
usually produce good results when turned loose on my
own. This time I had been given a real challenge. I had
been ordered to infiltrate a small town under control of
the Rebel forces. Once inside, I was to locate the local*

headquarters and the garrison commander. My mission was to "eliminate" him and cause as much destruction in his HQ *as possible. This was to be timed with an assault taking place on the west of the town by the main force.*

I was told I could go alone or select anyone I wanted to accompany me. In an urban environment another set of eyes would be a great help, so I chose one of the best soldiers I could think of. Corporal Brian Saulnier and I had worked together for a couple of years and I had a great respect for him. He was always cool headed under pressure and I trusted him. Together, we had slipped into town and were working our way towards the centre.

In the meantime, the battle had begun on the west side of the village. As in most urban combat, the fight had quickly degenerated from a well-planned, step-by-step operation, into a confused, fluid street battle. Attack and counterattack. We could tell from the ebb and flow of the sounds of battle that it was not going smoothly. As Brian and I slunk down alleys and crawled through basements, we often saw large groups of enemy troops rushing forward to counterattack. Occasionally stretcher parties would stagger past pulling out the wounded and the dead. . . .

We had been in Germany for two weeks. So far no one was impressed. It was July and it had been raining for two weeks straight. We had all been cooped up in our buildings and tempers were growing short. By day we cleaned equipment. The Patricias, who had been obsessed with the state of our equipment back in Winnipeg, had left a right mess here in Germany.

As a question of professional rivalry, we trusted the Patricias only slightly more than we did the Van Doos, and we didn't trust the Van Doos at all. Each regiment has a unique personality and differing sets of values. Often, we would all approach the same problem with completely different requirements in mind. Many times, these differences of opinions would cause mild friction between the regiments, but it was all trivial stuff.

With regard to character, the three regular regiments have individual identities. The Patricias, even before the scandals of Somalia, were considered an irresponsible bunch of cowboys who always caused more problems than they solved. The Van Doos were unfathomable; their units seemed to belong to an entirely different army. Nothing they did ever made any sense to us. For ourselves, the RCRs are easily the most anal-retentive outfit in the Forces. Obsessed by the details, we often miss the big picture. With a regimental rule of "Never Pass a Fault," we often spent great amounts of time debating the best way to lace our combat boots or some other inconsequential point. Still, this dogged attention to detail made for a Regiment proud of its traditions and determined to stick to them. Even with people shooting at us, as we were to discover several years later.

Life in Germany quickly grew on almost all of us. There were always the occasional holdouts who would barricade themselves on the base and refuse to venture out into the scenic countryside. For the most part, though, we all began to discover the wonderful chance we had been given by the Canadian taxpayer.

The base at Baden Baden was one of two in Germany. CFB Lahr was the main base for Canadian Forces in Europe. It comprised an Air Force wing of CF–18 fighters and the main elements of Four Canadian Mechanized Brigade Group. 4CMBG was Canada's premier fighting formation, located, as it was, in the heart of NATO's major concern.

The base at Baden was normally referred to as CFB Baden-Soellingen, after the small village of Soellingen, found at the southwest corner of the airstrip. Located on the banks of the Rhine river and below the hills of the famous Black Forest, it was a beautiful location. Nearby was the ancient Roman bath town of Baden Baden. This small, scenic town was renowned for its hot springs and was the playground of the rich and famous.

Twenty minutes to the south and across the Rhine was the French city of Strassbourg. Two hours' drive south was the Swiss border. Bavaria, and the Austrian Alps, were four hours drive to the east. I once spent a four-day weekend in St.Tropez, on the French Riviera, because it was only an eight-hour drive to the south. All in all, it was a great way to spend a few years.

The people of Germany were tremendous. Most of us found that beneath sometimes gruff exteriors there were hearts of gold. A practical and hard-working culture, I admired them greatly. After working with the German Army, and in particular their paratroops, the Fallschirmjaeger, I often commented that I was glad they were on our side now. Their troops were dedicated and tough. Their equipment, some of the best in the world. The German Air Force and Navy were often left operating aging equipment, but the Army was always well taken care of.

I believe that, for the most part, the German populace appreciated our presence. Among many, I will record two incidents that show these feelings well.

In 1988, I was reading the base newspaper, the *Der Kanadair*. Among the letters to the editor was a note from a Canadian family that was living in a small German village, several kilometres north of the base. Well after midnight, when the community was all fast asleep, the family heard their doorbell ring. The husband, answering the door, found a young German woman standing on his step. The woman was upset and very cold. The man, a Canadian Forces member, tried in his best German to find out what the problem was. It seemed that the young lady's car had become stuck in a snowdrift and she couldn't get it out. She explained, in English, that her father always told her that, "If you are ever in trouble and on your own, look for a car in a driveway with a Canadian licence plate. They will always help you." So the young lady had sought out a car with the easily recognizable red-on-white Canadian military plate used on all our personal vehicles, and rung the bell. Sure enough, the Canadian family got her warmed up, pushed her car out of the snowbank and sent her on her way. This family decided to let the rest of our small Canadian community know about the German father's advice in the local paper. Thinking about it has always made me proud.

The second incident took place during an annual exercise involving most NATO countries. "Fallex," as it was called, normally took place in September and involved hundreds of thousands of troops, all ranging over the German countryside staging mock battles. By law, German civilians couldn't interfere with military activities unless there were special circumstances. Since all German men have military experience, as a by-product of universal conscription, the tanks rolling through their streets are no surprise. In fact, as a country bordering the former Warsaw Pact, most were probably happy to see the annual show of NATO muscle.

During our first Fallex in 1988, November company was happily ensconced in a small German village somewhere in Bavaria. We had arrived in the town in the early morning and had taken up hasty defensive positions as we reacted to the "Big Picture." While we lounged on our APCs in the noonday sun, a small drama took place before us.

A local German farmer marched out of his house and began hammering a sign into his lawn which read "Canadians Go Home." Two Canadian troops walking by were dumbfounded when this individual started yelling at them and pointed at the sign. Somehow an argument, in German and English, ensued. One of the two soldiers was a great big character named Hadu. The other was a smaller private by the name of Edwards.

As the argument intensified between the hulking soldier and the irate farmer, fingers were pointed and there was a bit of shoving. In the middle of all this, the farmer's wife came out of the house to see her husband toe-to-toe with a large foreign soldier. Thinking her husband was being attacked, she rushed out onto the lawn, yelling at the soldier. The ferocity of her attack made the two combatants reel back. The big Canadian, feeling a little sheepish, fell back under the onslaught.

This continued until the wife noticed the sign. Then she stopped dead in her tracks, grabbed the sign and, beating her husband over the head with it, chased him inside the house. Later she came over and apologized for his behaviour and, if I recall correctly, offered the two soldiers some biscuits. The latter is hard to verify because the moment any of the delicious Bavarian pastries were offered, they were consumed before your comrades found out and demanded a share.

There were many other instances of the population of Germany showing their respect and appreciation for us. We were regularly invited into homes for a meal, or brought steaming jugs of coffee and bread by the wives and mothers of busy German households. There were always the small fringe elements courting the media and demanding NATO withdrawal of forces, but as a whole we were well thought of.

Certainly, we tried the patience of the locals at times. On one occasion we almost started an international incident when an armed group of Canadians hijacked a forty-passenger school bus. The story is as comical as it was probably terrifying for the bus driver. No doubt it also left an impression on the forty elementary school children stranded high in the Black Forest hills.

Very often during training we would transport our troops in rented buses to reduce wear on our military vehicles. The German companies that dealt with the Canadians became quite used to us and there were never any problems. The drivers would sell beer from a cooler at the front of the bus and look after us well. We became so used to using these buses that we often considered them all as part of the organization.

On this occasion, a platoon of troops was returning from a week in the hills on a patrolling exercise. They were dirty, tired and loaded with weapons and equipment. Camouflaged and moving silently, they made their way to a parking area where they were to rendezvous with a bus which would take them back to the base. Unfortunately, their bus was late. Even less fortunately, another bus had just unloaded forty school children who were off to view a local waterfall. It was now waiting in the same parking area, as the soldiers approached.

From out of the thick forest emerged twenty-five heavily armed troops. To the German driver, whose company had no dealings with the military, these men looked like terrorists. They quickly boarded the bus and the platoon commander said simply, "Baden Kaserne." The driver, not saying a word, closed the door and headed for the Canadian base, known, as are all military bases, as a "Kaserne."

On arriving at the Kaserne, the Canadian troops dismounted and the bus driver immediately sped off. Finding a phone, he quickly called the German Police and reported a hijacking. The Polizei, as the German cops are known, are a highly efficient and, when necessary, diplomatic force. Very quickly they discovered the mistake. The Canadian troops were so used to the use of these buses, it never occurred to anyone that a bus, in the right place at the right time, with an apparently willing driver, was the wrong bus. Speaking no English, the driver simply did as he was told. Oops.

The Germans were always forgiving though. I am not entirely sure why, even to this day, they had such a large place in their hearts for us. I recall on one exercise we pulled into a small German town and the company began to look for places to bed down for the night. Myself, with my driver, Corporal Steve O'Shea, pulled into a driveway beside a small farmhouse with an attached barn. It looked like a good place "to go to ground," as the army calls sleeping. We looked in the barn and discovered it had been renovated into a recreation room. A combination sun room and living room. Amazed at our luck we moved in. While we were unloading our kit, the owner of the house came out and was surprised to find us in his yard. We had been driving a Jeep as opposed to an APC, and he hadn't heard us arrive. He looked a little worried. Fortunately Steve was fluent in German and told him who we were. Steve asked him if he minded if we used his "barn" to sleep in. The farmer, an elderly man, thought for a moment and then shrugged his shoulders and went back into his house. We took this for an "OK" and moved in.

Several minutes later, the farmer appeared with a jug of coffee and some bread. He sat down with us and, after the introductions were complete, told us that the last time any soldiers had come into his house it was 1945 and an American soldier had kicked in his door. We talked, and as he became more comfortable with us, he told us more of his wartime experiences. He had been a Panzer driver in the German army of World War Two. After serving on the Russian Front he had been invalided out of the military due to a leg wound. We talked quite a bit, with me trying my best to carry on a decent conversation in my limited German.

I was often amazed at the reception we received from the Germans. If we were to pull into some Canadian farmer's yard and set up shop in his barn, we would likely be quickly introduced to his shotgun. Yet these Germans allowed us to come into their peaceful rural lives and cause much disruption without a word of complaint. Amazing people.

One of the most unusual changes to the battalion in Germany compared to Winnipeg was the Rest Easy and Kit Shop. In the absolute centre of the north part of the base was a large concrete building consisting of a snack bar and games lounge at one end and a kit shop at the other. The Rest Easy, known to us as the "Foxhole," provided inexpensive and completely unhealthy food, as well as that one absolute necessity: coffee.

The kit shop was a marvel. Run by the unit and staffed by injured personnel, it was a gold mine. Having secured the area distributorship for Survival Aids, a British outdoor and military supply company, it became an immensely profitable asset. As Gore-Tex burst on the military scene, the kit shop outfitted, at reasonable expense, the entire battalion in this new wonder garment.

There were U.S. military items, British kit, German stuff, everything. When the battalion travelled, the kit shop would follow and set up business. We sold to anyone with money. The combined profits of these two little businesses made our battalion one of the wealthiest in the Forces. Each year the battalion would throw an all-ranks ball in a ritzy Baden Baden Ballroom. There were Christmas parties, well-funded sports teams, gifts for spouses and an all-round fund for morale building.

Some might wonder why we were buying our own kit. If you had asked me prior to our deployment to Germany, I would have been curious as well. Up until then, my only kit purchase was a thirty-centimetre-long *kukri*. This Gurkha fighting knife was to be my constant companion and good luck charm throughout my career. More on the kukri later. Other than this one item, I was convinced that, in Canada, we were the best equipped army in NATO. This completely innocent belief was shattered when we reached Europe. Surrounded by armies that took fighting and equipment seriously, we learned that our "You can't have it if it isn't made in Quebec" procurement system was seriously flawed.

I am not saying that all of our issue kit is useless but, like always, we are constantly planning to fight the last war. If you were to compare a Korea-era Canadian soldier with a soldier of the late 1980s, you wouldn't have found too many differences. When you consider that up to two-thirds of casualties can be non-combat wounds, you would think we would learn a lesson. Compared to the Brits and Americans, we were poor country cousins.

We still wear World-War-Two-issue steel helmets in an age in which every other western army is wearing Kevlar. Our rucksack, an ergonomic nightmare on its own, isn't compatible with our webb gear. The Department of National Defense still insists camouflage doesn't work. The only up-to-date gear we have was bought only in large enough numbers to equip our troops overseas.

A good friend of mine was in the Gulf War guarding a military hospital. When the Scud alert siren went off, he climbed into his chemical protection suit and pulled on his gas mask. This was a new mask that was just coming on line with the Forces. Despite thorough testing, it suffered the minor problem of having the eyepieces fall out when you pulled it on. That is exactly what happened to Gary. So there he sat in the bunker with everyone else, cursing our supply system and praying it wasn't a chemical attack.

So our kit is not quite up to scratch. This was never more apparent than to those troops who have had to serve in the Balkans, the Gulf or in Africa. We all quickly discovered that our kit will do in a dry, cold environment, but in any other climate it is unacceptable. Add to this problem an overabundance of media in these areas and you have a public relations disaster. A couple of thousand miserable Canadians standing beside their comfy U.S. counterparts does not look good on the evening news. So now, when you get off the plane in Yugoslavia, you get issued a Kevlar helmet, Gore-Tex jacket, Gore-Tex boots, a new assault vest and all the other goodies to bring you up to international standards. Of course, when you leave, you have to turn it all in again because there is only enough for the troops in theatre. Back in Canada, none of it is on issue and is not an authorized dress in most units. All of which means you are back to the same old stuff.

If you compare our kit to that of the U.S. forces, it will be immediately assumed that we, as a country of lesser means, cannot afford the good gear. In the Forces we all acknowledge this fact. We have to do more with less and we do. Without all the high-speed items, we still have some of the best troops in the world. What often gets under our skin though, is the way the Forces spends the money it does have. All across Canada on military bases, you see huge, shopping-mall-sized buildings going up to house units which are quite comfortable in their existing structures. In England, the military is quartered in buildings that are fifty, a hundred or even two hundred years old. They constantly renovate what they have because they spend their money on weapons and equipment. In Canada, we can spend thirty million dollars on a new building for a unit that was doing fine in its old buildings before, but we can't decently clothe our troops.

As a description of the balance between issue and store-bought kit, I will describe my normal field dress for an exercise in Germany.

I always preferred a toque to a bush hat in the field. Yet the issue toque was unacceptable. I wore a U.S.-issue black toque with a fine wool weave. I never wore our combat jacket, because it was useless. Designed to look good while you were standing still on a parade square, it is neither waterproof nor windproof. Instead, I preferred a combat shirt and several layers underneath. Military issue underwear is universally discarded, and I wore a British Navy mesh undershirt. Above that, I would wear a French undershirt with full-length sleeves and a hood. Then came a British issue Gore-Tex suit beneath my combats.

On my back was a U.S.-issue, large Alice pack. Inside that was a Survival Aids polypropylene bivvy bag liner in place of the issue sleeping bag. A Survival Aids Cobra bivvy bag and a U.S.-issue poncho liner rounded off my sleeping gear. For cold nights, I kept a Norwegian sweater and a pair of Northern Ireland leather gloves. I always topped off my ensemble with a British mesh scarf for that extra swaggering look.

Nor was I alone. Excepting young soldiers who haven't learned their lessons yet, no good Canadian soldier wears all his issue items. Fortunately, in Germany we had enough financial benefits to have some disposable income. Inevitably, a large amount of this went into kit and equipment. Initially, the Commanding Officers, Regimental Sergeant-Majors and Company Sergeant-Majors would not tolerate these non-issue items. Then, after several stints in the rain-soaked Black Forest, they would show up with the Gore-Tex boots and bivvy bags as well. The unspoken rule has always been, as long as you look like a Canadian soldier on the outside, everything else is your own choice.

The British and American armies go one better; as long as your uniform is in the proper camouflage pattern, then it is acceptable. Take a good look at some pictures of British troops in the Falklands War and you will see what I mean.

Unlike in Canada, where our training was isolated from our NATO counterparts, we were constantly shoulder to shoulder with many other militaries in Europe. It became impossible to not take a good look at the kit and equipment of our allies and even our adversaries. To collect a bit of this and a bit of that became natural.

Training in Europe exposed us to many experiences not available in Canada. Many of our troops went over into France and took a French Commando Course. This was a confidence course for the French Marine Commandos and the French Foreign Legion. It consisted of a variety of training phases including rappelling, patrolling, urban combat and escape and evasion. The program featured a memorable obstacle course that took place high off the ground. At one point in the course, candidates are required to jump from a platform twenty metres up in one tree to a platform several metres lower on another tree a few yards away. All without any safety apparatus whatsoever.

In Senelager, a British base in northern Germany, soldiers are placed in a long trench with machine guns firing half a metre over their heads. Then on command, the soldiers must crawl over the top of the trench and worm their way fifty metres forward. During the entire period the machine guns continue to fire only centimetres overhead and explosives are detonated in pits along the route.

This type of battle simulation is not permitted in Canada due to excessive safety restrictions. Yet it is typical of the type of training our allies regularly conduct. I can honestly say that it took a fair bit of courage to crawl over that lip and into the fire. The experience definitely provides a glimpse into the fury of battle.

At a Fallschirmjaeger base in Nagold, Germany, an old M–48 tank is used as a confidence builder. First you squat in the middle of the road and the tank steers directly at you. As it closes, you must put your hands out to touch it. As it hits you, you fall backwards and let it roll over you. Next you must stand in a sewer entrance only waist deep. Once again the tank approaches. At the last moment you must duck down and let it roll over you. Finally, the real test. The soldier lies in a shallow trench only twenty centimetres deep and fifty wide. Your body is nearly flush with the road. Then the tank slowly drives its track right over you. I could feel the tread touching my stomach as it passed.

The most interesting and valuable type of training available in Europe for infanteers must be FIBUA. Fighting In Built Up Areas, as it is called in Canada, is essentially the practice of fighting in towns and cities. This type of warfare is distinct from any other and requires immense skill and discipline to conduct successfully. There are no training sites of this kind in Canada, although we constantly hear of plans to construct them.

This type of training is essential for several reasons. In the old days of the cold war, it was envisioned that if war should break out in western Europe, a sound knowledge of urban combat would be essential. The Warsaw Pact, numerically superior, would probably try to thrust deep into Germany and link up with massive airborne bridgeheads. Because fighting in villages and towns bogs down an offensive, the Warsaw Pact forces would attempt to bypass these obstacles and try to fight NATO in the open where their numbers would have been an advantage. NATO's defence was based on the plan of defending every little village, thus forcing the advancing enemy to commit to small fierce battles everywhere along his front.

For anyone who knows Germany well, this was a good strategy. In most of Europe, it is difficult to drive more than two kilometres without passing through a small village. By defending every village and sowing the open areas with mines and obstacles, it was hoped that the West could hold up the Warsaw Pact long enough for help to arrive. Therefore, fighting in towns and villages became essential to Western defences in Europe.

In the days after the fall of the Berlin Wall and the end of the cold war, western armies still find themselves in places such as Sarajevo, Kuwait City and Mogadishu. With the global trend towards urbanization, a thorough knowledge of urban combat techniques is essential.

The German government solved this problem by selecting a typical, small German village and moving out all of the residents. Now a ghost town, complete with a castle on a hill, it has served as a FIBUA training sight ever since.

The Americans, having the money but no town, built a recreation of a German village in their Hohenfels training base in Bavaria. In England, a typical English village was constructed in Warminster. Everywhere, fake villages are popping up.

To the average soldier, these places are like a military version of Disneyland. Everyone is equipped with a laser system similar to the "Laser Tag" games found in most cities. The soldier's helmet, chest and back are covered in a series of sensors linked to a small control box worn on a harness over the soldier's kit. The soldier's weapon is fitted with a laser device that fires one laser pulse every time the weapon fires a blank. In the laser emitter is a key. If the soldier is hit by another laser, in effect shot, a loud buzzer on his harness emits an annoying screech until the key is removed from his rifle and placed in the harness. With the key out of the rifle it can no longer fire the laser. The key turns off the buzzer, but if the soldier removes it in an attempt to fire his weapon again, the buzzer goes off until the key is returned. The summary effect is that once you are shot, you are out of the battle. Soldiers can fight their way through the town and actually see who is winning and who isn't. This is a great test of individual combat skills. It is a horror to the officers.

In the normal Canadian training style everyone fires off their blanks and, as long as you followed your drills, you can consider your attack a success. No one loses. With the laser systems it is possible, and probable, that an officer will watch his command wiped out in an ill-planned battle. The instant feedback, so essential to the individual soldier building his skills, can be a nightmare for the officer who has his command decimated and must explain the loss to his superiors.

In a large training area in the American southwest, called the National Training Center, an entire battlefield is dedicated to this type of training. Careers are made and broken. If a battalion commander is making a mess of a battle, his brigade commander may very well fire him and have the second-in-command take over. This system has the effect of producing an officer corps of extremely competent leaders.

The Canadian Forces have no laser systems of their own available for unit training. In Germany, we had to borrow them from the U.S. military. It has been mentioned in trade journals that we are planning to purchase these training aids, but their use may be limited. Very often, Canadian officers, hoping to avoid embarrassment, have instructed their units to issue only enough batteries to run one-third of the laser systems. The rest of the soldiers cannot be "killed" and an embarrassing loss is averted.

On some occasions, though, we have gone full bore, with everyone properly outfitted and supplied. Normally, a CO will task his sub-units, the rifle companies, to attack each other. One company will defend the town while two or three others attack. Occasionally, we will attack American defenders or vice-versa.

In one exercise, November and Mike companies attacked one hundred U.S. defenders. After the assault was over, the Americans described our soldiers as crazy. We had rolled right over their defences and "wiped them out." Typically, Canadians make up for their lack of sophisticated equipment with sheer aggression. Americans tend to prefer to hold back and let the technology do the work for them. When we combine this with encouraging initiative at the lowest levels, we have a formidable force. Also, we aren't slaves to tactics. All levels of commanders are encouraged, within limits, to think and plan for themselves. A Russian general once wrote of Canadians in a Soviet military journal, "The Canadians are difficult opponents; they seem to have no desire to follow their own doctrine."

Typical of this style, my new company commander in Germany was never satisfied doing things according to the book. His name was Major "Karate" Clyde Russell. A Newfoundlander, he got his nickname by giving the occasional lesson in manners to young Air Force officers who got a bit too big for their britches in the mess.

Major Russell was an excellent OC. He was not a "ring knocker" (a military college grad) and made no concessions for political reasons. Tough and honest, he displayed the typical Newfie characteristic of common sense, which is frequently missing in the officer corps. The Major always set a good example for the troops who served under him. He was always easy to pick out from a distance due to a most peculiar style of walking with his head canted to one side, and a bouncy step. In the dark, on sentry duty, you always knew when the OC was approaching.

Major Russell's leadership style matched his slightly unusual character. He always led from the front and constantly challenged his soldiers. Never becoming familiar with his troops, he always maintained a quiet and detached manner that was difficult to penetrate. You never knew what he was going to do next. His goals were always achieved by whatever means necessary. Rules, operating procedures and norms meant nothing if they failed to achieve the desired results. An unconventional thinker, he was successful within the battalion because he would always do what needed to be done, not what was commonly accepted.

For example, on several exercises Major Russell kept a bagpiper with him in battle. In the misty early morning light, the piper would sound the attack with an echoing rendition of "Scotland the Brave." While machine guns chattered and artillery simulators exploded, the piper would play away, reminiscent of the days of the Lord Lovat and his Number Four Commando crossing the beaches of Normandy. In the smoke and the confusion of the fight, the piper would signal the consolidation with "Blue Bonnets over the Border."

During Fallex, a single company amongst divisions and army corps was insignificant. While our battalion sat in some forest in Bavaria, the Big Picture often moved on without remembering us. Major Russell was never satisfied with sitting around. The only option for the battalion would be patrolling its locality to ensure its security. Not satisfied with sending out small recce patrols,

Major Russell tasked me to spend the entire exercise slipping through "enemy" lines to locate targets for the company to attack. I was given a jeep and two troops. Corporal Steve O'Shea drove and Corporal George Myatte acted as signaller.

On one patrol, I left my jeep on the friendly side of the front. Taking George with me, the two of us passed through the 2nd Armoured Cavalry positions, guarding our front lines, and slipped into the enemy defenses. After passing through the forward posts, we patrolled into the enemy's vulnerable rear area. Several close calls later, including one high-speed retreat into an electrified cattle fence, we located an anti-aircraft radar site. We reported to Major Russell by radio. He was waiting with the company near the front lines. Two hours later we linked up and led the company fighting patrol in to attack the site. The position was wiped out and the company returned to friendly lines with two prisoners we had found wandering around in the dark.

I remember this patrol well, because, as the company was assaulting the target, I was lying in a hedge with a U.S. captain who was along as an observer and umpire. Noting my unusual dress and the fact that I was operating well behind enemy lines, he asked if I belonged to some kind of special forces. I replied, quite matter-of-factly, that we were all trained for this sort of work. I was smiling secretly in the dark because we as Canadian soldiers take great pride in our varied skills. American troops usually have one specialty and that is it. We, having far fewer troops, are expected to be proficient with all the skills, weapons, radios, vehicles and equipment in the inventory. I'm sure that captain went home with a new respect for Canadian troops.

Throughout the month-long exercise, we were out there doing a sneak-'n'-peek for the OC. Often, my patrol would spot the enemy counter-attack or find the unguarded track that allowed Major Russell to pull off some seemingly impossible task. These small victories would bring great praise to the company and increase our esprit de corps. Unlike other officers I had served, Major Russell was never shy about sharing the limelight and credit with his troops.

On another occasion, the company was out in the Black Forest on the annual two-week battalion patrolling exercise. All the companies in the battalion were ordered to search the hills for a small group of terrorists. In the first week, Major Russell moved the company up to our patrol sector and established platoon patrol bases. From these bases our patrols scoured the hills.

During one patrol, we located a small terrorist position on a junction of trails. My four-man patrol hid in the bushes half-a-dozen-metres from the target while our platoon moved into position to attack. Linking up with the platoon several hundred metres away, I described the position to our platoon commander, Lieutenant Sullivan. I outlined how I thought the attack could be done, based on my knowledge of the position. He agreed and we quickly swept across the terrorist outpost, destroying the target.

Yet, at the end of the first week, the terrorists' main base eluded all the companies' search efforts. As normal, Major Russell devised an unconventional scheme to locate the enemy stronghold. I was brought before the OC with Sergeant Roger Stuedle, a soldier of German descent. Together we were briefed on the OC's plan. The whole operation was against the rules, he explained. We weren't to discuss our activities with anyone. The plan consisted of Roger and me dressing in civilian clothes and, riding mountain bikes, wandering through the mountains like tourists, searching for the enemy. We hoped to find some sign of the terrorists by blending in and not raising their suspicions. I borrowed two wigs from the local theatre club and we tucked 9 mm pistols into our belts. We borrowed mountain bikes and, thus equipped, cycled off into the hills looking for signs of the enemy.

The plan was for us to keep an eye out for a chance contact with an unsuspecting terrorist unit. We knew they were using certain civilian vehicles and were constantly watching traffic. We also stopped in local shops and Gasthauses asking for any information on sightings of strangely dressed soldiers. The Germans are quite sharp and a group of soldiers rarely goes unnoticed for very long. Each day we would rendezvous with the rest of the company who were continuing their search with normal patrols.

Finally, on the morning of the second last day, Roger and I spotted some old APC tracks heading up a small road. We followed them to a large field where some Germans were having a picnic. The track had climbed a large hill and we were both exhausted from the bike ride up. There was no sign that we were getting any closer to the terrorist camp. Certainly, with a large group of Germans nearby, this had to be a dead end.

Roger was fed up and said that we should turn around. These

tracks were old and could have been made months ago. We knew the terrorists had a stolen APC, but Canadians, Germans and Americans exercised all over these hills. Anyone could have made the tracks. I was determined to follow them, despite the slim odds. Time was running out and it was the only lead we had.

At one point, Roger started back down the hill, but he saw I wasn't following and turned around. When he caught up with me, he tried to convince me to turn back. While we were standing there arguing, a terrorist, dressed in British camouflage, stepped out of the treeline twenty metres away. Both of us froze. We didn't have our wigs on due to the climb and the heat. The terrorist was facing the other way but if he turned, he might recognize us as soldiers. We quickly dragged our bikes into the treeline. After slipping our wigs on in a ridiculously haphazard fashion, we leaned out and peered up the treeline. The terrorist was gone.

We were standing in a treeline that consisted of extremely thick underbrush and ten-metre-tall deciduous trees. It was impossible to see more than a short distance. Sneaking through the trees was out of the question. We would make far too much noise in the thick underbrush and, if seen, two civilians plowing through the woods trying to hold their wigs on would be highly suspicious. Our only alternative was to move up the treeline. So we mounted our bikes and, with me leading, bicycled slowly along the edge of the forest. As we passed the area where the terrorist had appeared, we noticed a well-trodden path heading back into the forest. We bicycled along the treeline for about a hundred metres, then stopped and pretended to take a water break. Roger and I agreed. There was no reason to have an observation post here; there was nothing to watch. According to the map, these woods covered a narrow spur protruding out from the hills. It meant that there was only one good approach and steep slopes on three sides. A good place to put a hidden camp. The terrorist we had seen had been quite casual; he wasn't patrolling. All the facts fit. This must be it!

We decided for one more pass and headed back down the treeline. As we approached the trail entrance two terrorists stepped out of the trees and headed directly for us. There was no turning back, so we bluffed it.

As I bicycled between them, as any obnoxious German would do, I muttered, "Guten tag," and kept my eyes on the ground.

Roger grunted something behind me and we left them in the field behind us. Neither one looked back. If they suspected us, we could expect an alert and we would probably be chased down with vehicles to prevent our reporting.

There was no sign that they were suspicious, so Roger and I sped down the hill and out of sight. We followed a small trail around the base of the hill and spotted signs of foot movement off the spur. This had to be the base of operations for the terrorists. On the far side of the hill we found a small road heading into the trees on the spur. On it were APC tracks. That confirmed it. We decided to beat it before our luck ran out and headed off to the rendezvous.

Major Russell was delighted and that night marched the company into position and swept through the terrorist camp. The operation was a success and was another feather in November company's cap.

I had many other interesting experiences with November company, including a mini SAS selection in Wales, rock climbing and spelunking in the UK and Bavaria and other enjoyable tales. It was a great time to be a young soldier.

I must briefly include one other major event that occurred during my time in Germany. Prior to leaving Canada, I had been dating a young lady by the name of Karla. After I arrived in Germany in 1988, she flew over for a visit. We got along pretty well. She was bright and full of life. Very lovely. We really enjoyed our time together. When it looked like she was going to return to Canada, I decided I didn't want her to go and proposed. We were married in the summer of 1989 back in Canada. When she married me though, she also married the army. Considering what lay ahead, I think I was pretty lucky to find her—a great woman.

Chapter 5

RECCE

DARYL AND I *were cold. It was only 0530 hours and the sun hadn't made an appearance yet. Together, we stood in the battle-scarred hut that formerly housed the Jugoslav National Army sentries guarding this chemical warfare base. Now, they were dead, probably buried somewhere nearby, their fancy little prefabricated hut riddled by small arms fire.*

Shivering in the brisk night air, under a single floodlight, we were guarding the main entrance to our new base. Not that we would be terribly effective if anyone wanted in. Unwilling to admit we were vulnerable in any way, despite recent attacks, the commanders wouldn't install even basic barricades. There were no defenses for the sentries, no vehicle obstacles, nothing. We did have an MI13 parked beside the gate, but it could not be moved easily and served only to block our view of a large portion of the approaches. So, Daryl and I stood there with our C7s and watched . . . and hoped.

While I was standing there, I became aware of a rustling in the forest behind the APC. Immediately, I could feel my heart rate accelerate and my senses sharpen. I froze and listened carefully. Nothing.

I looked over at Daryl. He had heard it too. I nodded to him. He gave me the hand signal for enemy, a fist out-

stretched with the thumb extended downwards, and I shrugged.

I crouched low and signaled Daryl to skirt the APC and take up an overwatch. Knowing I was silhouetted against the floodlights, I ducked into the shadow of the APC. Slowly, I worked my way to the rear. Behind it, the tree-line fell away into a small defile which was now enclosed in an impenetrable veil of darkness. As I reached the end of the APC's hull I took a deep, relaxing breath and held it, listening.

There it was again! Someone was definitely out there in the forest. I could hear a rustling in the leaves on the forest floor.

I let out my breath and took another, then I leaned out from the APC to have a look. I couldn't see much. Being under the lights had ruined my night vision. Slowly, I pulled my head back. I had a flashlight, but if I turned it on, it would give away my position and the fact that we were aware we were being stalked.

Suddenly, there was a burst of motion from the forest. I swung my weapon out and prepared to fire. I heard Daryl moving at the same time. This was it!

A rooster!

Out of the trees walked a rooster. Behind it, I could make out two other chickens pecking about for breakfast. Bloody hell!

As the tension of the moment broke, I burst out laughing. Daryl was chuckling to himself as well. Those were some lucky chickens. Too bad we hadn't offed them. They would have made a nice lunch.

———

In the spring of 1990 I had made my decision. Life in a rifle company no longer held much interest. I wanted to go to Recce platoon. I wrote a memorandum to Major Russell asking for a transfer to the Battalion Recce platoon as soon as possible. I got the memo back with a minute saying I would be going at the first opportunity.

Shortly thereafter, I was tasked out as an instructor on the next Basic Reconnaissance Patrolman Course. Successfully completing this course was a requirement for posting to the Recce platoon.

Technically, I shouldn't have been an instructor because I didn't have the basic course, but I had been qualified in Combat Intelligence the year before and had amassed a fair bit of recce experience. I believed I was a least capable of contributing as an instructor and I attended all the classes I could. I wrote all the tests and passed them all. As an ISCC graduate, I was already trained in basic patrolling and navigation. Combined with my record of employment to date, and my test results, I received my basic qualification with the other graduates.

Several weeks later I was told I would be moving over to recce in June. I couldn't have been happier. Finally, I would be out on my own, with my own detachment, doing things my way. No more waiting around for everyone else to make up their minds.

In a rifle company, the platoon commanders wait for the OC to give them direction, the section commanders are told what to do by the platoon commander, then they turn around and order the number one rifleman to fix bayonets and charge a machine gun. Initiative is encouraged, but generally action occurs within the framework of a set of specific drills. Master Corporals, as section second-in-commands, do not have a great influence on the course of a battle, except by individual action.

This is, of course, an oversimplification, but it is essentially correct. The rifle companies are designed as fighting units and require discipline and order to be effective. The commanders wield their units to deliver sharp but decisive blows. Anything less than this strict rule of conduct would produce a haphazard melee and would cease to be effective. Success in battle requires that everyone knows the plan well and does his part to ensure its success.

In Recce platoon on the other hand, small teams of highly trained specialists move about the battlefield conducting their missions of gathering information or keeping vital areas under surveillance. Orders often come by radio and a detachment can be on its own for days or weeks at a time. Once it receives its mission, how it accomplishes the task is up to the members of the detachment. There are no officers and no sergeant-majors watching over your shoulder. As long as you continue to produce results, your methods are your own. This was exactly the type of work I had come to enjoy. Give me a mission and leave me to my own devices to sort it out.

One of the great aspects of reconnaissance work in the Canadian forces is that officers do not conduct reconnaissance missions. They are exposed to patrolling in their basic training and, if they are very lucky, get to attend the Advanced Recce course. However, they still do not conduct reconnaissance patrols. This specialty is the sole preserve of the non-commissioned ranks. It is the one battlefield activity where officers must sit back and let go.

After arriving in Recce platoon I had only a few short weeks to prepare for my first major exercise as a Recce Detachment Commander. Fallex 1990 began in late August with our battalion's deployment to the U.S. base of Hohenfels in upper Bavaria. Here, I was to find out that conducting recce in a mechanized battle group was not just a matter of sneaking through the woods. In fact, it turned out to be a very high stress and intricately performed ballet of move and countermove.

The days of sneaking around in the bush weren't over, but now we had a much wider and more vital role in the actions of the battalion. I was challenged, I was learning and I was happy.

To carry out our tasks, each three-man detachment was equipped with a Lynx reconnaissance vehicle. This was basically a cut-down version of an M113. It was lighter and, consequently, much faster. Each detachment also owned a jeep and a mountain bicycle. Using a combination of these three modes of transport in addition to our "Black Cadillacs" (our feet), we could manage most missions assigned by the battalion. Often, we would be inserted into an area by helicopter. Versatile was definitely an accurate description of our outfit.

A typical action would begin before sunrise. Recce platoon, mounted in jeeps or Lynxes, would cross out of friendly lines several hours before the scheduled advance. We would have a short head start to scout routes and locate the first enemy positions.

Recce Platoon normally consisted of six detachments, grouped in pairs. Each pair, known as a Group, would have a lane marked out on the map that they would have to sweep, looking for signs of the enemy. The lane could be up to several kilometres wide. Behind the dets would be two Headquarters APCs. These would contain the Recce platoon commander in one and the platoon 2IC in the other. These two would take alternating bounds forward, trying to maintain radio contact at all times with their fast-moving dets.

The drill was complex. Your group would race up its lane, checking anything that the enemy would likely mine or occupy.

We also had to check roads and bridges to ensure they could take the weight of the forty-ton tanks that would be following.

If we were advancing up a road, checking the way for the forces to follow, our drill was fairly simple. Each vehicle would take a turn bounding forward. While one was moving, the other was covering and observing. Using binoculars to scan the ground ahead, we would watch for any tell-tale sign of enemy activity. If we came to an extremely dangerous area, a large field or an intersection, we would stop and I would dismount. Moving forward with my binoculars, map and weapon, I could scan the area for any dangers. Contact was maintained with the vehicle via a small headset radio I purchased for the purpose. This way my vehicle remained hidden safely out of sight of the enemy.

If we spotted any bad guys, a race against the clock began to complete a long list of actions. Immediately on spotting the enemy, I would signal the command, "Contact!" Transmitting over our radios, my message would be relayed from our vehicle to all of Recce platoon. The air would go dead until I finished my report. Now I had approximately thirty minutes to complete all my duties. First, I would send a detailed report of the location of the enemy. I included his size, what equipment he had and what he was doing.

My companion detachment would pick out the spot on the map and immediately try working its way around the position. Meanwhile, I would call in an artillery mission on the target. Next, I had to prepare a plan of attack.

Back in the HQ vehicles, the platoon commander was relaying my report to the Commanding Officer, who would in turn task a company to attack it. Then the platoon commander would flip over to the company frequency and give the OC a report. Then he would flip to the artillery net and send in my fire mission.

Meanwhile back at the enemy location, my partners and I were scouting out a safe place where the company could form up, out of view of the enemy. We also had to plan out where the company could put its fire base, usually a couple of tanks, to cover its approach to the enemy position. Then we had to check for minefields, ditches, swamps or anything that would provide an obstacle to the attacking company. During this time my signaler would be constantly monitoring the enemy and directing artillery and mortar fire on to them.

By now the company was on its way and calling for details. We had to let them know the route to the safe area. Sometimes I had to send my vehicle or another det for a link-up with the approaching company to lead them in. Once the company arrived, I would either visit the OC and brief him on what I had discovered or report to him by radio. Rarely, an OC would move up to my location and have a look for himself. On many occasions, the OC would totally ignore Recce altogether and go off and make his own plan.

Here lies the rub. Because officers have no extensive training in reconnaissance tactics and employment, they are often unprepared to utilize the information a recce detachment can provide. Having spent long months in schools learning combat tactics, they do not feel comfortable taking recommendations from mere NCOs on possible deployment options for an attack.

The best officers, and consequently the most successful, would always listen to whatever information recce could provide. Some would even ask questions. What does this ravine look like? Can I get my tanks across this river? Could I use this feature as my firebase? These officers would take all our recommendations under consideration and then formulate a plan. Fifteen minutes later the attack would go in. From moment of first contact by the recce det until the attack began could be as little as forty minutes with a good rifle company.

As soon as the company had received all the help we could provide, we would depart, swinging around the enemy position and taking up the search again on the far side for the next enemy emplacement.

For the officer who ignored us, the process could take much longer. In one instance a detachment under Master Corporal Jeff Elgie sat up on a mountain observing the enemy buzzing around in a forest on the next hill. He went through all his drills, preparing everything for Mike company to make its attack. He offered to link up with the OC to brief him on the enemy. OC Mike didn't feel the urge to listen to Jeff and proceeded with his own plan. He dismounted his troops and, detailing his plan to his platoon commanders, they set off to sweep the enemy position. Except for one critical error: they were attacking the wrong hill.

Mike company disappeared into the thick woods on a similar hill several hundred metres away. Jeff called up Recce HQ and informed them of the misdirected attack. The Recce platoon commander, Captain Dave Ready, tried to raise the OC of Mike but couldn't reach him. Jeff, a little exasperated, went down and found one of the Mike company platoons wandering around in the woods trying to find the enemy. He explained the OC's mistake to the platoon commander but was told that no one was in contact with the OC and that he had no idea what was going on. Jeff, feeling he'd tried, went back up the hill and watched as the enemy, somewhat confused, watched Mike company's attack strike an unoccupied hill.

Soon enough, OC Mike came up on the Battalion radio net and announced that there were no enemy on the position. He advised the CO that he was continuing his advance. Jeff, feeling a little insulted, called up Captain Ready and explained how he was still staring at the enemy and that Mike company had botched the job.

Captain Ready was in a difficult situation. No one listens to the recce radio frequency except Recce platoon. So far, no one knew that Mike company had made a major mistake except Recce. I was listening to the whole affair from my vehicle a couple of kilometres away. To report the error to the CO, Captain Ready would have to broadcast on the Battalion net, letting everyone in the unit know that OC Mike had just screwed the pooch.

The embarrassment it would cause OC Mike would be considerable, but the facts were that the enemy were still blocking a main route of advance. There was no choice and Captain Ready came up on the Battalion net and told the CO that Mike company had attacked the wrong hill. Before the CO could comment, OC Mike got on the net and told the CO that Recce had been wrong, that there were no enemy at the grid reference given. The CO, a little confused, asked Captain Ready to confirm the presence of enemy at the target.

"Six Niner, I have a det with eyes on the objective right now, over," he said.

The conversation had now come down to a confrontation between two officers on a battalion-wide frequency. In the Canadian army, any captain with career aspirations doesn't criticize a superior officer in front of the battalion and the CO. Still, facts were facts and Captain Ready was not backing down.

"Niner, this is One Niner, my company has just cleared that feature and there were no enemy in location, over," countered OC Mike.

"Niner, this is Six Niner, callsign One has attacked the wrong hill, over," replied Captain Ready. Well, the cat was out of the bag now.

The CO, callsign "Niner," came on the air and ordered Oscar company to attack the correct hill. Mike company was to move into reserve. Immediately, OC Mike tried to salvage his pride and offered to go back and do the attack right.

"One Niner, this is Niner. You had your chance, out," replied the CO. The matter was closed for the moment.

Later, at the next CO's meeting for all commanders, OC Mike blamed Recce for his company's failure. We had given him the wrong map reference. We should have contacted him and corrected the navigational error, anything, but it wasn't his fault. I don't know what Captain Ready's response was, but I doubt he would allow himself to be drawn into an argument. The final result was a great animosity between Recce and OC Mike for some time to come. Of course, this usually worked to the detriment of Mike company's performance. In Recce though, we made a point to work just as hard for Mike as we would for anyone else. We had done nothing wrong and were all professionals.

Without the benefit of attending expensive staff colleges, a good recce NCO had to become thoroughly familiar with battalion-level tactics. Not only did we plan company level attacks but we also had to be constantly planning on a battalion, and occasionally a brigade level. As one company was attacking an enemy stronghold and another company was preparing to attack a second position, Recce would be worried about likely enemy responses, avenues open to counter-attacks, where the enemy would withdraw to, where his guns were and all the responses the CO would have to make to react to these considerations. In essence, we had to develop a thorough knowledge of modern tactics at a level far above that normally associated with our rank levels.

In the free-play battles of Fallex, where entire one-hundred-thousand-man armies were ranging across western Germany, a single battalion's success often depended on the professionalism and intelligence of its recce elements.

I recall our entire Canadian Brigade being held up at a river; the far bank was in the hands of the opposing forces. In these war games umpires would assess losses to any unit found to be outmanoeuvred by its enemy. Forcing a crossing of the river might have caused massive casualties within the brigade. For us in Recce, it was a race against time to locate a suitable, unde-fended ford for the battalion and possibly the brigade.

In this situation, the opinion of a corporal may very well alter the actions of the brigade, and possibly the division behind it. It wasn't just the ford either, it was the approaches to it and the classes of vehicle it could take. Could trucks cross as well as tanks? Was it defendable? What was the enemy strength on the far bank? All these questions would run through the recce sol-dier's head before he sent his report. Offering the location of a ford would not be enough. By the time engineers arrived to con-firm the report, the momentum of the advance might very well be lost. The commanders would need information and, in the high-speed world of modern mechanized operations, a tactical decision of this magnitude may very well depend on "Master Corporal Bloggins" out there in Recce Detachment 62A.

After being involved in enough situations of this nature, Mcpl Bloggins quickly loses any great concern over the problems involved in dealing with difficult company commanders. Diplo-macy is still required, but Mcpl Bloggins is quite confident in his ability to plan a company attack even without the expensive schooling.

Sun Tzu, a Chinese military philosopher from many centuries ago, wrote that "Every battle is won or lost before the first blade is struck." The wisdom of this saying is its implication that it is not massive combat power that wins the battle; it is the thorough knowledge of your enemy prior to the fight that wins the day. The commander who simply lines up his forces and advances towards an unknown foe is doomed to failure. Proper intelligence collec-tion is essential to preparing for every battle. The Battalion Recce platoon is the CO's best tool for collecting intelligence and prepar-ing his companies for the battles that await them.

It was during my first few months with Recce that the battal-ion received its first war tasking. On 2 August 1990, the Iraqi army crossed the border into Kuwait and began the Gulf War. In Germany, surrounded by the forces of NATO and the Americans, there was among Canadian soldiers an immediate sense of impending action. In fact, many of the units heading for Saudi Arabia departed from bases in West Germany. As the days passed and American units shipped out, rumours flew as to what the Canadian commitment would be.

All of us stationed in Germany followed the debates and statements from Parliament concerning deployment of Canadian Forces closely. We knew that if any fighting units were sent, they would come from our brigade in Germany. Canada had only two units at that time capable of deploying at short notice for combat operations; the Airborne and the Brigade Group in Germany. Knowing that the upcoming battle would be a fast-paced desert war, an armoured unit would be best suited and that meant us.

I began to research everything about the Iraqi's military, culture and terrain. All of us in Recce spent a lot of time in our platoon bar after work drinking beer and speculating about whether we would get to go or not.

For those civilians living in the big cities back in Canada arguing over who forgot to take out the trash or what the vjs on MTV were wearing this season, it may be hard to fathom that their fellow Canadians were sitting in Germany longing for a chance to get involved in a shooting war. This is one of the main reasons that the Forces is so often at odds with the civilian world. The type of individual who wants to be a combat soldier or fighter pilot is not someone who suits up in the civilian world. Soldiers are not identical, but they all share that same desire to challenge the world and dare the gods. A couple of centuries ago, they would be the explorers of new lands, the soldiers of fortune seeking wealth and fame abroad, the conquerors of people and places whose exploitation built our wealthy society. The same society that, now prosperous, shuns its benefactors as immoral, antisocial and unenlightened dinosaurs, badly in need of some sensitivity training.

Yes, we wanted to go to war. Why? I always compared our situation to that of an athlete who trains and trains to compete in a marathon. He spends his life torturing himself to prepare. If he never runs a single race, then his life was wasted, wasn't it? For a soldier it is the same. We train and train, causing all types of long-term damage to our bodies. If someone offers us a chance to "run a marathon" then you can be damn sure we will want to do it.

To the civilian, this desire must seem ludicrous. I have watched debates in Parliament over sending our troops overseas and into harm's way. The politicians rant on about how dangerous it will be for our innocent young men and women, as if the last thing the military wants is to hear a shot fired in anger.

In days past, the government, wanting to avoid the political fallout over ordering its troops into battle, asked for volunteers. South Africa, both World Wars and Korea, all began with calls for volunteers. If today's vote-conscious politicians haven't the courage to commit to a battle, they might try asking the country's soldiers. Not the careerist senior officers at National Defense Headquarters, but the soldiers out in the combat units. Back in the summer of 1990, if you had asked for volunteers, I'm sure there would have been no shortage.

Of course, life isn't that simple. Maintaining the integrity of units and finding qualified people for each piece of high-tech equipment would make this process difficult. The underlying point is, we would have volunteered. Naturally, our volunteering would probably have done no good. It would only serve to increase the gap of understanding between those in uniform and our incredulous populace.

In today's special-interest, issue-conscious, we-are-all-victims-of-something society, where does that leave the adventure-loving soldier? What morally corrupt special-interest group do we belong to? Who knows?

In any event, we could only sit and wait. We all read the news clippings of U.S. requests for our participation and the lukewarm Canadian responses. As the days dragged by, our hope for a major deployment waned. Rumours flew and everyone listened when someone said he had the inside scoop.

It was much later that I learned the story behind our Gulf War involvement. I ran into an old friend who had been one of the individuals responsible for formulating our military options. He explained to me how the government selected our contribution to the first major post-World War Two test of the western alliances. The initial plan was to accept the U.S. request of army combat units. Our commitment was to be either a Division or a Brigade. The government turned to the military and asked for a study of these possibilities. The military put together a team to formulate a response.

In Baden-Soellingen, we were told that the government had let the Americans know of our intent to deploy the Fourth Canadian Mechanized Brigade Group in Germany and possibly another Canada-based brigade to form an understrength division.

There were two immediate problems. We had no way to get our

troops to the Gulf, and no easy way to supply them once in theatre. Neither our units in Germany nor those in Canada could reach the war zone without help. The U.S. was busy moving its own forces and would have difficulty moving the Canadians as well. Still, they said they would do it. No problem, we were told; they needed the support of their allies and would work something out.

Except for one small issue. They didn't want us to bring our own tanks. "Your Leopard tanks will be the only ones in theatre," they explained. "This means tons of extra spare parts and equipment to be moved." Also, our German-built tank's 105 mm main gun fired a different shell than the U.S. 105 mm tank guns. It meant shipping in special ammo as well just for the Canadians. No, our tanks would impose a logistical nightmare.

In answer to this problem, the Americans offered to give us enough of their much more modern M1 Abrams tanks to equip our tank units completely. After the war, we could work out some arrangement to keep them. A deal of one dollar a tank was suggested. We could also leave our ancient M113s behind as well, if we wanted to, and replace them with the U.S. Bradley Fighting Vehicles. This was the newest thing in infantry transport and was almost a light tank in itself.

Meanwhile back in NDHQ, the planning wasn't going too well. The consensus was to plan for ninety days of combat. In actual fact, the battle only lasted one hundred hours, but who would have guessed? Better safe then sorry. The problem was that if we sent a brigade and had to replace estimated casualties, according to the best figures we would need to mobilize every militia soldier in Canada. That would not go over well with our "come out when you feel like it" militia reserves.

If we deployed a division it would be even worse. With the best-guess combat losses, we would have to institute national conscription to replenish our losses. Now that definitely would not go over well at 24 Sussex Drive or in downtown Toronto.

While the politicians were mulling this one over, someone must have mentioned the tank problem. Although our forces would leap into the world of modern fighting equipment with one inexpensive bound, it would mean that we would be committed for the future to buying more U.S. equipment and spare parts. Once we had these tanks and infantry combat vehicles in our inventory, we would need the spares and replacements for years to come.

I can see most politicians balking at this. The needs of the Forces are secondary, or even less, when compared with the political damage caused by not buying products built in Canada. All those members whose home ridings included defense contractors would have a tough time explaining that political fumble to wealthy political contributors. With no bargaining power to negotiate production licences in Canada after the war and already having the vehicles in service, we would be backed into a corner.

The government was in a quandary, no doubt. If they showed solidarity with their allies by contributing combat troops, they had to take the U.S. equipment. If they took the U.S. equipment, they lost the political support of influential Canadian contractors. If they sent even a brigade, they would need to call out the militia, which in Canada, is a volunteer-only organization. If they didn't send troops they would lose an immense amount of influence with their economic peers. Even the tiny island country of Britain was sending twenty-five thousand troops.

There was also the realization that if we sent troops and equipment, a lot of it might be destroyed. This meant buying more. Also, scenes of wailing mothers crying over lost sons and daughters, or left-wing lobbies decrying the actions of the militaristic West, would not go over well in the next election.

As in any difficult political situation, the answer was compromise. A solution was needed that would show some support but not endanger political careers or political funding. In an ideal bit of political waffling, it was decided to deploy twenty-four of our high-tech CF–18 fighters. These are cutting-edge combat aircraft that also make up a large portion of the U.S. air arsenal. Combined with fighter pilots that can outfly anyone in the world, these would be an excellent contribution to the coalition.

The problem with this plan was that they were damn expensive to replace. The government has never had any plan in place to replace lost aircraft. Therefore, we demanded the condition that our aircraft would not be ordered to fly into hostile airspace. We would patrol the Saudi border and release other coalition aircraft for offensive operations. That way, we couldn't lose too many planes. Our other contributions would be two warships, safely kept out to sea, and a couple of small combat units to guard hospitals and secure rear areas.

Back in Germany, this was the word. Our fighter squadrons

would be on their way to Saudi Arabia to join the coalition air forces. There would be an infantry company sent with them to guard their aircraft.

———

On the parade square, the CO, Lt Colonel Fenton, gathered the battalion. He explained the government's position and announced that an infantry company would be going to provide local security. We all waited with bated breath for the announcement as to which company would be going.

"I have given this careful thought," he said, "and I have chosen Mike company to go." He explained his decision briefly, noting that Mike company missed Cyprus in '86. "I wish them well," he finished.

A great cheer went up from the battalion. Out of all the forces at the military's disposal, they had chosen 3RCR! We were quite proud. Although recce hadn't been selected, it wasn't out of the question that a sniper team or a recce det might go along as an attachment. The important thing was that we would be getting involved in our first war since the Airborne had fought in Cyprus in the early seventies.

Later, another platoon was selected to fly to Bahrain and defend an installation there. We also found out that Charles company of 1RCR, back in London, Ontario, was on its way to secure a hospital and prisoner-of-war compound near the Iraqi border. The best part was that those cowboys, the Patricias, didn't get any work at all. The Van Doos did a rotation after us at the airfield, but it was the RCR that got the lion's share of the infantry taskings.

Recce did end up providing a sniper team to Mike company. A couple of good friends of mine got the nod. My contribution to the whole war effort was helping to train the Air Force personnel to use their personal weapons.

The standard Canadian individual weapon is a C7. This is basically a U.S. M16 rifle with a few modifications. It is produced by Diemaco in Toronto, Ontario, and is an excellent weapon, easily handled by even inexperienced troops. Like all military weapons, to be really effective its sights need to be adjusted to the individual shooter. To do this, each soldier is issued his own rifle. He notes its serial number and that is the only rifle he uses. The soldier takes his rifle out to a range and fires groups of

rounds through it. Because each shooter holds the rifle a little dif-
ferently due to height, weight and musculature, the sights must
be tuned to the individual's style. If a soldier wants to hit what he
is aiming at over fifty metres distance, this process is essential.

Therefore, we took the Air Force people out and instructed
them in the handling of weapons, some characteristics and how
to shoot them properly. We explained that they must memorize
their own weapon serial numbers so that after the sights were
zeroed to their individual styles, they could always use the same
weapon.

"If you want to survive any fighting, this is essential," we told
them.

For the Air Force types I was instructing, I used the example of
the Marine guard on duty when a car bomb was driven into the
Beirut barracks in Lebanon. The Marine on guard had failed to
stop the explosive-packed van and by the time he managed to contact someone who knew what to do, it was all over. I explained
how any of them might be on front-gate duty or even wandering
around when terrorists attacked. If they wanted to hit their targets
and prevent a disaster, they needed to know their weapons and
ensure they maintained them.

All this went in one ear and out the other. After arriving in the
Gulf, all the weapons were thrown into a trailer and locked up.
There they sat collecting dust. If they had been needed in an
emergency, the plan was to just hand out any weapon to personnel as they arrived at the weapons trailer.

The next couple of years went by quickly. Recce platoon was
what you made of it. I loved my work, sometimes staying late at
night in my little intelligence office making blow-up posters of
Russian tanks or reading U.S. training documents. Life was good.
Unknown to all of us at the time, our lives were about to under-
go some drastic changes.

In Germany, during the close of 1991, our other battle over
cultural and philosophical differences was drawing to a close.
The Cold War was over. In Berlin, Checkpoint Charlie was a
tourist attraction. Our state of readiness was declining monthly.
Already, politicians back home were talking about closing our
European bases. For us in Germany, that would mean an end to
our new lifestyle and a return to the "Motherland." For myself, I
did not relish going home. I liked Germany. I loved the people,

the food and the less hectic pace of daily life. Career-wise, where were we going to be exposed to the wide cross-section of foreign forces and their experience that we had in Europe? Humping a ruck over the plains of Shilo just did not compare to the highlands of Wales or the mountains of Bavaria.

I also knew that I was probably going to be promoted to Sergeant soon and that meant leaving Recce platoon. I would have to return to a rifle company to do my time as a Section Commander or some other less interesting job. I hated the thought of leaving Recce. I began to consider leaving the Forces. I didn't really want to stop being a soldier. It was my profession. I just didn't see much room to grow. One option that always teased me was the French Foreign Legion. There was a recruiting centre twenty minutes away in Strassbourg. I had no qualms about being a mercenary. Historically, the best soldiers were often mercenaries. Prussians serving with the Austrians, Germans serving with the Spanish, Swiss working for everybody. Most of our precious western military history is based on the mercenary calling.

It has only been in the last few years that the title "mercenary" has taken on criminal overtones. In actual fact, the profession of arms, like most other careers, crosses borders quite regularly. If a stockbroker is dissatisfied with his employer, he will most likely seek better terms elsewhere. The soldier is the same. In the Commonwealth, military professionals often move between national armies. Australians abound in the British Forces, Kiwis are throughout the Australian army. British troops often serve in Oman or the Sultanate of Brunei.

Today, Britain, France, India and a host of other countries all employ foreign soldiers as a matter of course. Some countries such as Nepal derive a large portion of their national income from exporting soldiers for foreign service.

I have always gravitated towards unconventional warfare, but unfortunately Canada had no Special Forces at that time. The Canadian Airborne Regiment was a possibility, but I mistakenly thought of them as only Parachute Infantry and not true "Special Forces."

Perhaps a stint in the Legion's 2 Foreign Parachute Regiment (REP) would keep life interesting. Maybe I could head for England and try SAS selection. I had also read in *Jane's Defense*

Weekly that the Australians were in need of troops, so I wrote their Ministry of Defense and corresponded with the recruiting department. During my last visit to London I had visited the Princess Gate, scene of the SAS's raid on the Iranian Embassy. While wandering around this neighbourhood, I looked up the Omani embassy and had stopped in to speak to their defence attache. In most British newspapers you can generally find advertisements for British soldiers to serve in Oman. He wasn't in, so I wandered off on my scenic tour.

As 1991 was ending and 1992 began, my mental wanderings about career options were interrupted by a large mess developing elsewhere in Europe. Slovenia and Croatia were both breaking away from the Yugoslavian Republic and the United Nations was getting involved. Our thinking was that, combined with the troubles in Czechoslovakia, the Baltic states and western Asia, we could be facing a greater threat of war then ever before. If any of these battles spilled over into NATO countries, that would be a declaration of war. With the proximity of Greece, Austria and Italy to Yugoslavia, we all paid close attention to the developing situation.

Little did I know that within a matter of a few months, my career was due for a big change. By the spring of 1992 I would find myself out of the doldrums of peacetime service and dodging sniper fire in my new blue beret.

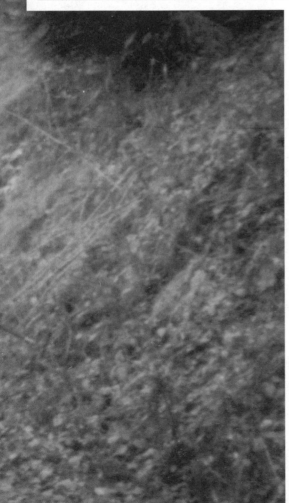

Overleaf: Troops from 3 RCR Recce Platoon mounted in a now-out-of-service Lynx reconnaisance vehicle in Germany. A cut-down version of an M113 APC, it was the standard transport for Canadian mechanized recce forces. JAMES DAVIS

Left: Recce troops on patrol in Germany. Canadians prefer three-man patrols as opposed to the four-, five- and six-man patrols common to our allies. JAMES DAVIS

Above: Pte. Rob McVeen at rest in the snows of Shilo, during the fall of 1986. His weapon is a now-outdated FNC2 LMG. JAMES DAVIS

Left: Mock terrorists from the Light Infantry Battalion capture air force flight crew during escape and evasion training at Petawawa. UNKNOWN

Above: Water flows past the carriers of November company 3 RCR on exercise in Germany, 1990. JAMES DAVIS

Right: Trooper practises his rapelling during house-clearing training. JAMES DAVIS

Patrolling the "dead zone" in Sector West. Large tracts of Croatian countryside were left lifeless as a result of "ethnic cleansing." MARTIN SPRIGGS

Left, top: A UN patrol navigates past a wrecked T-55 tank in Sector West, Croatia, 1992. MARTIN SPRIGGS

Right: UN checkpoint at the north end of no-mans-land in Pakrac, Croatia. Manned only by day, it reverted to Croat control after dark. MARTIN SPRIGGS

Left, bottom: Author being promoted to the rank of Sergeant in Croatia by his CO, Lt. Colonel Hatton (L), June 1992. UNKNOWN

Recce Platoon in Yugoslavia. Standing L to R: Sergeants Eric Hobbs, author, Jerry Williams, Jeff Elgie, Kevin Donovan and Warrant Officer Mike Sullivan. Seated L to R: Corporals Glen Faubert, Carl Fletcher, Winston Hewlin, Chris Sainsbury, Dave Predo, Glen Whitten, Master Corporal Wayne Nicholson, Captain Dave Ready, Corporals Brent Bannerman, Dave "Horse" Horochuk, Greg Alkerton, Glen Willis, Daryl Ballentyne, Pete Ainsworth and Dion Henn. UNKNOWN

Chapter 6

INTO YUGO

I STOOD ON THE SUMMIT *of the mountain. Beside me stood a Major from the Irish Army. Together we gazed out over the beautiful scenery of the city of Sarajevo. Nestled in a mountain valley, it reminded me of Bavaria or even British Columbia. There was a bit of haze in the valley far below us, but from our perch, we could see well out into the mountains to the west.*

The sun was shining and it was a warm summer's day. It was easy to forget for a moment that a war was on and in a few hours I would be back down there dodging bullets again. Unless, of course, I turned around to see the Ukrainian counter-battery radar vehicle ten metres behind me.

The Irishman, I don't recall his name, and I were speaking about the war here and the Troubles in Ireland. It was a philosophical conversation, a respite for us from having to face the day-to-day mess the UN was up against within the city below.

"You will have to remember what you see here," he said to me after a long pause, while we admired the scenery. "Remember it well, so that when you get home to Canada you can tell people what happens to countries when they break up."

I didn't respond to him. I was considering his words.

*"It's your responsibility, you know," he continued.
"I've seen it in my home. If your Quebec province tries to
leave, this may be the result," he finished, nodding
toward the city.
"I will . . . ," was my weak response.
We stood there for a moment, saying nothing.
"This your first mission?" I asked him.
"No, my sixth," he answered.
"How are you enjoying it?" I asked with a grin.
"Wonderful," he responded. "Actually I quite enjoy
working for this General MacKenzie of yours. Do you
know him?"
"Nope, first time I've met him," I said.
"Well, I'll tell you, I've worked for quite a few
commanders now with the UN and none of them even
compare with your MacKenzie. He's terrific. Probably the
only one who could handle this mess."
"Really?" I responded. "He seems pretty good." I
hadn't met a General officer before that I had any respect
for, until him.
"It isn't just me either," the Irishman continued,
"everyone thinks that. Even the press. I have a friend in
the BBC here. He was telling me that with most missions
they just wait around hoping the commander will screw
up, so they will have something to report. MacKenzie
hasn't made a single mistake though. My friend also
said that no one would report it anyway, even if he did."
I was quiet for a moment. Then I began my tale.
"Actually, he has already saved my life once. . . ."*

It was mid-February 1992 when we received the Warning Order for
a deployment to Croatia. In military parlance this meant, "Get
ready." Rumours had been circulating, but it wasn't until Major
Devlin, OC November, addressed the company that we knew for
sure.

Of course, what we knew for sure was sketchy. What we did
know was that our brigade had been put on standby to place an
undetermined number of troops at the UN's disposal for operations in Yugoslavia. Major Devlin made it quite clear he didn't

want anyone starting rumours. He would pass on information as he received it.

For most of us, there was a mix of elation and disbelief. We were excited at the prospect of deployment to a war zone but frankly suspicious of the Canadian government's determination to follow through. No one wanted to get his hopes up too high. Still . . .

"Fail to plan, plan to fail," I always say, so I began to research the country of Yugoslavia. I had a distinct feeling of déjà-vu from the Gulf experience. "I hope this one turns out better," I thought.

As the days went by, the situation became both clearer and more confused. It was decided to send an infantry battalion, but which one: us or the Van Doos? Then all seemed lost when the Van Doos' CO, Lt Colonel Jones, was appointed as commander of the formation. Everyone said, "I told you not to get your hopes up."

We began to train anyway. If the Brigade commander suddenly needed more troops, we wanted to be ready to go. As we entered March, there was still no clear picture as to what was happening. Lt Colonel Jones was on his way to Croatia for a week, to make a plan. Who was going would depend on what he found there.

Back in Baden, we began sorting out our wills. It is important to note that, at this time, Canada had not been involved in ground actions for more than twenty years. The Gulf war fiasco was not any standard to measure by. Not since the Airborne Regiment battled in Cyprus in the early seventies had we seen any real fighting. Cyprus of the last few years didn't count either. That conflict had become a long drawn-out stalemate marked only by occasional taunting by both sides. Somalia wasn't to become an issue until the fall of 1992. Were we ready? More importantly, was Canada and our government ready?

I dug into every thing I could find about Yugoslavia. I searched every periodical for photos, articles and, especially, first-hand accounts. I had a big board set up in the common area where I put up all the photos I could get. I got ahold of an English–Serbo-Croat dictionary and phrase book and started studying the basics of the language. I spent many long nights in my office preparing colour sketches of uniforms, equipment and the countryside.

It was a high-spirited time. Life became very focused in those days. All the daily distractions of social commitments, fixing the broken sofa leg, taking out the trash, faded away before the needs of the moment. The community fell in behind the operation as well. Wives formed committees and base clubs held supporting events to keep the families' morale up. Even the normally intransigent base facilities such as the photo shop and the base supply people suddenly had the time of day for us lowly grunt types. Normally, if I wanted a photo from a magazine turned into a slide for a presentation, I would have been laughed out of the Photo Technician's office. Now I could bring him bags of stuff to be duplicated and he would spend half the night getting it done.

This underlying feeling of commitment to a real event made our already-close Canadian military community even tighter. Life took on a new meaning and it affected all of us, from the lofty Base Commander, down to the wives and children.

Eventually, word came back from Lt Colonel Jones on his scouting trip. He envisioned a combined team of RCRs, the Van Doos and the Recce Squadron of Hussars. This latter outfit was basically a duplicate of our infantry recce platoon, mounted in Lynxes and normally employed in a forward screen role for the tankers.

In Baden, this made us feel better and, once again, even more confused. RCRs would be going, but in what capacity? Would it be like the Gulf, where the Air Force wanted us to do their laundry for them? Even worse news was the inclusion of the Recce Squadron. That meant they would get any recce role in theatre and we would not be required.

The choice of the Recce Squadron really pissed us off. We saw it as an attempt to include as many units as possible as opposed to sending just the required troops. This is what turned Desert One and the Grenada invasion into disasters for the U.S. military. Everyone wants a piece of the pie. Also, we saw Recce Squadron as not nearly as flexible an organization as ours. You needed a crowbar to pry their asses off the seats of their tracks. Armored recce units are designed to move fast and keep their mobile tanks from running into any nasty surprises. Although the "Black Hats" sometimes got out of their vehicles to do the occasional observation post, you needed to hold a pistol on them to get a rucksack on their backs for a long dismounted patrol. We, in infantry recce, were obviously a much better choice. We were effective in both roles.

I think, in retrospect, we were just a little jealous. None of us wanted to be left behind. We clung to the hope that they would need both types of recce forces. Let the tankers have their mounted recce role. Frankly, no self-respecting infantryman, even Recce troops, wants to be cooped up in those big, noisy tracked vehicles. We all felt far more comfortable with a ruck on our back and a rifle in our hands, out there in the safety of the darkness. The tankers could keep the vehicles. They were welcome to them.

I began studying the local language. I carried my little book around and whenever I spoke to other members of Recce, I tried to speak in Serbo-Croat. I intended to be at least able to read a sign or get the gist of a conversation in theatre. Fortunately, I can pick up languages fairly well and I was hoping to make a lot of progress before I ever reached Croatia.

Eventually, near the end of March, Lt Colonel Jones announced his plans for the upcoming operation. He intended to form his unit based around two overstrength companies. About one hundred men overstrength in fact. The first company would be based on Alpha company of the Van Doos. The second was to be formed on November company of 3RCR. Each outfit would be about two hundred and twenty in strength. He based his decision on the nature of the terrain. The area in which we would be operating was a thumbnail-shaped pocket of Serbs remaining inside Croatia. Called Sector West, this pocket had as its base a bridge crossing the Sava River. This river marked the border between Croatia and Bosnia-Herzegovina, presently in the hands of the Serbs and the remnants of the Yugoslavian National Army (JNA). The pocket extended northwards into Croatia for about sixty kilometres and was about twenty kilometres at the widest point.

The entire southern area was bisected by a major road. The CO planned to deploy A company west of the road and N company to the east. Eventually, we would be joined by an Argentinian Battalion to cover the north end of the sector and Jordanian and Nepalese Battalions to cover the south. That would leave us to handle the most contested territory in the centre of the zone. Until the other forces arrived, our unit would be responsible for a thousand square kilometres of ground.

The zone was roughly divided between Serb and Croat forces. Twenty kilometres south of our planned base in Daruvar, Croatia, was the front line of the fighting. Here, in the village of Pakrac, was the northernmost extent of the JNA lines. The Serb forces held all the ground south from Pakrac as far as the river. Any Serbs north of Pakrac were behind the Croat forces front line. By consolidating their defences with their backs to the river as an escape route, the Serbs had halted the Croat advance. The situation was basically static at the moment with both sides digging in. Minefields were everywhere and artillery duels common. The JNA forces had large quantities of tanks, artillery and engineering equipment but suffered from low morale and poor leadership.

The Croats, flushed with their recent victories and rapid advance, continued to threaten the Serbian JNA enclave. Despite their enthusiasm and relative inexperience, the Croats knew they could not defeat the heavily armed Serbs once they had dug in. With many Serb families trapped in the pocket, the JNA would probably fight fiercely to defend their last refuge inside the new Croatia. Added to this situation were bands of Serbian Chetnik guerrillas roaming the mountains in the eastern half of the zone. These extremists were known for their long beards and animal ferocity.

The Canadian plan was for the two companies to set up platoon-sized encampments across the Croatian-held areas to prevent the murdering of ethnic Serbs trapped behind Croat lines. As soon as possible we would try to establish lines of communication into the Serb pocket to reassure them that the UN was in place. Eventually, the UN hoped to insert itself between the two opponents and negotiate an end to the fighting.

To cover this wide area, the CO planned to utilize four recce platoons in addition to his two overstrength companies. He would use both the Van Doos Recce platoon and our Recce platoon to carry out missions for the Battle Group HQ. Each rifle company would also form its own recce platoon to help patrol its own area. While the rifle companies manned checkpoints and searched vehicles, the four recce platoons would range across the zone "showing the flag." The CO was bringing along a platoon of Combat Engineers to handle the mine clearance problems. There would also be the usual service and support elements to handle transport, rations, fuel and equipment.

This was all we wanted to hear! We were going! Even more importantly, we were going as a formed platoon and not broken up within the force. No less impressive was the fact that we would no longer work for November company. We were back to being an independent outfit, responsible only to the CO and his HQ.

The whole thing would get off the ground in less than three weeks. We needed to be in theatre by mid-April. I went home that day feeling as happy as I had been in years. I tried not to walk around with an idiotic grin on my face though; this was serious business. In addition to my elation with the mission, I also felt a little sorry for the tankers because they were staying behind.

"Well, better them than us," I thought.

Now there was even more work to be done. Equipment needed to be sorted out, vehicles painted UN white, personal affairs settled . . . so much! I needed to redouble my intelligence efforts now. I was alive with purpose! All of us were, running around with a great sense of urgency, everyone pitching in. Even the occasional officer got into coveralls to help prepare the vehicles. It was a great time to be alive.

As the sun rose in Baden-Soelingen on the morning of 11 April 1992, there was excitement in the air. The morning was cool, the sky clear and the sun bright, all promising a good day. Soldiers, lugging bags of last-minute personal gear, were strolling across the North Marg headed for their unit stores. Wives drove them in to work. There they said their goodbyes, for tonight the men would not be coming home for supper. Today they left for the former Yugoslavia.

Someone had decided to leave the Recce Lynxes behind and replace them with regular MII3s. So, in the last few days before departure, Recce had to collect a whole new batch of vehicles from different outfits. These tracks were in various states of serviceability, but with hard work we got them working and properly kitted out on time. Once the vehicles were warmed up, the drivers drove them up to the Recce stores building for final loading.

Once there, the weapons and electronic surveillance gear was loaded on board. Along with the regular gear, there was a wide assortment of extra kit. Each carrier was filled with its share of recreational items. I had brought a collection of power tools, hammers, nails and assorted building gear to use in improving whatever hovel we were expected to live in. Another vehicle held the platoon television and VCR. We also had a complete stock of products for our platoon canteen including chocolate bars, pop and about thirty cases of Heineken beer.

The atmosphere was relaxed, but with an underlying current

of anticipation. There were two schools of thought on what awaited us: those who still couldn't believe the Canadian government had the balls to send us into a war zone; and those who expected another boring Cyprus-style six-month drinking binge. I have always believed in preparing for the worst case scenario so that I am never caught in a situation I am not prepared for. After studying the conflict in Yugo, I had the distinct feeling that it was definitely not going to be a boring Cyprus-style tour. I wasn't sure what to expect, but I knew better then to believe that all we would see was a lot of Turk–Greco-style finger pointing.

Once the vehicles were ready, we mounted up and headed for the railhead outside the base. November company had begun loading its vehicles on the train that was to take us south at about 0200 hours. Recce was due to load at 0730. We weren't complaining.

Once we reached the railhead, the tracks were loaded one at a time onto the flatbed railcars. At the front of the train were five sleeper-style passenger cars. These would be our living space for the next little while. Our train would carry two hundred and fifty troops and more than fifty vehicles, both M113s and trucks.

A few wives had shown up for one last glimpse of the boys before they mounted up and departed. Prior to mounting up, we were gathered together at the loading ramp for a briefing about the trip. We were told that the trip was expected to take between thirty and forty hours. We would travel east to Munich, then turn south into Austria. Once we had passed through the Alps, we would enter Slovenia, one of the breakaway Yugo states. After Slovenia came Croatia.

As we stood there listening, I scanned the faces of the troops. My most vivid recollection is that of a young officer across the circle from me. His name was Drey and he was a lieutenant. He stood out from the crowd because, clutched closely under one arm, he held a great big fluffy pillow. Encased in a glowing white pillow case, it stood out like a sore thumb. I remember thinking, "Here we are headed off to war and he brings a feather pillow!" The embarrasment of it! However, after several months of sleeping on a rolled-up combat jacket for a pillow, I began to envy that young officer.

On completion of the briefing, we boarded our train cars. Recce was given one entire car to itself. With our total platoon numbers at twenty-one, we made ourselves quite at home in a car made for forty-eight passengers. Each compartment featured two benches, one on each side of the compartment. These doubled as beds. Folding down from the walls were another two cots on each side. With a total of six beds to a compartment, we settled in nicely for our voyage.

The train pulled out at 1230 hours and we all stood at the open windows watching as we slipped away from our home in the quiet heart of Europe. As night fell on our speeding train, I took out the journal a friend had given me. In it, I recorded my first feelings about the whole enterprise: *"For myself, I am calm. I feel lucky to be part of this adventure. Whatever lies ahead, I know I am surrounded by twenty of the best men I ever met."*

As morning dawned on day two, we were moving south through Austria. The sight of the Alps made for interesting viewing as we wandered back to the kitchen car to collect our breakfast. With a steaming mug of coffee in one hand and a deliciously greasy bacon-and-egg sandwich in the other, we watched the scenery slide by. Most of the troops had brought along a bottle of something or other. Jerry Williams passed around a nip of Irish Cream for our coffees.

At noon, we reached the Slovenian border. None of us knew what to expect, so we watched for signs of battle in the local countryside. Much to our chagrin, there was no apparent signs of fighting. Slovenia appeared to be a typically peaceful European state and showed no signs of recently having overthrown its government. There was no overt military presence, which, to a military mind, meant that the new government had the support of its populace.

Yugoslavia had been a country prepared for guerrilla warfare. Despite its communist government, it was extremely westernized. The populace had a fairly high standard of living. There were good schools, televisions and Levi's jeans. Anyone could travel out of the country on vacation if he or she wished. Imported products were not held in contempt by the leadership. Basically, the pre-war Yugoslavia could have been any left-leaning western European state.

Because of their liberal ways, the government always had a great fear of the Soviet Union. When both Hungary and Czechoslovakia had drifted too far to the right of the communist spectrum in years past, the Russian-dominated Union had swooped down and crushed their governments. Yugoslavia, under the iron discipline of Marshal Tito, had been determincd to prevent the same fate for their own progressive version of communism. Consequently, unlike their unfortunate predecessors, the Yugoslav defence assets were spread in small allotments around the countryside. Their was no centralized command that could be targeted and destroyed. In its place was a system of weapons caches hidden in the mountains and forests. All men in the country were trained in basic military tactics and, in event of invasion, would fade into the mountains to resist. It was in this fashion that the Serbs had resisted forty divisions of Germans during World War Two.

These irregular formations were supplemented by the Yugoslavian National Army (JNA), who provided the traditional military forces. The JNA was a conscript force, drawing their recruits from across the cultural spectrum of the country. Officers were, for the most part, ethnic Serbs and provided political reliability to the military.

Therefore in 1991, after the fall of the Soviet Union and the death of Marshal Tito, the separate provinces of the Yugoslavian Republic were in a good position to separate from the Serb-dominated federation. Every village literally had access to a supply of modern military weapons, including anti-tank missiles, explosives and mines. When the province of Slovenia announced it was separating in the summer of 1991, the government's defence policy was turned against the JNA. The JNA forces were quickly routed. The well-armed Slovenes simply surrounded the JNA bases and demanded surrender. Realizing they were hundreds of miles from Serbia and surrounded by a determined, well-equipped and trained foe, the Serb officers acquiesced and were allowed to leave the new state.

So, as we travelled through the peaceful countryside, we were a little surprised to find no signs of a struggle. The whole affair had been a well-managed coup and had done no visible damage.

A sense of anxiety was growing in us all though. We wanted to get to Croatia as soon as possible. The imaginings of our destination could only be laid to rest by our arrival. Drifting through this quiet Slovenian landscape only served to heighten our feeling of anticipation.

The most interesting development during the whole trip so far had come shortly after crossing the Slovenian border. While the train paused to be inspected by the local authorities, we had been placed next to a similiar train carrying Czech troops to their UN sector in the west of Croatia. We were meeting our former enemies for the first time. For the past forty years, these men had been our sworn opponents. We would have destroyed western Europe to prevent their kind from taking it.

You wouldn't have known it that morning. Without the politicians preaching hate, we were all just grunts on our way to an uncertain future. We reached across and exchanged the international currency of soldiers: beer, food and pornography. As the Czech train pulled away, we wished them luck. I think, from looking in their faces, that they held similiar feelings to ours about the whole affair.

We finally reached the Croatian border at 1800. The locals seemed quite happy to see us. To them, I think our presence was a sign of international recognition of their quest for independence. All along the route we would find civilians waving gaily at the train. The sight of fifty glistening white military vehicles, all proclaiming "UN," and five carloads of smiling Canadian troops must have made a good impression.

As the sun set, we reached the capitol of the new Croatia, Zagreb. Here we found a pleasant European city going about its business. Here and there we noticed uniformed men, but there were no automatic weapons or armoured vehicles. Once again, we could find no signs of fighting.

Because the sun was setting and it was only a couple more hours to Daruvar, our destination, it was decided to halt the train for the night. No one wanted to arrive in the dark. From all reports, fighting was likely anywhere from thirty kilometres outside the city to the Bosnian border, some fifty kilometres to the south. The train pulled into a large railyard and we dismounted some armed guards to secure our equipment.

While I watched the sun setting, one of the boys was talking to a Croat policeman nearby. The policeman asked where we were going and the soldier replied, "Daruvar." The policeman just smiled and said, "War."

The train was on its way just before first light. Once again, we sipped hot coffee and ate our breakfast while observing the countryside. There was no liquor today; in several hours we would be unloading the vehicles into an unknown situation.

As the train progressed, we finally began to see signs of warfare. Houses scarred by bullet holes, mortar impact scars on the paved roads and more soldiers. As we neared Daruvar, I remember passing five Croatian soldiers standing at a level crossing. One of them had a mine detector out and appeared to have just finished clearing the railway crossing. They stood there, quite relaxed, grinning at us while we passed.

Finally, we entered the outskirts of Daruvar. As the train slowed to a crawl, we had ample opportunity to examine the massive damage to some of the buildings. One three-storey apartment block beside the tracks appeared to have had its rear wall simply sliced off, revealing the shattered interior of the building. Nearly every building showed signs of small-arms hits and some houses had been gutted by fire as well.

When the train halted, we gathered our kit and dismounted into a small courtyard beside the tracks. We were immediately formed up into a hasty parade and briefed on the upcoming events. The vehicles would be dismounted and, as soon as possible, we would be on our way to our different camps.

For the next few hours we offloaded our vehicles and sorted them out. Once Recce's tracks came off, we parked them in the courtyard and mounted our machine guns. We did a radio check and, when everyone was ready, we moved out into the surrounding village streets. The local populace seemed to be moving about fairly calmly. From this, we assumed there to be no immediate threat. Still, we kept our guard up.

We headed south out of Daruvar and climbed up into the hills south of the town. Our M113s' engines roared and our tracks made a terrible racket on the pavement. As we passed children and women in the streets, they would inevitably cover their ears and small children would cry. With our radio headsets on, the sound was somewhat muffled and we concentrated on the terrain around us.

This part of Croatia was primarily rolling, forested hills. There were homes and farms all along our route, but a good three-quarters of them had been destroyed. In the remaining houses, women hung out laundry, children played and farmers worked in the fields using only their hands. Ten minutes up the road from Daruvar we came to the gates of our new home, Camp Polom.

Camp Polom was formerly a JNA chemical warfare base. During the fighting, the Serbs manning the base defenses had held out for a short while. All around the base were signs of a fierce struggle. All of the buildings were pocked by small-arms hits. Many of the walls had large holes in them, which I assumed to have been caused by tank or rocket fire. As we drove into the camp, we could see large areas which had been cordoned off because they were filled with unexploded munitions. Canadian Combat Engineers had arrived ahead of us and had already begun the task of clearing the buildings and grounds of mines and booby traps.

We were led to a small area on the north side of the camp. Here we would park our vehicles and set up our modular tents. Dismounting from our carriers, we were met by a Sergeant-Major from the Engineers. He gave us a quick briefing on the camp layout and its dangers.

"This base had some type of chemical warfare role," he said. "The area you are in now is the base administrative side. Out that-a-way," he gestured behind him to the south, "is the ammunition dump."

We all just stared back at him. He definitely had our attention.

"This is an example of how the JNA liked to think about chemical warfare," he said, holding up a rather silly-looking gas mask with an elongated nose piece. "This was designed for use by a donkey. The Yugos seemed to use donkeys a lot for hauling their gear around the mountains." This certainly fitted in with a guerrilla mentality, I thought.

"Stay clear of any areas marked with white mine tape," he continued. "There is quite a bit of unexploded ordnance around here. In fact, don't even step on the grass if you can help it."

We all glanced down at our feet to confirm we were on a paved road. Then our eyes naturally wandered over to the grassy slope beside us. Was death lurking there?

"Behind your tent area, there is a gap in the wire. The Croats bashed through there with a tank. The area is littered with unexploded RPG rockets they fired at it. Guess they were too close. Anyway, as the story goes, once the tank was in it basically shot up the base."

I glanced up at the main buildings. "So those *were* tank hits," I thought to myself. Having never seen what a tank would do to a house, it had only been an educated guess.

"We get a lot of shooting here, mostly at night. They don't seem to be serious about it, just testing us, I think."

The Sergeant-Major went on to explain the sanitation rules and the duty roster. He finished by saying it was a bit too early for lunch, but we could head over to the mess tent to get a sandwich if we wanted.

Warrant Officer Sullivan wanted to sort out the site before we started setting anything up, so he told us to go and get a snack. We all wandered over to the mess tent. There wasn't much laid out except for a couple of loaves of bread. We found some peanut butter and dug in.

We were in love. The bread we were eating was the most succulent bread in the world. I had thought German bread had been good, but this stuff was incredible. It was soft, and moist, and even the crust almost melted in your mouth. We wolfed down all the remaining loaves. It was a feeding frenzy, and I don't remember even feeling particularly hungry. As long as they kept serving this bread, my morale wasn't going to suffer.

The rest of our first day was spent setting up our tents and getting our carriers unloaded and ready for work. We heard occasional firing. None of it was serious. We just went on about our duties and by nightfall were comfortably ensconced in our big tents.

As night fell, so did the temperature. It became quite cold in our unheated tents and everyone was rummaging through his kit for a warm sweater. We had no duties that first night and the boys just played cards, listened to Walkmans or wrote letters home. I sat with the other NCOs, having a beer and chatting.

Occasionally, we would hear shots. There was considerably more shooting after dark than there had been by day. On one occasion, a single bullet cracked close over our tents. We all wandered outside, trying to locate the shooter. We stood in the dark waiting for another round, hoping to at least figure out if there was a threat, or if it was just a drunken Croat having a laugh at our expense. We weren't too worried about being hit. It was dark and the locals didn't have much in the way of night vision equipment, or so we were told. No other shot followed, and our morbid fascination with the idea that someone was shooting at us waned. We did hear some distant artillery fire and wondered who was on the receiving end. Eventually, we lost interest and moved back to our beers and conversations.

Suddenly, in plowed Captain Ready.

"November Company is being mortared!"

We all sat up, suddenly very alert.

"Their camp's been hit. They're evacuating and should be on their way here now."

Up until that moment, none of us really thought that either side would target us. We were Canadians, for Christ's sake. Who the hell would want to shoot at us? It was that little shell of emotional security we all pulled close to our minds, the safety blanket that prevented us from danger. We were the UN! For all those that had thought this to be another lazy Cyprus tour, the party was over.

Having nowhere to put the November company troops, it was decided to remove all the tables from the mess hall for sleeping space. During the afternoon, the engineers had erected a huge beer-hall style tent that now housed our eating area. It would easily accommodate November company's two hundred-plus troops.

As I left our tents to head for the mess hall and give a hand, I heard a loud thunderclap. "Mortars," I thought, and quickly ducked down behind a carrier in the dark. When no other shells followed, I raised my head. I could see through the door of the well-lit mess tent that the sound had come from someone dropping a six-foot wooden table onto the concrete floor. The echoing sound had been magnified by the still night air and it had startled me. Glancing quickly around to make sure no one had seen me cowering, I headed once again for the mess hall.

After finishing the job of prepping the mess hall, we all shrugged and, with nothing else to do, went back to our tents. We were all on alert, but that only meant no sleeping. As the minutes dragged by, we waited for some word as to what was happening. Finally, Captain Ready showed up and said that November company was not coming in. The mortaring had stopped and they would remain in location, rather than risk a move by night. We didn't want the local Croat forces hearing artillery and then a large number of tracked vehicles moving in the night. They could well assume a Serbian assault was under way and move to engage the unfortunate November company.

Eventually, everything calmed down and we were stood down. Having nothing better to do, and a long day ahead tomorrow, I went to ground.

The story of November company's experience came out over

the next few days. I was not there and my knowledge of the
incident comes only from accounts given by friends of mine who
were involved. I will recount the tale because it had a profound
effect on us all.

November company had left the railhead in Daruvar and
headed south into the hills towards Camp Polom. Several kilometres short of the main camp, the company swung southeast on a
well-paved road and headed for the town of Sirac, some three
kilometres from Polom. Here, on a soccer field, they made camp.
The vehicles were lined up parade-square fashion, in neat straight
lines, and were unloaded. The troops set up tents and enjoyed a
fine supper prepared by the company cooks who had brought
along a field kitchen. Everything was NATO standard.

Of course, it was standard for a relaxed administrative camp
somewhere back in Germany, not an active war zone. There were
no defences established. No slit trenches dug. No weapons sighted.
No emergency plan. November company might have got off the
train in Manitoba, for all the concern they displayed. Not that anyone in the entire Battle Group had done any better. All of us arriving that afternoon expected . . . what? Certainly not an attack.

After supper, the troops began wandering off to their tents and
climbing into their sleeping bags. Some hung around the canteen
sipping pop or munching on chips. There were several poker
games going, as there always are.

As the sun grew near the horizon and the air became still, the
troops of November company were treated to a display of firepower by some unknown faction. Nearly a kilometre away, several mortar rounds impacted, throwing up great clouds of dirt
and debris. Most everyone moved to where they could get a better look. Someone was getting plastered. A minute later several
more shells landed a bit closer. More troops gathered to have a
look. They had all seen mortar fire before, but not fired at people. They were just glad that it was someone else getting the crap
knocked out of them.

Four more rounds impacted only four hundred metres away.
This was getting close. Those guys had better watch it! Those
things could get dangerous inside a hundred metres. Some of
those in the crowd began to get a little nervous. "If these clowns
weren't more careful, they were going to hit us," they thought!

Four more impacts hit only two hundred metres away. "Could

they be walking their fire onto us?" many of them thought. Quite a few started walking towards the APCs, the only shelter available. Even a direct hit shouldn't damage a carrier.

In the CQ's tent, two Sergeants were watching the display. They began to realize something was wrong and began walking towards the carriers like everyone else. Sergeant "Smith," as I will call him, began berating Sergeant "Brown" because the latter began to jog towards the carrier. He wasn't afraid, was he?

The next salvo landed at the edge of the camp, fifty metres from the two NCOs. Sergeant Smith, no longer teasing Sergeant Brown, nearly bowled over his partner in his haste to reach the safety of the M113s.

They were aiming at us! Now rounds began to fall on the camp as the gunners got the range and bearing. Great gouts of earth were thrown up from the explosions of the bombs. The concussions compressed the air and sucked the breath from your lungs. Pandemonium reigned as troops threw themselves in the dirt or sprinted for the tracks.

Reaching the rows of APCs, everyone realized they were locked! Normal Standard Operating Procedures. Only the drivers had the keys. Everyone crawled under the carriers or got behind them, waiting for someone to get a track open.

Private Edwards, a quiet and unassuming Native Canadian, climbed up on his track. The only way to unlock an APC is through the driver's hatch located on top of the vehicle. While Edwards fumbled with the lock, a mortar blast sent him sailing from the top of the carrier. Other drivers edged up onto their vehicles, trying to unlock them and reach safety. Edwards, shaken but undeterred, climbed back up onto his vehicle.

Finally, one of the drivers got into his track. He dropped the rear ramp. Suddenly, fifty soldiers tried to cram themselves into the one vehicle. Sgt Smith, recovering his composure, ordered the troops out. It was his track.

One by one, the vehicles were opened up. The panic still wasn't over. The carriers had been parked parade-square tight, in some cases with only centimetres between them. As the drivers raced to get out of the impact area, they bounced off each other's vehicles and ran over fences, equipment and trees. Troops inside were thrown about as the drivers made a headlong dash to get clear of the area. One vehicle ran over the electrical generator. The drivers were driving with their hatches down and using vision ports only. Since we never practised this and the view was extremely limited, everyone was running nearly blind.

Finally, the vehicles and their stunned cargo made it away from the camp. The officers tried to restore some order. The company recce platoon commander tried to lead his platoon away in the darkness without any lights on. Using standard combat procedure to avoid giving yourselves away, he intended to lead his platoon to safety.

It was at this point someone realized the implications of a move, by night, so soon after a mortar bombardment. Normally, attacks are preceded by mortar and artillery fire. This very well might appear to the Croats up the road to be a Serb assault.

Still, where was safe? Had the Croatians mortared us or was it the Serbs? The nearest Serb lines were over ten kilometres away and mortars usually only have a maximum range of about eight. If it had been the Croats, well, we were all living inside Croat territory! Where do you run to?

By the time order was restored, the mortaring had stopped. The decision was made to just sit out the night, and wait for dawn.

Back in Camp Polom, things were just beginning to quiet down when word came that now A company headquarters had been hit by artillery fire. They were roughly eight kilometres to our west. It seems the Croats had moved some Russian-made 122 mm self-propelled guns to a position very close to the company HQ. They had fired on the Serbs and, in retaliation, the Serbs had fired back, hitting A company.

While we were all standing around Camp Polom wondering if the whole place had gone mad, a small car drove up to the front gate and the passenger fired a couple of rounds at the sentries. Then it sped away before the startled Canadians could return any fire.

So went our first night in Croatia. "Welcome, my UN friends!"

The next morning, as an extremely cold and grey dawn broke, November company examined the damage. Many of their vehicles had been hit. The CQ's truck had been riddled by shrapnel. Some of the tents were only metres from the shell holes. A sense of awe filled the troops. This was battle. One-sided, but those rounds had been meant for them. Amazingly, no one had been hurt. In a streak of luck they had all escaped reasonably uninjured.

Private Edwards had been hit in the buttocks by a small piece of shrapnel. The medics took care of it without any problems. Considering his heroic efforts, it was an ungracious place to receive a battle wound.

At Camp Polom, we all rose with the sun and prepared for our second day in this wonderful place. Reports of the night's actions were filtering in and Captain Ready headed off to get some information on the situation. When he returned, he gave us the poop as he understood it. The situation was pretty much the same. Protests were being lodged with both sides, but neither the Croats nor the Serbs admitted to firing on us. As the Platoon Commander finished, he asked if anyone had any questions. Apparently, I was the only one.

"Sir, what are the medevac [emergency medical evacuation] procedures if one of us is seriously wounded?" I asked.

Since last night, I had been thinking about the implications of fighting breaking out between us and any of the local forces.

Captain Ready opened his mouth as if to give an answer, but none was forthcoming. As several of the troops were still standing around, and the issue was an important one, Ready felt obligated to answer.

"I don't know," he said, "but I will find out."

A short while later he returned from HQ and announced that, at the moment, there was no medevac plan. For now, all we had were our medics and our medical officer.

"So, if one of us were seriously wounded, say in need of surgery, what would happen?" I asked.

He was clearly becoming a little frustrated. I am assuming it was because this kind of talk could hurt morale if it became widely known. "They'd probably drive you to Zagreb, I guess."

I nodded and walked away.

So, we must be either the most confident army in the world, or the stupidest. How could we deploy to Croatia without any proper medical coverage? A three-hour drive to Zagreb was not promising in the event of a serious combat wound. Hell, even an attack of appendicitis could kill you in three hours!

We had failed to bring helicopters and had no hospital. This was one of those moments when I had serious doubts about our officer corps. It was quite apparent that we, as an army, simply would not react to any threat until we had been hit by it once. Fail to plan, plan to fail!

Actually, this whole line of thinking got me around to what would happen if the Croats turned on us. At some conference table in New York or Geneva, I'm sure that this idea wouldn't even occur, but out here in Sector West, we had already been attacked three times in less than twenty-four hours. To me, it was a serious question, one that would nag at me for some time to come.

The next few days passed quickly. We had to go into Daruvar and provide traffic sentries for an arriving train of Van Doos. My det was sent to an intersection in the centre of town. We found out quite quickly that the place was a leave centre for Croat troops rotating out of the front lines. Everywhere there were soldiers. Or those pretending to be soldiers. One character looked like a carbon copy of a Rambo film, complete with sleeveless t-shirt, headband and a huge knife on his hip. All of them seemed attracted to us. Soon, we had hundreds of locals gathered around, staring at us. Not unfriendly, but merely curious. "Who are these UN soldiers?" they seemed to be asking.

We found over the next little while that the locals, not being professional soldiers, felt a little intimidated by us. We had all the kit, we were disciplined and were obviously tough. These men had been fighting for several months but were still not professionals. They scavenged for uniforms and had a wide variety of weapons. As soon as these men could, they would be back to their wives and old haunts. Up until our arrival though, they had been winning a war against a former oppressor who had been far better armed then they. No doubt, the Croats felt a great pride in their accomplishments. They were the Kings of the Hill.

Enter the UN. We had shown up only after the worst of the fighting was over. Now, with our high-tech kit and our cocky attitudes, we had undoubtedly left these "liberators" feeling like a rag-tag bunch of amateurs in their cast-off camouflage and sandals. We had suddenly displaced them from being in control of the situation and were now getting the international credit for being the saviors of the Croat people. The Croat army had been doing fine before we arrived. No doubt many of these soldiers resented us and the implications of our arrival.

Of course, for others, it meant that we would take over the front lines and they could return to pick up the pieces of their lives. In truth, we weren't in Croatia to defend the Croats or replace their fledgling army. We were there to ensure the Croats weren't murdering Serbs and vice-versa. The sooner both sides went home, the better, thought the UN.

Many of the Croat soldiers milling about the square stared at us while they sipped Cokes. Local citizens went about their business, shopping and relaxing in cafes that lined the square. The morning town bustled with activity and in the middle of it sat a thirteen-ton APC painted day-glo white and sporting a loaded .50 calibre machine gun manned by an alert foreign soldier.

Eventually, the local children approached us. All soldiers are suckers for kids and, soon enough, they were hanging around us in knots. Once the ice was broken, the occasional Croat soldier would stroll over and attempt to talk to us. I had been making progress with my Serbo-Croat but wasn't ready for a conversation.

The topic that always bridged the gap between us and any local troops we encountered was weapons. If we wanted to talk to the local troops we would go up to them and ask them about their weapons. Soldiers are always proud of whatever arms they are carrying and quite willing to show them off. To the Croats and Serbs, our M16s represented all the Hollywood action flicks they had been watching for years. No one in the country had these weapons, and they were all curious.

We, quite willingly, showed them our weapons. We would usually remove the magazine and show the troops that the weapons we used were loaded. Then we would make a show of letting the Croats see how many mags we were carrying. We wanted to make sure the Croats knew that we were combat troops and well armed. Occasionally, we would allow a local to handle the C7 to test its weight. They all admired them for the "cool" factor the M16 held amongst their comrades.

Conversely, we would take great interest in local weapons for other than friendly reasons. In Recce, we used these exchanges of weapon admiration to gain insight into the status of the local forces. We wanted to know if the weapons were Yugoslav in origin or were they imports? If so, from where? As days went by, Romanian variants began showing up in large numbers. Also, how well were the weapons maintained? Most importantly, how much ammo did they have? The majority of the magazines we saw removed from weapons held fewer than five rounds. Did this mean ammo was in short supply? Also, when shiny, new rounds showed up, we wanted to know from where. Intelligence gathering was our business. After a while, it becomes a difficult habit to break.

The rest of our time was spent getting our living quarters sorted out. We had been given an old ammo warehouse in the ammo dump to use as a shelter. The only problem was that the roof had been destroyed when the Serbs had blown up the contents prior to losing the base. Even more disconcerting was the presence of thousands of small plastic vials of chemicals. This having been a chemical warfare base, we were curious as to what they were. A medic corporal came down, had one look and pronounced them safe. Rather doubtfully, we swept the place out and mopped the floor several times.

The ammo dump covered an area of about ten hectares. Most of it was thickly wooded and through these trees ran a single road in a large circle. Spread out along this route was a mixture of concrete warehouses roughly thirty metres by twenty in size and underground bunkers. In one area, far back in the dump, there was a huge crater. The retreating Serbs had stacked up a huge pile of mines, ammunition and God-knows-what-else. They had blown up the whole mess, scattering debris for hundreds of metres and leaving a huge crater.

In our building's area, near the main camp, there were four of these concrete warehouses. One belonged to the Van Doos Recce platoon, the next was ours, the third was badly damaged and missing its roof completely and the last one belonged to the Combat Engineers. We had originally been given the building with no roof at all, but Warrant Sullivan sorted that out immediately. We received the second building, with most of its roof intact. Immediately, we got to work scavenging the materials we needed to complete our building.

We needed roof tiles and wooden beams. Some items we took from the damaged building next to us. Others were liberated from different sources. There had been a wooden building in the middle of the ammo compound. One night the boys backed up a truck to it and came away with all its roofing. The next night they went back and took the rest of the building. We also took some tiles from the engineers' roof because they hadn't moved in yet. We knew the engineers would just replace their roof anyway, so we figured we were just giving them a hand.

The platoon had been told it would start patrolling on 30 April. The plan was for the two Battle Group Recce platoons to patrol the southern Serbian enclave while the companies covered their own areas. Before we could enter the enclave, UN Liaison Officers (LOs) would have to negotiate our crossing sites in no-man's-land. Then the crossing sites would have to be manned by UN troops. All this would take time, so we used our leisure hours to make our home as comfortable as possible.

We added a hot water shower and a weight room. We built a bar inside and liberated some kitchen equipment so that we could do some of our own cooking. Out back, we built a patio and a fire pit with bench seats. Jeff Elgie had brought some seeds and planted a garden with tomatoes, corn and potatoes.

On 20 April, the Croat forces began an offensive twelve kilometres to our south in the area of Pakrac. At this time, the town was contested ground with the Serbs holding the south side and the Croats the north. Anticipating the UN troops coming in and stabilizing the situation soon, the Croats hoped to sieze control of the town. However, the Serbs held the hills south of the town, and with extensive amounts of mortars and artillery in place, the Serbs were in a good position to hold.

On 24 April we were alerted for a possible operation in A company's sector. A Serbian woman had approached some Van Doos and told them the Croats were coming to destroy her village that night. She asked the UN to protect the villagers. Our rules of engagement were a little hazy here, but it was decided to make our presence felt, hoping this would serve to discourage the Croats.

Recce platoon was on standby to react to any threats caused by our interference in the Croat plans. This was going to be our first combat mission and we were hyped up. The Van Doos might get involved first, but we would be called if there was fighting or a serious threat the Van Doos couldn't handle. Everyone was keyed up and ready to go.

At 2000 hours the phone rang. Everyone of us froze. Captain Ready took the call. After he placed the phone down he turned to us.

"Stood down," he said.

We all sagged. We had been practising intravenous drips and

as soon as that was done we all cracked a beer. We looked around at each other. So far, no one had reacted badly to the threat of action. Everyone had seemed ready to go. That was good. We drank some beer and put on a movie. The picture was *Pretty Woman*, starring Julia Roberts.

This film enthralls soldiers. Training in Wales earlier, all the troops were seeing this movie. Guys kept saying it was a great film. Everytime it comes on, soldiers everywhere just can't seem to resist it. I had imagined it to be some kind of woman's picture and not worth watching. Finally, back in Germany, I had rented it and, I almost hate to say it, loved it.

I think, deep down inside, most soldiers are romantics. We believe in the virtues of old: honour, duty, courage and love. This film has all of these, hidden inside a romantic comedy. We envy the hero, a super-rich corporate pirate who has it all. We also sympathize with the prostitute, as played by the lovely Julia Roberts. Since this line of work is the only one older than soldiering and is only slightly better regarded by the public, we empathize with her attempts to achieve respect.

Whatever the secret, we went from adrenaline-pumped combat troops, ready for action, to a bunch of teary-eyed romantics, guzzling beer, in a matter of an hour. I wrote in my journal that night about this film and our reaction to it. The end of the entry follows: *"Just another reason I love being a soldier. We may not be the smartest, or the wealthiest, or the most respected men in the world, but we are the finest. All that is best in men."*

––––––––––

A couple of days later we began to do some patrolling in November company's area. This was a chance to get out and practise our skills and also have a look at the countryside. Getting a feel for an area means spending a lot of time observing the lay of the land and meeting the people. Only when you are in tune with your environment are you able to detect changes in it. A subtle change in the attitude of the locals could alert us to problems in advance. You can learn to read the signs pretty quickly and get a sense of when the locals are friendly, tense or frightened.

We began patrolling down into the southern portion of November company's sector. The majority of this sector was high, forested mountains and the southern boundary ran east-west along the Pakra River valley. This narrow valley also marked the line between the Serbs and Croats in the area. Running along the northern bank of the river was the Dragovic road. The Croats were established in platoon-sized strongpoints along this road, covering the Serb-held Cukur hills on the south bank.

On our first patrol out, we began to get a sense of what was going on in this country. Travelling east from November company's HQ in Sirac, the land became dead. In village after village we could find no signs of life. The whole area had been wiped clean. Almost every house had been destroyed. Barns had been razed. All the animals in the farms had been slaughtered. The whole area smelled of death.

We would drive along the Dragovic road and then turn north into the hills, heading for the small villages that dotted the hills. Every one of them was empty. We would pull up into the centre of a village and stop. Immediately, that sickly sweet smell of rotting flesh would hit you. From our vehicles, we would search the windows and doorways, but no one ever emerged.

Where had all these people gone? Was the smell of rotting flesh just the cattle? At each village I would make a note on my map, "Dead."

On one of the side roads, we ran into a group of Croat soldiers blocking the route. They insisted we turn around. We weren't allowed into this area. Our curiosity was piqued, so the next day another detachment under Sergeant Kevin Donovan approached the site from the rear. Before the Croats could react, he was in their position. What they found was field artillery, hidden in the trees. The Croats didn't want us to know about this equipment. They didn't trust us and thought that we might inform the Serbs.

In a nearby Croat position, the road was blocked by mines and a sentry post. No one was allowed up this road. Some pressure had been applied to the local Croat commander and our patrol, with Sergeant Jerry Williams in the lead, was tasked to go and have a look. When we arrived, there was some last-minute haggling and then we were waved forward. The Croats had pulled two anti-tank mines from the centre of the road over to the sides to allow us to pass. The trail was narrow though, and this allowed a gap of less than a third of a metre on either side. Either one of these mines could destroy our vehicles. The Croats could have moved them further, but it was a challenge of sorts and we weren't about to let them intimidate us. If they got one-up on us once, they might be tempted to try even more. Like spoiled children who are always trying to test where the line is drawn, these Croats wanted to see if we would back down.

Jerry just told his driver to take it easy and, with my vehicle following close behind, we edged between the mines. The Croats watched closely, not wanting to appear frightened of an explosion. We found nothing of great interest. Obviously, whatever had been there was now gone, hauled away before we could see it. Still it was a victory in the battle of wills for us.

Another test of wills took place several days later. While my patrol was working up in the hills east of Sirac, 71 and 71A detachments under Sergeant Eric Hobbs and Master Corporal Wayne Nicholson were patrolling the Dragovic road as it turned southwest towards Pakrac. We could not yet get closer than a couple of kilometres from Pakrac. There was too much fighting. We would patrol the road up to a point three kilometres from Pakrac and then turn around. 71 Patrol had been tasked to drive down the road and turn around. The area was under constant surveillance by both sides and tensions were high.

Back in 72 Patrol, we were halted on the side of a road doing a navigation check, when we heard Wayne's voice come over the radio.

"69er, this is 71A, we have a problem, over."

"69er, send, over," replied Captain Ready from his command post.

"71A, I am surrounded by a platoon of Croats. They have a machine gun pointed at us and say we are under arrest. If we try to move, they say they will shoot us, over," said Wayne's calm voice over the air.

Immediately, we forgot what we were doing and concentrated on the situation developing to our south.

"69er, send your Loc Stat, over," replied Captain Ready, asking for his location state.

Wayne read off a grid and both Jerry Williams and I plotted it on our maps. It was about a twenty-minute drive away.

"71, this is 69er, what is your status, over," asked Captain Ready. He wanted to know where Sergeant Hobbs was in relation to 71A.

"71, we are approximately figures one hundred metres from 71A, over," replied Eric.

"69er, this is 71A. The locals here want 71 to close up with us, over," reported Wayne.

This meant trouble. As long as 71 remained some distance away with their .50 calibre machine gun pointed at the Croats, 71A had some support. It was an insurance policy. If 71 pulled up close, the weapon would be useless and the troops would be outnumbered and outgunned.

"69er, this is 71A. The local commander has given me a piece of paper. It says we are under arrest. He says if we try anything, he will shoot. They have deployed another machine gun to cover our 71 callsign. He wants him to pull up now, over," said Wayne, still quite calm.

"71, yes, I can see the other weapon now, over," injected Eric.

Suddenly a new voice appeared.

"71A, this is Sun Ray Minor," it was Warrant Sullivan on the air, "you tell him to stick that note up his ass, over!"

Jerry couldn't wait any longer. "69er, this is 72, do you want us to move to 71's location over?" he asked.

"69er, no, 71 move up to your other callsign and wait. I am going to contact higher and have him send a Lima Oscar [Liaison Officer] to your location, over," responded Captain Ready.

"71, roger, they don't have the authority to arrest us. Correct? Over," asked Eric.

"69er, no, over."

"71, roger, out."

I got down from my vehicle and walked over to Jerry's track. I climbed up and asked him what he thought. Jerry was a quiet type, very smart, and had good instincts. I enjoyed working in his group.

"Not much we can do," he replied, deep in thought.

"Shall we head out or brew up here?" I asked.

"Yeah, let's have a coffee," he replied.

I called back to Daryl to get the water on. We stopped and brewed up fairly often. It was down to a drill. This time though, it was an excuse to monitor the radio. We had good comms here. That might not be the case if we moved. As we travelled through the valleys and hills, we would often lose contact. At this particular moment, we wanted to hear every word on the net. I could imagine our guys down there in a Croat version of a Mexican stand-off.

About half an hour later—I am sure it was much longer for the boys in 71—Captain Ready came on the net and reported he was en route with Croat military police. While we drank our coffee, the Croat police intervened and told the Croat troops they had no authority to arrest us. After much argument, the Croats allowed 71 patrol to leave.

Jerry and I both breathed a sigh of relief. I told him that I thought it had been a mistake to move 71 up. You can't give in to the locals. Holding one carrier a hundred metres back was an insurance policy. Moving it up was dumb, I thought. Of course, I wasn't there, and could easily make that call while sipping coffee twenty kilometres away. Jerry and I agreed. If things looked suspicious, I would hang back far enough to provide some covering fire. From there we would take it as it came, reacting to the situation.

I was convinced that there had to be some give and take in negotiations, but you never just threw in your cards. In the days ahead, I took quite a few personal risks to defend this point of view. If every time the local forces challenged us, we backed down, our credibility would be shot. "Threaten the Canadians, and they'll scurry away with their tails between their legs," sort of thing.

Later on, when the story was told in full over a beer, I recognized that you can't second-guess another commander. Eric and Wayne had made their call and the situation was resolved peacefully. That was the aim. Not having been there, I could only guess what my response would have been. Also, I was only the 2IC in our two-vehicle patrol. Jerry had the final say, but I felt I had made my feelings on the subject clear.

While we were back in camp and not out patrolling, we had other duties to perform. One was front gate security. This was where the infamous "Attack of the Chickens" occurred. Our platoon shared the duty with all the other groups on base. We spent a lot of hours out there, standing in the cold night air. Eventually, our protests were heard and a bunker was constructed at the front gate.

The unit also began hiring large groups of locals to work on the base. This was done to accomplish a three-fold aim. To prevent the local community from making up all sorts of rumours about what went on behind the wire, we allowed the locals to come and work on the base. They had free access to most areas and established good, friendly relations with the UN troops. Secondly, we paid them a wage that in Canada would seem like slave labour but locally made them quite wealthy. Workers were paid in deutschmarks, which was a hard currency. The local currency was worth almost nothing. When we arrived, the Croat dinar was worth 120 to one mark. By paying the locals a high wage in a stable currency, they would in turn be able to buy products on the local market and in doing so help to re-establish the Croat economy. The final benefit came in purchasing products for the UN troops from the local producers. We had a standing contract for bread for the mess. We also purchased building materials, recreational gear and comfort items.

The local marketplace was always full of UN troops buying local products. I still have two big wicker chairs I purchased in the Daruvar market for about $15.

One contentious issue was canteen products. The Van Doos had brought down thousands of crates of pop and Heineken beer. They wanted to sell a single can of Heineken to us for DM 1.50. That meant, for our canteen to make a profit, we would have to sell it for DM 2.0. This was outrageous. Especially when we could buy the local Croat beer for 29 German pfennigs a bottle (about twenty cents Canadian).

The local product, named Staroccsko, was not the best beer we had ever consumed. Still, the price was right. Warrant Sullivan found a little shop in Sirac that would sell him crates of the stuff, so every couple of days he would stop in on the way back from patrol and pick up a few cases. We would buy a couple of token cases from the Van Doos to keep them from getting suspicious. Actually, I don't doubt they knew. Across the battle group, Starocesko was the beverage of choice.

No doubt some self-righteous, bone-headed do-gooder will take offense at the concept that we actually consumed any alcohol while in theatre. How could troops with guns and bullets be drinking? Well, for four thousand years soldiers have lived with three facts of life. They will mount most anything that moves, drink anything that resembles alcohol and die in huge batches before they grow old enough to take the time to enjoy life properly.

Despite the best efforts of the social scientists of the world, we found alcohol to be a great stress reducer. After a particularly dangerous day, we would need to unwind and let go. Unfortunately, the type of lifestyle we live tends to produce macho types who don't show emotions well. After enough beer, though, people

let down their guard and will talk about it. The secret is to be surrounded by good friends who want to listen. We would watch
each other. If someone seemed to be walking too fine a line, the
Warrant would have a couple of the boys get him drunk and
encourage him to let it out.

Of course, this wasn't a permanent solution. As long as we
were in theatre, the stress was constant. This technique would get
us through until we could get away on a seventy-two-hour pass or
two-week leave block. Unlike the rifle companies, who manned
checkpoints or operated roadblocks in static locations, we were
always traveling up dusty little trails and into unknown areas. In
the back of our minds was always the question of when we would
hit that anti-tank mine or booby trap. Not if, when. Each day
when we went out, we just tuned out those little voices, because
we had a job to do. At the end of the day, we would have a couple
of beers and talk about it. The next day, we were ready to go
again. Some of us didn't drink. Many were hitting the weights and
running. They were laying off the beer to train. Often, I wouldn't
have a beer for weeks. Still, it was always there if I needed one. If
it got to be too much, I could get myself happily plastered and let
go of some built-up stress. If we hadn't had this release, I don't
think we would have made it.

For the troops on missions today, there is a rule of no alcohol in
theatre. I laugh. This rule is only to please the politicians. The
troops still drink. You can't stop them. Even the officers will have
their little stashes. What the rule does accomplish is that it covers
the asses of senior officers and politicians should an incident occur.
It is always easy to blame the alcohol and in doing so prevent any
career implications for those in charge. It also usually prevents anyone from examining the deeper cause or finding a better solution.

The excuse-makers will counter with the fact that the army
deploys teams of social workers to work with soldiers to measure
their stress and provide counselling. Every soldier knows not to
talk to these clowns. One good friend of mine admitted to a
counsellor once that some of the things he had seen had bothered
him. Immediately, he was identified as an emotionally unstable
character and was categorized as a danger to himself and others.
He was prevented from carrying a weapon and, since he was an
infanteer, this meant he could not do his job. We all knew this
guy. He was stable. I trusted him with my life, no question. To

some university-trained psychologist, he was one of the few to admit to stress. Textbooks or articles for journals could be written about his case. Miraculously, according to the counsellors' reports, my friend suddenly suffered from cold sweats, recurring nightmares and all the symptoms of Post Traumatic Stress Syndrome. Of course, he wasn't experiencing any of these and tried to explain the fact to his counsellors. His protests were put down as due simply to his state of total denial. The longer he claimed to be fine, the worse they were convinced he was. It took years to finally convince them he was not nuts.

Could all his friends and co-workers be wrong? Was he suffering from PTSS? Well, the fact he successfully completed an advanced demolition course while he was supposedly suicidal, makes a good case for our side. Between all the opportunities he had to blow himself up or pull his releases while parachuting, he didn't seem to be too far gone.

Now, all troops know better than to tell these clowns anything. Back in 1992 in Croatia, we didn't have any of these teams coming around. They didn't exist yet. It wasn't until the boys got home and marriages started breaking up and a couple of guys blew their own heads off that these teams were formed.

At the beginning of May, we were still waiting to get down into the enclave. Negotiations were going slowly. While we were waiting, we filled our days with gate duty, home improvement and other little jobs. We had been watching the situation in Bosnia developing. The Bosnians were trying to break away from Yugoslavia as well. There was quite a bit of fighting going on down there. The Serbs were actively fighting the Muslims. The JNA was also supporting irregular forces fighting in the Krajina district in the west of Bosnia. The Croat army had a couple of brigades in northern Bosnia as well, fighting the JNA for control of the border areas. The entire country was a mess. The western Adriatic coast of the former Yugoslavia was in Croat hands.

This domination of all access to the sea encouraged the JNA to attempt to seize areas near the coast. The historic and beautiful town of Dubrovnik was being destroyed under intense artillery bombardment. Fighting raged everywhere.

In an attempt to secure their position, the Bosnian government asked for foreign military assistance. The UN began toying with the idea of sending troops into Bosnia. The main reason was that some bureaucrats back in New York had put our UN headquarters for our Croatian mission smack in the middle of Bosnia. Originally intended to be in a small city in northwest Bosnia called Banja Luka, it didn't work out. General Lewis MacKenzie had to take his command to the capitol of Sarajevo. Of course, as war broke out, Sarajevo became the prize, and all sides tried to seize the city. Because the UN was already in the middle of the whole Bosnian mess anyway, sending peacekeepers was a natural progression.

Back in Camp Polom, we were informed that we might be redeployed to Bosnia. It seemed the Canadians were the only troops in theatre with the resources to pick up and move south. Most of the contributing countries had sent infantry battalions with only small arms and a few logistic vehicles. Some, like the Nepalese, showed up at the port in Split with only a rifle and a spoon. No vehicles, no equipment, no tents or supplies of any kind. They expected the UN to provide everything. The UN had to buy up a large quantity of East German surplus vehicles and stores for issue to the Nepalese battalion. Unfortunately, most of these hill people had never driven a vehicle before and they crashed most of their new trucks in the first few weeks.

So Canada was it. With a Canadian UN commander already in theatre, it was a natural extension to send us. In Croatia, the situation was pretty much stabilized. Our resources could be better employed elsewhere. The Argentinians could easily handle our sector, when they arrived.

With these thoughts in the back of our minds we bashed on with our home improvement tasks. We cleaned up the demolished building next door so that it was like a roofless gymnasium and began playing spirited games of volleyball and floor hockey. We spent our days patrolling, doing duties, working around the home and having a beer while watching movies in the evenings.

On 6 May, I finally got a chance to go down south into the enclave. Van Doos Recce had begun patrolling down there the previous day and our det commanders were getting a chance to ride along with them. Eventually, it would be a rotating duty. The Van Doos Recce would go one day and then we would go the next. Early in the morning, Jeff, Wayne and I mounted up in the back of the Van Doos Recce tracks and headed south to observe their patrols and the situation in the enclave.

Our patrols would enter through the town of Pakrac. An arrangement had been worked out whereby a ceasefire was in effect by day and the UN could operate a single crossing site. On the Croat side, members of November company established a checkpoint each morning. After crossing through this point, we had to travel roughly five hundred metres along a narrow side street to reach the JNA roadblock. During the drive, we would pass the forward positions of both opposing forces. The area in between the checkpoints was a collection of burnt-out homes and businesses. On finally reaching the JNA barricades we would wait until everyone was caught up and then the JNA troops would lift the barrier and allow us to cross. At first, a Liaison Officer would be present at the Serb checkpoint to facilitate the movement. To get there each morning, the LO would put a radio on his back with a small UN blue flag attached to the top of a three-metre-long antenna. He would then walk the length of the street, passing through no-man's-land as he went. Eventually, this duty was assumed by November company troops. They would sit up at the Serb end sipping slivovicz with the Serbs and monitor the radios connecting them with the Croat side.

In this way, communications were established between the two forces. The Canadians would later install a field telephone that remained twenty-four-hours-a-day. Afterwards, if one side fired a few rounds, instead of retaliating, the opposing commanders would get on the phone to find out what was going on. This dialogue, it was hoped, would eventually produce a truce.

When I had hopped aboard the Van Doos carrier, the det signaler had asked me for my weapon. These guys tied their rifles to the seat post inside the carrier during patrols. I politely refused, preferring to keep it slung over my shoulder. I figured if we didn't need weapons, then the UN didn't need soldiers here, just social workers. I would keep my rifle close by. Always.

As we entered the enclave, I expected them to hand out the rifles, but no. I shrugged, if it was my day to die, then why worry? This was the attitude that I had been developing to handle the thought of mines or ambush. If fate had it in store, there wasn't much I could do about it. Still, I was determined that if my turn came, I would go down fighting with a rifle in my hand, not on my knees with a pistol in the back of my neck.

Actually, I also kept my big Gurkha kukri with me as well. When my two mags of ammo ran out, I figured I still had the biggest knife in town. Crocodile Dundee had nothing on me!

We headed south, splitting the six tracks up into two vehicle patrols. I was quickly stunned by the quantity of military hardware the JNA had. In the first few kilometres, I counted dozens of M84 and T55 tanks, mortars and artillery pieces by the battalion. These guys made the Croats look like farmers.

As we crested a small ridge south of Pakrac and headed downhill towards an old farm, I was shocked when I spotted an M84 tank directly in front of us, parked in the remains of a barn. What grabbed my attention immediately was the fact that, as we came in to sight, the tank's main gun swivelled to bear on us and began tracking our movement. The 125 mm round those things fired would cut through our vehicle like paper-maché and vapourize us all. The Van Doos seemed unconcerned. Not wanting to look bad, I said nothing. The tank's gun followed us until we were out of sight around the next bend. *Dobar dan*, my UN comrades! I hoped that gunner had enjoyed his little game.

The civilians we passed seemed very friendly and appeared to welcome us. I am assuming that our presence was the first sign that the outside world had not forgotten their plight. Everywhere were farms, beautiful country homes and delapidated but quaint little villages. We stopped for a while in the major town of the enclave, Okucani (Oak-a-chan-ee). We bought a bread roll from a local merchant and watched the local population go about its business. Everything seemed reasonably normal, but you could tell they were all on edge. There was an undercurrent of nervous tension. Knowing the Croats were only kilometres away and that no mercy would be shown to anyone, whether man, woman or child, would put an edge on anyone's day.

After a small conference among the Van Doos commanders, my patrol set off for the Sava River, fifteen kilometres to the south. On the way, we passed even more tanks and artillery pieces. Two kilometres short of the river we came to a completely destroyed bridge over a small canal running east-west. On the banks were four M84 main battle tanks facing down the canal in both directions. The bridge had been a modern concrete overpass and looked to have been brought down with a surgical charge. The expertise to do that was not the sign of amateurs. Yet, with all this equipment and skill, the Serbs were nearly wiped out here in Croatia. The adage, "One man defending his home is worth ten hired soldiers," must be true.

When we reached the Sava River, we stopped and had a good look. A large suspension bridge spanned the river. The water itself was approximately one hundred metres across and fairly swift flowing. On the south bank, in Bosnia, we could see military tents and soldiers relaxing. We knew they were fighting to the east and west as Croat units sought to cut off the enclave from Serbia. This must be a rest centre for them.

Not wanting to outlive our welcome, we headed back to the north and Okucani again. We travelled around a few of the side roads, but as we neared the JNA front lines we picked up a Serb Military Police escort. We were informed it would be dangerous to wander around on our own. The Serbs led us around several small villages and, once again, I was constantly amazed at the amount of tanks and artillery pieces scattered about the countryside. In one field, I could make out three batteries of heavy artillery and an ACRV artillery command vehicle. Ammunition was stacked around the guns and the equipment appeared to be well maintained. "With all this kit," I thought, "they should be able to roll over the Croats."

The reason they didn't was morale and lack of support. The JNA's morale was not the best. Their hearts weren't in the fight. Before the war, the JNA had conscripted soldiers from across the country. As the federation fell apart, large numbers of Slovenes, Croats and Bosnians deserted with their weapons to their new ethnic armies. The JNA was immediately thrown into disarray and the Croats took advantage, pushing the Serbs out of most of their country. These units gathered here in the Okucani enclave were only the remnants of the JNA. They had the equipment, but their chain of command was nearly non-existent. In one case a former corporal was now a Brigade commander. The equipment lacked trained maintainers and spare parts. Most of all, they lacked extensive support from the remainder of the JNA which, at this time, had its hands full in Bosnia.

We stopped and talked to some of the Serb troops. Mostly they just wanted to go home to Serbia and their families. They were conscripts and not professional soldiers. They hoped the UN could sort this out so that the Serb families trapped in the enclave could get on with their lives without the threat of Croat attack. I found the Serb troops a little easier to get along with. They may have been conscripts, but they were still soldiers. Unlike the cocky Croats, they did not have a long record of rapid victories to fill their egos.

As we prepared to set out the next morning, a half-dozen troops showed up from November company. They were bored and OC November had wanted to get some of them out and see the country. I had Grant Mason riding along with me. Grant was a master corporal and a former member of our Recce platoon. Standing six-foot-six easily, Grant was an impressive sight, but with both of us jammed into the rear hatch, it got a little crowded.

Every Recce detachment had its own little idiosyncracies. How it set up its vehicle was a matter of personal taste. Some commanders handled the navigation, the .50 cal and the radios themselves. Their signallers were little more than observers and coffee-makers. In my det, everyone had a job. In the Lynx, I had sat at the .50 cal and handled navigation and command. My signaller handled all the comms and backed up my navigation. Even the driver handled movement. I would tell him to get me to the next ridge, then forget about it. How he got us there was his business. I was more concerned with watching the surrounding territory for signs of the enemy. If someone called on the radio, it didn't distract me because the signaller handled it.

In an M113, we had to change around a bit. Our solution was that Glen, the signaller, would ride in the commander's hatch and handle the .50 cal. The reason was that, in this environment, I was often dismounting to talk with locals or check something out. This would leave the gun unmanned. So Glen became the gunner in the team. I took over the radios and moved to the rear hatch. This rear hatch was a large rectangle a metre-and-a-half long and a metre wide. I kept my rifle in a quick-draw scabbard on one side and a row of smoke grenades in a rack along the other. From here I could handle our maps and the radios and have a good view of the surrounding area. We kept our portable headset radios handy for when I dismounted. I also kept a small video camera in the back. I had painted it green and encased it in a green canvas and aluminum cover. To the casual observer it looked like a radio component or a weapon sight. I would use it to surreptitiously film items or points of interest. Held at my hip or even just sitting on the top of the carrier, it would record weapons and equipment as we passed.

So, on this day, Grant and I piled into the back of the carrier and, in our turn, we pulled out of the parking lot to follow the other Recce tracks to the front gate. Once out of the base we turned south and headed for Pakrac. Feelings were running high in the platoon. Everyone was excited about finally getting started with our real work. The south was quiet at the moment, but it was a potential trouble spot and we wanted to get in there.

The UN plan was to eventually get both sides to withdraw their big guns. The JNA would withdraw all its tanks, guns and assorted military vehicles, if the Croats pulled their artillery out of range of the enclave. The UN would occupy the whole area, providing security for both sides. In Recce, our mission was to locate and identify all the military equipment we could find. Once it was recorded, we would know roughly how much gear the Serbs had and count it as it left. Constant patrolling would assure compliance with the plan. Today, though, we were just to drive around and get a feel for the area.

We crossed without incident at Pakrac around 0900 hours and headed south as a platoon for Okucani. Once there, we split up with 71 going southeast and 73 going west. Our patrol, 72, had been tasked by radio after reaching Okucani to rendezvous with an LO and recce a new area. Following Jerry in his 72 callsign, we headed north to Donji Rogolji. As we passed through this village, we noticed an entire regiment of D30, 122 MM howitzers dug into a field just west of the town.

Turning south into the hills, we met up with the LO in the tiny hamlet of Bobare. It was Lieutenant Drey (the man with the comfy pillow). He was waiting there for us in a jeep with his driver and a truckload of Serbs. Drey explained the task. We were going to recce a route running out from the Serb-held area we were in now, south down a dirt track and into a Croat pocket in the hills. This Croat position had created a bulge in the Serb defenses that reached to within three kilometres of the main road from Pakrac to Okucani. We were to patrol into the Croat pocket and then out again to the south. By patrolling this route regularly we should be able to limit the Croat ability to threaten the Serb lines of communication.

The problem was that the Croats weren't playing yet. When

Lieutenant Drey had tried to reach the start of the trail yesterday, he had been engaged by machine gun and sniper fire. Today we were involved to provide security for him and the truckload of Serbs who were along to disarm their mines and booby traps on their end of the trail.

With Drey leading, we set off in a little convoy into the forested hills to the start of the trail. A few minutes later we pulled into a small glade in the woods. It was a junction of two trails, the southern fork being our objective.

Here, we all dismounted. Drey got together with us and the JNA commander. This guy was about forty and was missing a couple of teeth. He was friendly and very co-operative. He had been a corporal in the army before the war and when the previous battalion commander had heard about today's job, he had disappeared. This guy was now in charge of his battalion.

We made our game plan. From our glade, the trail turned left and went downhill for sixty metres where it turned right over a small creek. This section of the trail was mined and booby-trapped. The JNA troops would disarm all of these between here and the creek; then, with the JNA battalion commander in tow, we would move a couple of kilometres down the trail to meet up with the Croat forces in the village of Sirinci. Another Liaison Officer was at the other end, trying to negotiate with the Croats.

When everyone understood his duties, we set off. Jerry, Grant, Private Litchfield from November company (who had been riding in 72) and I all advanced with the JNA troops to remove the mines and booby traps. We left the vehicles in the glade for the moment and went forward armed only with our rifles. I kept in contact with Glen using a portable radio. We were expecting trouble and kept our eyes warily on the forests around us. The JNA troops worked quickly to clear the route. The sooner they were finished, the sooner they could get back to safety.

While they worked, Drey chatted with the JNA commander near the creek. As long as the Serb "officer" was there, the troops felt okay. Still, the moment they were done, they headed back up the hill and into the, largely imaginary, safety of the glade. Jerry had me call the tracks forward. I called Daryl on the portable and told him to bring up the vehicles. Slowly, the carriers came down the trail to meet us at the creek. From here, Jerry and I would walk about fifty metres ahead of the vehicles, looking for mines, booby traps or ambushes. The Serbs had supposedly removed all their mines, but who knew about the Croats? The vehicles would follow, with Drey and the JNA commander bringing up the rear.

The lead vehicle was 72, with Corporal Dave Horochuk, known as "Horse," driving and Corporal Glen Faubert on the .50 calibre. I gave Horse my video camera and he filmed us as we headed off down the trail. This was going to be a hairy one and, if we lived, I wanted it on tape.

Jerry and I stayed about twenty-five metres apart. Lieutenant Drey had driven down this trail the day before until he was shot at, so we walked in his jeep tracks. Of course, any decent enemy would mine the tracks and roll an old tire over the new dirt a few times to give an unbroken look to the trail. Still, this was what we got paid for.

We walked very slowly. I didn't worry about the trees around me too much. Faubert was behind me with the .50 cal to cover over our heads. I concentrated on the ground. Before I put my foot down, I would search the ground ahead for any sign of disturbance.

Once again, the incredibly high threat of stepping on a mine or being hit by a sniper ate at my subconscious. I'm sure all of us were tense as hell. I just asked myself, "Is this my day to die?" I always answered myself, "No, not today," and went on.

Was I scared? Yes and no. I did feel fear, but it was more like a warning from my subconscious trying to impress upon my conscious mind that this was a dumb idea. If that little voice got too loud, I had to make a conscious effort to choke it down, because lurking behind it is that primordial fight or flight instinct. As long as I concentrated, I really didn't feel any fear. If my concentration slipped, then I would feel a moment of panic before I pushed it back down deep. When I was being shot at later in the tour, I didn't feel fear because I was too busy. This job, though, was lasting a long time. With each step we headed farther and farther into no-man's-land.

I had to work pretty hard to keep my emotions under control. Whenever I felt I was slipping, I called Faubert on the portable and asked him, "How's it going?" The idle chatter had a calming effect. Our little patrol bashed on.

About halfway along, I spotted a roundish shape partly obscured by the surface dirt. I signalled to Jerry, who was up ahead of me, to stop. I then signalled Horse to hold up behind me. I knelt down and gently dusted away the topsoil. Underneath, I found a large rock. Standing up, I signalled everything was okay, and our little expedition continued.

Soon afterwards, Jerry spotted a hole in the trail that had, until recently, held an anti-tank mine. He pointed it out to me and I pointed it out to Horse. When his vehicle reached it, he stopped and shot some tape of the hole.

The entire trail was fifteen hundred metres in length. As we rounded a bend in the last four hundred metres, we saw a Canadian jeep sitting ahead of us. Around it stood the other LO and a couple of Croat officers. We pulled the vehicles up to their location. Lieutenant Drey brought the JNA commander forward. Everyone seemed relaxed, and the LOs, the Croats and the JNA had a short chat. When they were finished, Drey escorted the JNA officer back towards his own lines. We were told to mount up and follow the jeep. As I climbed aboard my carrier, Glen pointed out a position that two snipers had occupied about three hundred metres away on a hillside opposite us. They had been watching us make contact to make sure everything went okay. After a while, they had begun edging their way out. I couldn't see anything but Glen described them. He said one had on a yellow camouflage smock. I shrugged and pulled on my headset. Not much we could do about it now, except be careful. I did compliment Glen on his call. Spotting a sniper is no easy task.

The jeep pulled out carrying the LO and the Croat officer. We fell in behind. A little way up the trail was the completely destroyed village of Sirinci. As we arrived we could see that this place had been levelled. Waiting there for us were two grinning characters, one in a yellow smock. He was carrying a Dragonov sniper rifle. I looked over at Glen. Our eyes met. Good call.

As we stopped in the middle of the shattered village. Jerry got down from his vehicle and went to speak to the LO and the Croat officer. I stayed in my vehicle. While we watched, bedraggled soldiers began hauling themselves out of the rubble. I could see a large variety of different uniforms and weapons. These guys didn't have the look of the normal Croat troops. A couple of them came over to bum cigarettes. While we smoked and joked I realized they were all mercenaries. One of them spoke pretty good

English. Through him we learned that they were all mercs, mostly from European countries. We talked for quite a while. It was during this conversation that he asked us to jump ship and sign up. He went on to describe their pay arrangements and I was doubtful, but it was still an attractive offer. From the look of this village though, these guys had been pounded regularly by that regiment of artillery back in JNA territory. I'm not sure this was the best offer to take seriously.

Soon it was time to go. Some mercs jumped in a vehicle and headed off down the road, heading south, just ahead of us. Our carriers followed the LO in his jeep. We waved goodbye to the soldiers of fortune and headed out of Dodge City. Another kilometre south of this position was the remains of several houses collectively known as Licko Brdo. Here, the mercenaries had another position. They had the road blocked by wood cuttings and, beneath them, some anti-tank mines. While we waited, the volunteers removed the obstacle and the mines. Cautiously, we pulled through. Behind us, the mercenaries quickly replaced the roadblock. As we sped off, I turned around for one last look and got quite a shock.

A soldier had stepped from the trees behind the barricade. He was wearing sunglasses, but that wasn't what made him stand out. He was dressed head-to-toe in Canadian combat gear. Helmet, jacket, pants and boots. This guy had Canadian issue webb gear and was holding a C7 with a Leitz scope mounted. My mouth must have dropped open because this guy ducked back into the trees before I could get anyone else to look.

I called 72 on the radio and reported what I had seen, but we could not stop. The Serbs watched this stretch of road closely. If we acted suspicious at all, the JNA might suspect the Croat forces were up to something and open fire. My discovery would just have to wait.

In fact, very soon we emerged into a wide open field. In the distance we could see JNA tanks with their main guns pointed right at us. The LO carefully dismounted and began talking on his radio. He had his backpacked, Vietnam-era 77 set radio on, with his UN flag flapping merrily from his antenna. The LO was not very merry though. In fact he seemed terribly nervous. The situation was in his hands, and out of ours. The first sign we would have of trouble would be a hypersonic 125 mm tank round slamming into our track. After a short wait, we got the word to carry on and very quickly sprinted the remaining distance into Serb lines. Once back in the enclave, we had to cross a narrow bridge with a dozen mines scattered along its sides. We had only a few centimetres on either side and crossed very carefully. Once through, we were finally back in Okucani and grateful as hell.

We were told that tomorrow we would do it again.

After linking up with the other patrols, we learned that we were not the only ones to have had a bit of excitement. 73 Group under Kevin and Jeff had been exploring a country lane, when they suddenly found themselves in the middle of a Chetnik para-military training camp. One minute they are headed through more abandoned buildings and the next, Chetnik irregulars are charging out of doorways arming their RPG–18 anti-tank rocket launchers and charging their AKs.

It seems no one had liaised with these characters. Not surprising, since I don't think even the JNA was too proud of these radicals. Our guys stopped and tried not to look too aggressive. The Chetniks had heard about the UN coming, but no one had warned them to expect big armoured vehicles to roar into their midst during a siesta.

Kevin and Jeff did some fast talking and the tension lessened somewhat. The Chetniks weren't too happy about UN troops driving into their camp, but they at least lowered their weapons. They didn't unload them though. Jeff and Kevin, having seen all they needed to see, waved goodbye and pulled away.

Before pulling out of sight, there was one Canadian who wanted the last word. Croats wave with two fingers extended like a peace symbol. Serbs wave with the first two fingers and the thumb extended. To confuse the two is a major insult. Corporal Chris Sainsbury, 73A's signaller, was standing in the back of the rear carrier and he gave the Chetniks a great big Croat salute as the vehicles pulled out of the camp. The Chetniks, relaxing now, suddenly turned red with fury and some raised their weapons again. Fortunately, the vehicles were pulling out of sight. Their last view would have been Chris's grinning face. Later, Chris swore he did it by accident. It was generally decided not to visit the Chetniks again in the near future.

The next day was Sunday. This meant Sunday routine. There were no patrols and we could all sleep in. After brunch, we spent the day in our civvies and caught up on our personal administration. Today was wash day for me. You could send your laundry out to be cleaned, but everyone was getting their bags back with items missing. I figured I would just do it by hand.

Later in the day we had a platoon floor hockey match: NCOs versus the troops. The troops always beat us. This drove Warrant Sullivan nuts. He could not stand losing at anything. Back in Germany, the NCOs' side won every contest we had. Here in Yugo, the troops were undefeatable. They would needle the Warrant about it and he would be in a foul mood all day.

Some of the NCOs would rather have spent their spare time in other pursuits than the relentless quest for floor hockey victory, but the Warrant was a man possessed. He would make it quite plain we were all playing floor hockey and loving it, or else! Actually, it was fun and it was a great way to keep fit while burning off some aggression.

One Sunday, we ran the eight kilometres down to November company's position on the Sirac soccer field. We challenged them to a game and the Warrant told all of Recce that if we didn't win we would be running back as well. We had a truck with us for our reward, so we all were motivated to crush the rifle company slobs in the match. I can't remember who won, but we did get a lift back after having a few beers with the lads in November.

We weren't too impressed with their living conditions, so we invited the troops and NCOs up for a party at our Recce country club. The rifle company boys were limited to two beers per man per day and would welcome the chance to get out and relax a bit.

Like anywhere, the headquarters and administrative types always live a cushy life. If, for example, the Sony Corporation donated five hundred Walkmans to the troops in theatre, these would be grabbed up by all the headquarters REMFs who would see them first. This happened with everything. Good Samaritans back home would mail boxes of magazines and cookies for the troops out on the line. They would be addressed to "Any UN Soldier." Out in the cold and dreary checkpoints, manned by the working class rifle company boys, they never saw anything that the headquarters slugs hadn't rifled first. When it came to amenities, working for the HQ was as close to comfortable as you could get. Since Recce platoon was attached to HQ, we managed some perks, mostly due to Warrant Sullivan's efforts. We didn't complain too much about HQ. What would it have accomplished, except to draw attention to ourselves?

We were given a long leash, because we were an Anglo outfit in the middle of a Franco headquarters. No one from the head-shed would just "drop by" our building unless on official business. Living out in the woods, separated from the main camp, was also a additional bonus for us. The RSM didn't just wander in during the course of the day. In fact, I can't even remember the CO coming into our building.

So a chance for the rifle company boys to get away and relax a bit was an opportunity they would not miss. They could come up and we would lay on the beer and steaks. We had the senior NCOs up first. They brought their cots and, after a late night of celebrations, they crashed in our building. Trucks came to collect them the next morning.

Next, it was our soldiers hosting a collection of troops from across November company. The officers and senior NCOs had volunteered to cover their duties while they were away. The rifle company boys got to let down and have a good time without anyone looking over their shoulders.

Our little social club also attracted a few of the base types who would come over to work out on our weights or sit around the Pivo Pit, "pivo" being Serbo-Croat for beer. This included two of the women on base. They worked for the base transport section and were very fit soldiers. They wanted to keep their fitness up and would come down to work out. We all enjoyed the company.

I remember several times dozing in my cot several feet from the weight area. I would get a wafting scent of perfume drifting over on the still air. It would be one of the women working out. I would wake up with a smile on my face and pleasant memories. Occasionally, around the fire at night with a lot of beers down range, the boys might try to hit on these ladies, but it was never serious. We considered it bad form. They were fellow soldiers. Very pretty ones, but still soldiers. We didn't want them to stop coming around because the boys wouldn't leave them alone. In the end, we all got along fine. After a little time, it became a moot point. The girls all had boyfriends outside the platoon. These were guys they had been seeing back in Germany before deploying. So, with no romantic entanglements, it just made for a more interesting social life in camp.

I had always been in favour of women serving in the Forces. In training, I've seen women turn out to be the top shooters, best navigators and all-round better soldiers amongst large groups of their male peers. Many guys don't think women have a place in combat units especially. The common refrain is, "Well, if I get wounded, some girl isn't going to be able to carry me off the battlefield." I always laugh at that one. I weigh about a hundred kilos without my kit on. Not too many of my male peers are going to haul me off the battlefield either. The female soldiers with us in Yugo were as tough as the men and shared our hardships. As long as they don't ask for special compensation and do the job, I am quite happy to have them serving with me.

On May 15, something special happened. We had stopped in Okucani at the end of our route to await the other patrols. The carrier was parked near the centre of the town and, as usual, we were mobbed by the kids. We carried chewing gum and little Canada pins to give them, so the kids would crowd around and wait for their chance. I had handed out a few of these things to a couple of kids, but there was a young girl of about eight or nine waiting in the back. She couldn't push through the crowds of boys to get a pin. I waved to her and signalled her forward. The boys stepped aside to let her pass. She was shy, but with a smile or two, she came. I gave her my last pin. Then I gave the boys a hard stare so they would know to lay off her.

The little girl smiled and ran away. I shrugged and turned back to the job at hand. We were preparing to move and head to the link up when the little girl came running out from behind a house across the street. She ran as fast as she could to catch us before we pulled away. I saw her and told Daryl to wait. She ran up to the side of the carrier and produced a big yellow rose. It was for me and, really a little stunned, I bent down to take it.

"*Hvala*," I said, melting before her smile.

"*Molim*," she replied in a shy and gentle voice, then turned and sprinted back across the street. I looked around. Several Serb soldiers had been watching. They were all smiling. I could feel my cheeks burning red.

I told Daryl to go, and leaned back, staring at the rose. I admit, I was a bit shook up. To her, we were some kind of heroes, there to protect them. I took the rose and broke off a bit of the stem. Then I tucked the remainder into the webbing on my flak vest. I wore the flower proudly on my breast for most of the way home. I finally had to take it off because the wind was threatening to blow it away. When we got back to camp, I laid the little flower on the top hatch of our carrier. I hoped it would bring us luck.

That little girl and her gift left a deep impression on me. Three years later, in a spring offensive, the Croats rolled over the UN positions and seized the entire enclave. It was a lightning strike and the UN -disarmed Serbs were no match for the well-prepared Croats. The UN just got out of the way when the Croats approached. I remember seeing a picture of Croat troops on the news. They were standing in the main square of Okucani. That little girl would be ten or eleven years old. I can't help thinking that she is probably dead now. A broken little body in a mound of rubble. The UN failed to protect her. I failed. Even writing about it now, years later, brings up deep emotions.

On the night of 7 June, the CO left word for the unit to "prepare to move," and took off with his senior staff for Belgrade. We had a couple of guesses what it was about. The first, and most likely, was to move to Sarajevo and try to open the airport. The second guess was to protect Serb troops moving out of the enclave. Croat offensives in Bosnia had cut the JNA land route back to Serbia. They were now, in essence, surrounded. Only the UN and the remaining Serb troops held the Croats out of the enclave.

The final guess was a redistribution of units within UNPROFOR. In our sector we had four battalions of troops, including two reasonably professional units in us and the Argies. Sector West was fairly quiet now. The other three sectors were in far more difficulty than ours. Shifting us to the other trouble spot seemed likely.

Whatever the reason, all leave had been cancelled and the Battle Group began packing up. The next day we received word from Belgrade. We were on standby to go to Bosnia and open the Sarajevo airport. We were waiting on a vote by the UN Security Council as to when we would deploy, but we were assured it would be soon. Recce was also told to stand by to depart immediately for Sarajevo to provide security for the CO and his senior officers while they had a look at the area.

The platoon was electrified. Sarajevo! That was a war zone in a big way. Even the underlying concern over the extreme danger the mission entailed made our hearts race. Life was getting boring in Croatia. A new mission like this was perfect. Now we just needed the word to go.

On 10 June, Lt Colonel Hatton, the CO of 3RCR came around to Recce to visit us; he had been in country for a couple of days visiting his troops while they waited for the word to go. Accompanying him was Sergeant-Major Clarke. His first order of business was to call the platoon together. We expected the normal speech about what a good job we were doing, and so on. We liked Colonel Hatton. Too bad he wasn't in charge of this mission.

His first duty was some promotions. We looked at each other. Having the best troops in the battalion, it could have been anybody.

The CO called a name. "Sergeant Davis."

More than a little shocked, I walked up to the CO. One of the boys hauled out a camera. Here I was getting promoted to the senior NCO ranks and I was wearing a ratty Norwegian sweatshirt and combat pants. The CO shook my hand and, speechless, I walked back to my place. Next was Jeff. Two promotions to sergeant in one day!

Immediately, I became concerned. Promotion was the fastest way out of Recce platoon. If they told me I was reporting to November company tomorrow, they could have their rank back. There was no way, with Sarajevo looming, that I was leaving the platoon.

After the CO left, I went immediately to Captain Ready and Warrant Sullivan. Jeff was with me. We explained our concerns, and were assured that we would be staying in Recce for the rest of the tour. Yahoo!

---

18 June. A week has passed and we still have no definitive word on whether we are going or not. We do duty at the front gate and play floor hockey. The news from Sarajevo is sketchy. General MacKenzie and his column finally made it back into the city on 11 June. They had been forced to withdraw back in mid-May by fighting in the city. We had heard on Jeff's short-wave radio that there was still a lot of fighting going on. The General and his officers had been threatened many times and we heard a story about someone holding a knife to a Canadian officer's throat.

In Camp Polom, everything was a mess. No one was sure what equipment should go. Some people and gear would stay behind;

other stuff would be returned to Germany. At one point we were told that if we went to Sarajevo, there was no more ammo to issue. Our guys averaged about ninety rounds per man in Recce. I had seventy-five rounds. Going to Sarajevo with less than a hundred rounds per man was criminal stupidity, I thought, and I told anyone who would listen of my opinion.

It reminded me of the famous scene in the historical film *Zulu Dawn*. In this recreation of the battle of Isandhlwana in South Africa during the year 1879, a small British Army garrison is attacked by thousands of Zulu warriors. The well-disciplined Brits soon run low on ammunition; there are simply more Zulus than bullets. The ammo reserves are in a wagon controlled by the company quartermaster. He insists on following regulations and will only issue ten rounds at a time. Soon the Zulus overrun the entire garrison and the quartermaster is killed, defending a wagon loaded with bullets. Every British soldier is killed.

If you are going to send a soldier someplace and give him bullets, you might as well give him enough to do the job. If we got into a fight where we had to expend our few rounds, what were we supposed to do then, surrender? Not in the former Yugoslavia. Once we started a fight, we had better finish it, because there would be no prisoners taken. I don't know what the lawyers in New York thought, but I had seen first-hand how the local troops did business. I wasn't surrendering to anybody. It was for this reason that I kept the kukri close at hand. If my magazine ever clicked empty, I planned to charge swinging that big knife. Better a bullet standing up, than cut into little pieces, a bit at a time.

To be honest, I was starting to come to the conclusion that the UN, and the world at large, was missing a very important element here in Yugoslavia. UN peacekeepers are, in essence, international cops. Like our domestic counterparts, we were intended to enforce the laws as directed by the global government. In this case, the UN Security Council. To enforce these laws, we were equipped with weapons and patrol vehicles, similar to normal police forces. Here lies the rub: The implication of sending an armed "policeman" to enforce a law requires that failure to comply will result in some type of response, otherwise the laws will be ignored. Resistance will demand forcible compliance.

To accomplish this, police forces have a rule of one-upmanship. Raise a fist, they pull a billy club. Pull a knife, they pull a gun. Raise a gun, they call for back-up. You can't overpower the police. Yet here we were, surrounded by hundreds of thousands of potentially hostile forces, yet we had very few weapons, little ammo and no back-up. Enforce the commands of the Security Council? Ha! Good one, Boutros.

Our orders so far had made no mention of exactly how we were to enforce anything. In fact, we were pretty much told to step aside if the belligerents wanted to kill one another. If that was the case, what the hell were we doing? Why had they named us the "UN Protection Force"? The Serbs in the enclave agreed to remove the very weapons that were protecting their lives because they believed the UN would protect them. Unknown to them, our orders were to simply let the Croat forces pass if they really wanted to attack, which is exactly what happened. The end result was that we managed to defeat the Serbs for the Croats by preying on their faith in the UN. If that little girl with the flower died when the Croats attacked, then it was my fault and the fault of the UN's stupidity.

You can't fool soldiers for very long. The Serbs in the enclave, under the rules, were not permitted any weapons. Only their military police were allowed pistols. We all knew that these rules applied only to the Serbs and not the Croats. So, frankly, we developed an unwritten policy: if we didn't see it, it wasn't there. The Serbs would smile and play badminton as we patrolled by, but we all knew they had stockpiles of weapons inside their platoon houses. The tanks and guns were gone, but I will be damned if we would prevent these men from dying standing up with a rifle in their hands defending their families.

We weren't in conflict with any orders in doing this because, in Recce, we just observe and report. If the UN wanted to raid the Serb platoon houses, they would have to change our mission orders and rules of engagement. So we continued to patrol the enclave with a mutual understanding between the Serbs and us. Keep it out of our sight and you can have it.

Finally, unable to tolerate the vacillating, François Mitterand, the president of France, flew into Sarajevo airport on 28 June with little warning. He was escorted through the lines and into the city for a meeting in the Bosnian Presidency. Then he returned to the airport, met with the Serb leaders and flew out again. We in Recce all applauded his courage. Here was a national leader who went himself to a war zone to see what could be done. Three days later, a company of French Marine Commandos arrived at the airport to hold until we arrived. Mitterand definitely had our respect!

Finally, the embarrassed Security Council got off their big, fat bottoms and committed us. At twenty minutes past four on 29 June, Recce received the word to go. H-hour was midnight the next day. The clouds had lifted and we stepped lively! Sarajevo, here we come!

Chapter 7

SARAJEVO

L AST NIGHT AT 2000 *hours General MacKenzie raised the* UN *flag at the Sarajevo Airport. He immediately called for at least a company of infantry to head to the airport. At 0200 hours Engineer elements, A company Recce and A company itself departed for Sarajevo. The rest of us leave tonight. My packet departs the base at midnight.*

It is, at present, 1800 hours and we are listening to BBC *radio. Heavy fighting has broken out again in the city. Looks like it is going to be fun. Especially since Recce is supposed to be living in the former Holiday Inn downtown. . . .*

We departed shortly after midnight on 1 July. Our trip was to take nearly two days. It began with Recce escorting some large supply trucks in the battalion column. Before we traveled a kilometre from base, four had gotten lost and one broke down. So much for a smooth start. After I sorted that out, we headed south for the bridge over the Sava.

We crossed into Bosnia as the sun began to rise and, shortly after, passed out of the Bosnian–Serb lines and into those of the encroaching Croat brigades south of the border. Our entire trip after that was spent crossing a stretch of no-man's-land that separated the warring factions. On a couple of occasions, we ran into intransigent local militia who answered only to the local warlord. In many areas, criminals, psychopaths and other low-lifes had set up private kingdoms and surrounded themselves with armed thugs. One such group refused to let us pass until Lt Colonel Jones brought up snipers, machine guns and TOW detachments. Then they backed down. As we passed, we saw the usual black coveralls and mirrored sunglasses of the pseudo-soldier. Losers.

During the second day, my carrier broke down and was loaded on a flatbed for the rest of the trip. We drove through the first night, stopping to rest early on the second of July. After a lunch of cherries donated by a local farmer, we prepared for the last leg as the afternoon waned.

At about 1530 hours, we mounted up and moved off. As darkness fell, we could see paraflares and tracers soaring across the night sky ahead of us. We passed through quite a few checkpoints and finally, at 2330 hours, we reached the Sarajevo airport.

The entire place was right out of the movie *Apocalypse Now*. Under great arc lights, the entire Battle Group's vehicles were lined up in rows on the runway. People were running everywhere. French Marine Commandos strolled around the place and above us tracers continued to crisscross the sky.

It reminded me of the famous scene in that movie where the hero, a Special Forces officer, is wandering around an American outpost in the dark during an attack. Lights hang everywhere and paraflares cast an eerie glow. Trying to find out who is in command, he stops and asks a freaked-out Marine:

"Who's in charge here, soldier?"

"Ain't you?" replies the Marine.

The Sarajevo airport had the same surreal quality that night. Soldiers were everywhere, but no one seemed to know what was going on. Guys in helmets, clutching M16s, were running around aimlessly. Remembering another famous line from the movie, "Never get out of the boat," we just sat on top of our carrier watching the tracers and the flashes of artillery in the nearby city. People would run up and tell us something, and we would just nod or ignore them. I half-expected Captain Willard, the movie's protagonist, to wander up out of the dark in his tiger cams and tell us no one was in charge here.

Captain Ready called all the det commanders together. Apparently, no one knew what was going on. There was no place for us all to go, but staying on the runway all bunched up guaranteed an attack. The cushy go at the Holiday Inn was out of the question at the moment. When someone figured out what was going on, he would let us know.

Eventually, we moved into a large concrete building near the airport's entrance. This had been the customs warehouse and would provide some protection from small-arms fire. The remainder of the night passed quickly and, with the arrival of the sun, we were all up working. The cooks set up a feeding line and we all got some breakfast into us. Next we moved our vehicles into a parking area beside the customs building. Daryl went and checked on our broken APC later and returned to say that, once all the kit was unpacked, the mechanics could fix it up.

The platoon moved its kit to a large room on the second floor of the warehouse which was to be our new home. We shared this space with the Van Doos recce platoon. After getting our personal kit unpacked there wasn't a lot to do. A company was now tasked to defend the airport along with the Marine Commandos. November company moved out early in the morning, headed for an old JNA camp in the city's industrial district. Their task was to set up a distribution system in the city for humanitarian aid. For the two Recce platoons there was no immediate role, so we were tasked as Quick Reaction Forces in the event of an attack.

Planes started landing soon after first light. They would offload their cargoes and then get out because there was almost continuous small-arms fire crisscrossing the airfield. The pilots didn't want to hang around long enough for someone to start lobbing mortars at them. Later in the morning one of the troops was nicked in the head by a 7.62 round. Just a bit of broken skin.

Around mid-morning Daryl and Glen headed down to our carrier to sort out some kit and do some maintenance. I was only a couple of minutes behind them. As I walked across the distance between the customs building and the hangars, bullets would crack by overhead. I wasn't too worried. No one seemed to be shooting at me in particular, or if they were, they were pretty bad shots. As I arrived at the vehicle, two bullets zipped by within a metre of Daryl, Glen and me as we stood in front of the carrier. We ducked down and ran behind the carrier. A news crew was hanging around and, seeing us taking cover, rushed over to get our reaction. Daryl, tall and good-looking in a boyish way, handled the reporters well. He made no big fuss about it, as if we had been doing this for years. The reporters, wanting more, moved on for a better reaction. There is no angle in being calm under fire.

At lunch, another soldier was hit in the leg by sniper fire. Considering the volume of shooting, we were all quite surprised there hadn't been more casualties. Despite all this fire and the couple of wounded, we weren't too concerned. The airport was smack in the middle of various factions. We were also next to a suburb that was constantly being fought over. The majority of the rounds were strays from local fighting. That was what we were telling ourselves anyway.

Lord Carrington, the former British Foreign Minister, arrived by plane during the morning to attempt to negotiate a ceasefire in the city, but he was unsuccessful. He blamed the Serbs for being unwilling to comply. I think the Lord may have been a little too optimistic. Croat forces had been advancing steadily on the city, intent on linking up with the Bosnian Territorial Defence Forces (TDF). The Serbs were already shifting some of their equipment to deal with this threat and any local ceasefire wouldn't include the Croats. Thus, the Serbs were quite unwilling to give up the fight, with the Croats threatening their flank.

By the end of the day we were all a little tired. The frantic pace of the last few days had worn us all out and we all looked forward to a good night's sleep. By the light of a Coleman lantern, Captain Ready gave us his O group. Over a warm Starocesko, he outlined the situation and gave an account of the day's events. His final instructions sounded promising. It seemed General MacKenzie was no spineless slouch of an officer. He instructed Colonel Jones to deploy snipers to defend his personnel if he saw fit. The rules of engagement were, if there was a threat to us or our equipment, it could be engaged. Since our recce platoon held the only snipers in HQ, we would get the nod. Once again, Van Doos recce had shown up without qualified people. Apparently, there was only one qualified Van Doos in the whole Battle Group. Oh well, more work for us.

In fact, the sniper engagement rule applied for any of us spotting a threat. This was recce work! We could set up observation posts and try to spot the locals who had been shooting in our direction. Once spotted, we could direct a sniper of our own to their location and he could make the call.

Sniping is still a valuable military art. Not the local brand of shooting women and children, but military sniping designed to cause havoc prior to an attack or lower morale by piling up the casualties. Because it is once again the domain of the non-commissioned ranks, it is often overlooked by Canadian officers, the Van Doos being a case in point. To become a sniper, selected individuals had to pass one of the most difficult courses in the military. Then, on posting to a Recce platoon, they became unit snipers. It remains one of the least publicized, but most coveted, jobs in the infantry.

Tomorrow's work would be counter-sniping, and our sniper teams would have a look and make plans for our employment. We all went to bed looking forward to the dawn.

Our slumber was interrupted at about 0200 hours. Without warning, the entire building suddenly rocked in an intense explosion. I was instantly awake and looking for signs of a collapsing roof or who knew what? The fight or flight instinct was surfacing quickly and I choked it back down. Another explosion shook the building. I felt as though my hair was being lifted by the concussion. I had never been on the wrong end of heavy artillery up until now, but I knew the sound immediately. I rolled out of my cot and pulled my boots on. As I did, I looked around me. Everyone else looked either dead or asleep, probably pretending to be asleep. Most had pulled the covers up over their heads as if to shut out the sound. Kind of like children hiding under their covers to escape the monsters.

I couldn't believe it! Here was that stubborn Canadian determination to refuse to believe anyone was aiming at us. Another series of impacts shook the building and I didn't know if they were targeting us or not. I knelt near an open window and tried to see where the rounds were hitting. Seeing nothing, I headed for another window and gazed out over the airfield. When another volley landed, I could see no hits on the airfield. The rounds must be falling on the TDF positions in the suburb of Dobrinja, one hundred metres across the street from our building. The blasts were fantastic. Each time the air seemed almost to solidify for an instant, and you would feel the vibration course through your bones.

Dion Henn, one of the boys from 73 group, came over to watch with me. We sat there in silence listening to the artillery.

We climbed out onto the roof of a first-floor extension and joined some Van Doos in observing the fireworks. We were all mesmerised. The rounds were falling several hundred metres to our north. Probably big 122 mm and 153 mm artillery rounds, I figured. Impressive.

The show continued until about 0400 hours, when the gunners up in the hills had finally had enough and went to bed. In the stillness of the night air, I couldn't help but think about being in Sarajevo. People were fighting and killing one another very close by. No matter how you looked at it, we were in a war. We hadn't joined the fray yet, but how long could we avoid it?

With these thoughts on my mind, I went back to my cot to grab a couple more hours of rack time before reveille.

As day two dawned on Sarajevo, we prepared for another challenging time. After breakfast, Daryl and Glen headed down to our carrier. The part we needed was supposed to be available this morning. I headed down to the hangar at about 0900. On my way there, I cut through the back of the maintenance sheds. I noticed a crowd had gathered near our Badger. This was a big Engineer vehicle with a dozer blade on the front and a back hoe mounted on the rear. Basically, a modified Leopard tank, it was the biggest piece of machinery in our inventory at the moment. The engineers had been using it to plow the top layer of dirt off all the unpaved ground around the hangars. This was meant to lift any mines that had been laid there.

I walked up and saw some of the boys hanging around in the crowd. I asked Horse what was happening.

"The driver was plowing along when suddenly this hand flops over the blade. The guy freaked," explained Horse.

Apparently, a corpse had been buried in a shallow grave recently and the plow had unearthed it. When the driver saw the hand, he lost it. The vehicle was backed up to expose the corpse folded in half with its feet resting on the back of its shoulders. They had to take the driver away. Now a crowd had gathered to see the remains and take pictures.

I didn't bother. I've seen enough stiffs in my life. The corpse was immediately named "Bernie" after the movie *Weekend at Bernie's*. This nickname stuck and in the days ahead all corpses were referred to as Bernies. To some, this might sound disrespectful, and it probably was, but when faced with this type of situation your sense of humour is one of the only defences you have. For us there was nothing malicious about it, we just needed to make light of a depressing fact of life in a war zone.

The sniper fire continued through the day and our snipers set up observation posts to counter the threat. We were all ordered to wear our helmets due to the combined mortar/sniper threat. I was in a fix, because I wasn't sure where mine was. We hadn't worn them once since arriving in Yugoslavia. I knew it was in the carrier somewhere and had to go down and dig around for it. Once I had found it, I went up onto the roof to see if I could be of use, but the orders were to keep all but the snipers off the roof to limit the number of targets.

As the day passed and no counter-sniper work materialized for us, we became a little downhearted. Here we were in Sarajevo and everyone else had work to do except us. Even the Van Doos recce platoon had some task down at MacKenzie's UN HQ in town. Slightly depressed, we went down to supper, which by this time was being served in another part of the customs complex.

At 2130 hours, Captain Ready came into our quarters and announced he had found a job for us. The next morning we were moving down to UN headquarters in the city to work for the staff there as a security team. Our title would be "Intervention Force" and we would be at the disposal of the operations cell in General MacKenzie's HQ.

We were all pretty excited. We would be away from the airport and closer to the action. Also, we would be away from the Van Doos for a while. The job would last seven days. I couldn't have been happier. My carrier was fixed and we had a mission. Life is good.

We rose at 0600 hours and packed up our kit. As we pulled out of the airport we turned left onto a two-lane road and headed for the city. Everyone was glad to be leaving the airport.

UN headquarters was located in the city's former telephone exchange, the PTT building. A sprawling office complex, it consisted of two floors underground with parking garages, two storeys of office space with cafeteria and a four-storey tower for the executive offices. The tower was mostly glass and was not in use due to the danger of flying shards. This was our new home.

UN headquarters had previously been just down the street in a garishly painted, multi-storey complex referred to as the Rainbow Hotel. During the initial battles for the city, when the UN was forced to withdraw, the building was smashed and gutted. As we drove past, we could see the burnt-out hulls of Canadian military jeeps and UN trucks abandoned during the retreat.

We pulled into the PTT buildings parking area and lined up our carriers. We were about two kilometres from the airfield and in the outer area of downtown Sarajevo. During the trip, we had crossed out of Serb lines and into the TDF-held zone. Most of the buildings en route had been smashed or burned. We had passed several ten- and fifteen-storey luxury hotels that had been built for the 1984 Olympics. They were now gutted. The Hotel Sarajevo was now a blackened shell and each of these buildings was now home to a host of snipers who used the high perches to harass their opponents' lines. Across the street from the PTT was the Olympic housing complex. These ultra-modern apartment blocks still appeared to be in fair condition and probably housed a large number of Sarajevans.

As we shut down our carriers and pulled off our headsets, we were greeted with the sounds of a major battle going on several hundred metres away. On the other side of the Olympic village, machine guns and small arms hammered away at something. We all looked towards the French sentries manning the bunkers around the complex. They didn't seem concerned, so we relaxed.

Captain Ready dismounted and headed into the building with Jerry, Eric and Kevin to find out where we would be staying. The rest of us waited in our carriers. Glen kept a hand on the .50 while scanning the buildings around us.

They soon returned and led us into the foyer of the complex. Here we found a sandbagged bunker manned by a French soldier. We turned right and headed up a staircase for . . . guess where?

That's right, the tower. We would be staying in the offices of the former CEO of the phone company high up in the glass tower. At the moment, we only had the key to one of the outer reception offices, so Dave Predo and I went to a row of wooden cabinets separating us from the main office. Sure enough, the interior wall of the cabinet was wood, so with a swift application of a size eleven boot, we created a new doorway into the executive suite. Everybody found a corner and dumped his kit. We had the entire floor to ourselves, consisting of one large office and conference room, plus three smaller offices. One office became the Op centre and TV room; the rest were sleeping areas.

We settled in and Captain Ready briefed us on our new duties. We were to be prepared to react to any incidents that might occur, such as a hostage taking or a similar crisis. We would also provide VIP security for the headquarters. A secondary task would be to collect information for the use of observation posts and sniper teams. We all felt that this was a good use of our platoon. "Special jobs" was what we did best.

We were also briefed on the nature of the headquarters. The building was home to a motley collection of organizations. At the top were General MacKenzie and his staff. His 2IC was a Colonel Petrounev, a Russian Airborne officer. His staff consisted of a mixed bag of UN member nationalities. There was a Dutch signals element, a British medical team, a French security platoon and an assorted group of observers.

The observer team was headed by a New Zealander, Colonel Richard Gray. Under his command were observers from Russia, Ireland, Canada, France, Holland and various others nations. There was also one Swiss major who had no job; he was just there to watch. For his efforts, he was receiving $14,000 U.S. dollars a month. All tax-free and on top of his normal salary.

Mixed in with this military lot was the civilian side of the house. The United Nations High Commission for Refugees (UNHCR) was located in the building. There were also representatives of numerous Non-Governmental Organizations (NGOs) such as the Save the Children Fund and the International Red Cross. Finally, there were the interpreters, who were, for the most part, local college students.

Oh, and I can't forget our Swedish cooks. Of course, I use the title "cook" rather loosely. I don't think I will ever eat another bowl of borscht again.

In the first two days, the platoon did a variety of uneventful escort jobs, usually out to the airport or downtown to the Bosnian Presidency. There was always a lot of shooting going on and we generally dodged bullets every time we went out.

The French platoon on duty had three VAB armoured cars for getting around. These were big steel-bodied vehicles with a machine gun mounted on the roof. The locals loved shooting them up and, on our second day there, one of the VABs rolled in with a string of fifty-calibre hits along one side. Both the French crew and we Canucks were impressed with the fact they didn't penetrate the armour. Our APCs were aluminum as opposed to the French steel hulls and we knew we wouldn't have been so lucky.

The city of Sarajevo is essentially one long strip. It occupies a narrow valley, surrounded by mountains on three sides and an open plain at the fourth. The airport was out in the plain at the southwest end of town. From the mouth of the valley, the city stretched eastward four kilometres into the surrounding hills. The city was at no point wider then a kilometre along its entire length. At the eastern end was the old city, the downtown core centred on the Presidency. Through the centre of this valley, and consequently the city, ran a small river called the Miljacka. The Bosnian forces held on to most of the city. Surrounding them in the hills on all three sides were the Serbs. Their positions looked down on the entire city. It was from here that their artillery and mortars rained on the TDF.

The Serbs did hold a small portion of the old city. They had seized all the buildings south of the river in the eastern end of town. This basically made the river the front line in the old city. At such close quarters, there was almost constant fighting in the downtown core. All of the north-south roads were open to sniper fire. This left the Bosnian seat of power, the Presidential building, only one hundred metres from the Serb lines.

Outside the valley, in the area of the airport, the situation was no better. The suburb of Dobrinja lay at the mouth of the valley. It consisted of about a square kilometre of residential housing. The Serbs held the eastern end of the suburb and the Bosnians had the western half. The south side of the suburb bordered the airport. There were some open fields between the houses and the rest of the city on the north side and a major road on the west. The Bosnian residents of this suburb were almost cut off from the rest of the city.

West of Dobrinja and the airport was a large flat plain of about twelve square kilometres. This was held by the Serbs as well. This left these Bosnians cut off from the remainder of the country.

Enter the rampaging Croat army. They had driven south to try to link up with the TDF in the city. By the time we arrived, the Croats were within sight of the city from the mountains surrounding the plain.

All in all, it was a confusing situation.

During the evening of our second night at the PTT, someone heard there was a phone we could use to call home. Glen had proposed to his girlfriend over the phone from a bathroom in Zagreb during a seventy-two-hour pass. He wanted to call and let her know he was okay. It was about 2000 hours and the building was pretty quiet. We didn't do any work in the city after dark—too dangerous. Glen walked down to the main building and began looking around for the phone. He couldn't find it and was standing there, scratching his head, when an old guy who had been reading a novel in the lobby asked him what he was looking for. Glen figured he was a janitor from the sloppy way he was dressed and figured he'd know the building pretty well.

"I heard there was a phone around we could use," he said.

"I think the French have one down in the basement," replied the janitor.

Glen thanked the old man and headed down to the basement. After waiting in line for half an hour, he was told that the phone was for French troops only. Dejected, he headed back upstairs. On his way up he passed the janitor again.

"How'd it go?" he asked.

"Didn't get on," Glen answered.

"There is another phone down that hallway, third door on the left," replied the old man.

Glen thanked him but didn't hold out much hope. The hallway he headed down was the operations area. It was where the duty centre and the main offices were. He walked through the third door on the left and found two Canadian sergeants sitting at desks, shuffling paperwork.

"Is there a phone around here I could use to call home?" he asked.

One of the NCOs looked up from his work and stared at Glen.

"No, the only phone here is in the General's office, and it's out of bounds," he stated.

Not surprised, Glen shrugged and headed back to his bunk. Again he passed the janitor reading his book.

"Any luck?" the old guy asked.

"No, they said it was the General's phone."

The old guy got up and motioned Glen to follow him. Glen fell in behind the janitor as he headed back down the Ops hallway. At the door to the General's office, the janitor turned and strolled casually past the two startled sergeants. As Glen walked by, the two NCOs eyed him carefully.

Inside the small, messy office stood the janitor with a phone in his hand.

"What's the number?" he asked.

Glen rambled it off and the janitor dialed it for him. When he heard it ringing, the janitor gave him the phone and left. Glen took the phone and, when his fiancee answered, had a good chat.

Later, as he left the office, he asked the sergeants who the old guy was, so he could thank him later.

"That was General MacKenzie," one of them replied.

———————

Back in our suite in the tower, we were watching tank and multiple rocket fire racing past our windows. When Glen showed up, he looked pretty embarrassed. When pushed enough, he related the entire story. We all had a good laugh. Later we found out that both Glen and General MacKenzie were from the same hometown. Small world.

While we were having a chuckle, Captain Ready came in. He called the det commanders together. We had a mission. It seemed that the owner of the PTT building was being held hostage by the Serbs. An ethnic Muslim, he was under house arrest in an apartment in the Serb-held zone of the old city. At 1300 hours the next day, we were going in to get him out.

"If the Serbs find out we have him, they will probably try to grab him," our boss explained. In the recent past, the Serbs had grabbed a few people under UN protection and gunned them down.

"If they try to take him, we fight," stated Captain Ready.

The operation would be led by Colonel Gray and would involve only our platoon. We would be going into the Serb-held portion of the city and they had never seen the UN in there. We had no idea what kind of reception we would receive. They didn't usually like us seeing their front line defenses. No matter, the headshed was determined to get him out. We were going to roll in, grab him and get him and his family out.

I looked over at Jeff. He gave me a little doubtful grin. This was going to be a hairy one. We briefed our troops and settled down to have a couple of beers and watch the fireworks. I could feel that little trickle of adrenaline starting to seep into my system. I was getting pumped. It was like the world's best cocktail: a shot of adrenaline, a dash of fear and a mix of excitement.

Captain Ready was talking about trying to do a really impressive job the next day so we might influence a few people to let us stay at the PTT instead of rotating back to the airport. After lunch the next day, we went down to the vehicles and began to prepare for the mission. As we were mounting our weapons, testing comms and checking, checking, checking, Colonel Gray came down with a couple of civilians. He explained that they were Serbs who wanted to be taken out to the Serb-controlled areas. Gray had made a deal with the JNA, that if we brought these people out, they would provide a guide to get us into the city. How much the JNA knew about our mission's objective, I don't know.

The Colonel was a gaunt figure, the strain of his duties was apparent in his grim features. As we started up and got ready to move out, he went to each vehicle and ensured that our weapons were loaded and made ready. This was against our rules of engagement, but everyone ignored those rules anyway. When he was satisfied, he climbed aboard Captain Ready's track and we were off.

To reach the Serb-held portion of the city, we first had to head out to the airfield. Once there, we cut across the runway and came up to a barricade and bunker blocking a service road. This bunker was being manned by guys from Van Doos Recce. Beyond the barricade was a straight stretch of road several hundred metres long. At the far end, the road turned left and headed southeast towards Serb lines.

The problem was a small village at the end of this stretch. Known as Butmir, this place was held by a very militant group of Muslims. They would often engage the UN troops at the airport and anyone trying to reach Serb lines, as we were now. The Van Doos moved the barricade and we were off. The APCs are not exactly performance machines, but we accelerated for all they were worth down the straight and around the corner.

At the time, I didn't think they had shot at us, but I was later to learn that above the noise of the APCs and with the headsets on over our berets, we couldn't hear any firing. Whether the Muslims engaged us or not, we bashed on blissfully unawares. After turning left, we headed down a long stretch of destruction before reaching the Serb lines, where we were greeted by a T55 tank covering the road. The Serbs had been expecting us and we passed without difficulty. From here, we wound our way along the Serb

lines to the town of Lukavica. Here we found the JNA headquarters. We pulled into the compound and all seven of our carriers
halted in front of their command post.

Colonel Gray jumped down and led out our Serb passengers.
They were greeted by several grinning JNA officers and the group
headed inside the building. After a short discussion, Colonel
Gray emerged with a JNA officer. As the Serb went to get his
vehicle, the colonel walked up to each vehicle and told us quite
clearly, "Be ready to fire at the first sign of trouble!"

We were already in contravention of our rules of engagement.
Our present orders allowed us to have a loaded magazine on the
weapon, but no round up the spout, especially on the .50. However, I don't think there was a single soldier from any contingent
who followed those rules. "Better tried by twelve than buried by
six," was our motto. Gray needn't have worried about us. We
were ready for anything.

I was beginning to have my doubts. We were about to enter the
most dangerous place in Sarajevo and yet we had received no
proper mission orders. Where exactly were we going? What was
the drill when we reached our objective? Who would dismount
and enter the building? What were the "actions on" (preplanned
orders for reacting to threats)? If we became separated, what
were the rendezvous coordinates? Who was in support? And on
and on.

Fail to plan, plan to fail.

With these questions still scrolling across my mind, we moved
off. I dumped all my worries into the mental trash bin and fixed
my attention on the job at hand. Whatever happened, we were
up to it. These guys were the best.

We proceeded northeast from Lukavica along a winding paved
road that followed the base of the hills. Eventually, we came back
into the city. Immediately, we became the focus of all attention.
The first thing we noticed was the fact that nearly everybody was
armed. Obviously not a quiet neighbourhood. Slowly, we drove
into the narrowing streets and closer to the front lines.

It was difficult to remain at the peak of alertness. So far we
had mostly seen women doing laundry while their men lounged
about, AKs in hand. There was nothing threatening about their
behaviour and we felt a little uncomfortable acting as if we were
entering a battle. Of course, that is exactly what we were doing.

After a short ride through the residential area, we arrived in the downtown core. As we pulled up to the first primary road paralleling the river, we were surrounded by Serbs. Not just JNA either. A large group of soldiers approached us wearing black coveralls with a large crest on one sleeve. These were the "White Eagles," a paramilitary group known for their ferocity. Here our JNA escort stopped and moved to speak with the locals.

Captain Ready signaled for our 71 and 72 groups to wait where we were. With 73 and 73A, he headed off to the left to confirm our location. With the JNA officer present, we weren't in too much trouble. As we waited, more and more soldiers began to arrive in the intersection. For the moment, they just watched and talked amongst themselves. Our guys stood firm, presenting a totally professional air of nonchalance. We showed no sign of fear and this, I hope, instilled a sense of doubt in the locals about their ability to take us on.

Fortunately, we didn't have to wait around to find out. Captain Ready returned and motioned for us to follow him. We turned left onto a wide street flanked by large buildings. We were traveling west, paralleling the river. Each time we passed an intersection, it opened us up to fire from the TDF forces one hundred metres to the north across the river. My vehicle was last in the procession. I turned around at one point, after passing an intersection, to see a long burst of machine gun fire impact in a building behind us. Up ahead, 79 halted. Each of our vehicles pulled over to the side of the road. Glen covered across the street, over 72's heads, and they watched over ours. This way, no one lurking in a window above could surprise us.

Now that we had stopped, I could hear the sounds of a major fight taking place around the corner by the river's edge. The TDF had probably heard our vehicles and thought they were JNA tanks moving. The intersections now became shooting galleries. A Serb irregular holding an old MG42 raced around the corner behind us and out of the line of fire. He was panting and appeared to have sprinted quite a distance. He looked up at me and grinned. Catching his breath, he jogged along the sidewalk and turned into a doorway. Probably headed for the roof, I thought.

I wasn't sure what was going on at this point. Up front, they seemed to be having some confusion about the address. Finally, we began to move. As we crossed intersections, Glen and I

ducked down a little. The TDF troops probably had no idea what
UN vehicles were doing in the Serb front line and targeted us out
of suspicion. Because we kept moving, they weren't scoring any
real hits.

One of the things I was quickly learning here was that it is
damned hard to hit a moving target. Especially in the local standard of fire discipline, firing bursts of automatic fire from the hip
or above the head. Still, a poorly aimed round can be just as
deadly as a well-aimed one.

Eventually, we split off on a Y junction and stopped in a rela-
tively peaceful, treelined side street. 79 wheeled about and backed
up to the doorway of an old apartment block. The rest of us took
up covering positions, watching the street and buildings around
us.

Now what?

Colonel Gray dismounted from 79 and hurried into the building, alone. I was stunned! He had no weapon because, by law, as
an observer, he had to be unarmed. He also had no radio and
was going into a building that none of us had any idea about.
Where was the apartment? How long do we wait? What happens
if someone intercepted Gray? I hoped Captain Ready had some
idea, because the rest of us sure didn't.

Actually, the start of a battle probably worked in our favour.
Everyone with a weapon was sprinting for the river and had forgotten about the UN guys.

We waited and listened. The fight wasn't a pitched battle but
more of a game of cat and mouse by the sounds of it. Soldiers
were opening up for brief bursts and then changing positions.
The enemy would return fire for a moment and then all would be
quiet again until the next burst. Because the fight was taking
place less than a hundred metres away, we almost had front row
seats. This was one time that I wouldn't have minded being up in
the cheap seats.

Colonel Gray came out of the building . . . alone. He stuck his
head into 79 and then headed back inside the building. Captain
Ready came over the air moments later.

"All callsigns, this is 79er, unable to locate the package, but
have found some non-combatants that want to come with us,
out."

Sure enough, Gray emerged with an elderly couple who were

quickly stuffed into the back of 79. Probably Muslims who wanted out of Serb lines. Well, at least the mission wasn't a total waste.

79 fired up and wheeled out into the street. In turn, we all pivoted and roared after Ready. Dodging fire as we went, our rescue mission finally linked up with our JNA guide, who led us back out of the city. He had no idea who was in the carrier, but he must have known we came for something. This was the most dangerous part of the trip. If he wanted to set up a road block to stop us and seize our cargo, he had ample time to have prepared it. Probably somewhere near the HQ in Lukavica I figured. We all kept up our guard and, as we passed the JNA barracks, the Serb turned in and we just roared by. Fifteen minutes later, we were back at the PTT. Gray dismounted, thanked Ready and led the Muslim couple away.

We all breathed a sigh of relief and relaxed. Our first hostage rescue was over. As we cleaned our weapons, each of us sat alone with his thoughts. I don't know about the others, but I was quite concerned about the way we had approached this mission. I was glad to have done it, but it was not a well-planned affair. In fact, it had the potential for a major disaster. We were all professional troops and knew our jobs, but this was not everyday work for us. We were all highly trained in seizing buildings and room clearing, but in this case we had been in an urban environment mounted in mechanized vehicles. Anyone who knows anything about urban combat knows that vehicles don't survive very long. Our drills and tactics were . . . well, non-existent.

I knew where it came from. As a mechanized recce force, we always moved fast and were used to thinking on our feet. Our normal orders process usually consisted of a radio message that said, "Move here and do this, out." That type of SOP wasn't suitable for this environment. We should have spent a couple of days studying the area and preparing for every contingency.

As I jumped down from the carrier and headed into the PTT, I was thinking of how best to raise my concerns with the rest of the commanders. As a very junior sergeant and group 2IC, I couldn't just blurt out that we didn't know what we were doing.

The situation resolved itself. Fate has a way of getting your attention, I have found.

We had dumped our kit and headed down to supper when a

warning order arrived. As we got back up to our bunks, we were informed we were going out again. The platoon had two missions. The Royal Canadian Mounted Police guys attached to our headquarters had just got the go-ahead for a POW exchange, and a column of French troops was arriving from Belgrade.

It was now close to 1700 hours and there was no way we could pull either one off before dark. So much for my concerns about a lack of proper planning. We grabbed our gear and headed back to the carriers.

Once at the vehicles, we had a quick briefing on the upcoming actions. 79 would establish a command post near Lukavica. Eric's 71 group would set up to cover a couple of high-rise buildings near the PTT that were known to house snipers. Our 72 group would go to meet the incoming French convoy and shepherd it through all the danger areas in the city. 73 group under Kevin and Jeff would take the RCMP officers and an LO to the prisoner exchange. All of this would take place in the exact same area we had been in earlier. There was no time for a lot of questions, so we mounted up and prepared our weapons.

The two RCMP officers arrived and mounted up in 73 and 73A. These guys were supposed to be advising the locals on how to establish a new, effective law enforcement system. However, since there was no law, these guys didn't have a lot to do. We liked them but were very envious. These guys made up to $75,000 a year over here. That didn't include their salaries back home. Up until we met them, we had been happy with our extra $1,300 a month in combat pay. If we were lucky, we would get home with nearly $8,000 in our bank accounts. Of course, we had to work pretty hard for our money. These RCMP guys didn't seem to do much of anything. C'est la guerre.

We headed off on the same route that we had taken earlier in the day. After dashing out of the airfield and making our way past the JNA headquarters at Lukavica, our 72 group stopped at a major road junction above the old city. 73 had stopped at Serb HQ to pick up the POWs, before proceeding down into the old city. As they passed us, we had a good look at a busload of terrified old men, women and children. Guarding them was a nasty-looking group of Serbs. So much for the prisoner of war theory.

The exchange was to take place at one of the many bridges over the river. As Kevin reached the river, all was quiet, but things quickly began to go wrong. There was no UN representative present on the Bosnian side of the bridge. To get the process started, the RCMP guys and a Liaison Officer had to sprint across the bridge and into Muslim lines. This left Kevin and his group alone with the Serbs and out of contact with the guys across the river. Not a good situation if anything went wrong. The exchange started with an old woman being dragged off the Serb bus and being sent across the bridge. Once she was across, the TDF released an old man. At this rate, with a busload of forty hostages (there were no soldiers being exchanged), it would take several hours. Darkness was already falling and things weren't looking good.

Back at 72's intersection, our carriers were parked fifty metres back down the road in the direction of Lukavica. I was dismounted with a headset radio. We weren't sure when the convoy was due to arrive, so we simply had to wait. As the light faded, a persistent drizzle began. The low, dark clouds hastened the onset of darkness and gave an almost claustrophobic effect to the night.

The UN didn't operate at night in Sarajevo. There was too great a chance for a mistake. Now, here we were sitting at an intersection, in the fading light, waiting for a convoy whose whereabouts we didn't know. I was even more worried about the boys down at the river. They were on the front lines. Bad, very bad.

While we waited, an occasional shot would zip by. We were on the side of a hill roughly four hundred metres from the TDF lines. The rounds went well above our heads and we weren't too concerned. As I waited in the dark at the intersection, a crowd began to form. Mostly locals with nothing better to do, they came and stood in the shade of an old bus stop and watched me. One of the men was very interested in my weapon. We had heard the locals often thought we had no bullets in our guns. Probably a result of UN propaganda downplaying our status as combat troops on a humanitarian mission. I didn't want any mistakes, so I called him forward. When he was close, I pulled off my magazine and allowed him a good look. Then I cocked my weapon and a round was ejected from the spout. The action of me cocking my weapon frightened him and he began to back away. I held out my weapon to him in one hand and motioned for him to touch it.

Nervously, he reached out to grasp the rifle. I never let go of it, but I let him feel the weight. He was very impressed and immediately stepped back. I don't know if he noticed my other hand on the kukri. I then made a big show of replacing the mag on my weapon and cocking it. I wanted him to be sure it was loaded. Now I only hoped he went home and told all his friends that we were well armed.

From this point things started to go wrong quickly. Several shots snapped over my head and my audience scattered. I got on my headset and reported some shooting at the intersection. Back in the vehicles, the message was relayed to Captain Ready in 79. Somehow the message got confused and he misunderstood it to mean we were under sniper fire. At about the same time, down on the river, a T55 tank pulled out of an alley on the TDF side of the river and fired a round at 73. It hit just above the carrier on the wall of a building which immediately exploded in debris and smoke. The tank quickly pulled back out of sight. Now machine guns opened up from both sides and the bridge was raked by fire.

The Serb guards freaked. They were not front line troops and wanted no part of this shooting stuff. They began herding the hostages back on the bus, screaming and kicking at them. Our guys felt sorry for the hostages, but were more worried about the UN officers and the LO across the river. They couldn't leave without them and were forced to watch carefully for any sign of the tank, hoping not to be around if it reappeared. Neither Jeff nor Kevin could fire their weapons because, if they had joined the fray with that big .50 cal, they would have called more attention to themselves than needed. The Serbs and TDF were just firing generally at each other and not specifically targeting them. They were just caught in the middle. All they wanted to do was get out of there.

The Serbs had done just that. The bus, once loaded, turned around and took off back towards Lukavica. Kevin, Jeff and the boys had to wait for the guys across the river. Just as they were thinking about dismounting and trying to get across the bridge, the RCMP officers and the LO came sprinting across. Machine gun fire chased them the whole way, but they made it. You can say what you want about the RCMP's involvement over there, but they definitely weren't short on bravery.

Jeff and Kevin could have covered their movement by fire, but where would they aim? This was our constant problem in the city. Firing goes on all around you, but from where specifically? In any normal inner city, there are a thousand windows and doorways in every direction. As UN troops, we couldn't just hose down entire neighbourhoods. We were permitted by the rules to target only specific threats. Once someone stopped firing at us, he was no longer a threat and could not be engaged. So Jeff and Kevin just held their breath until the runners reached them. Once they were on board, the two carriers pivoted and tore out of there just as more tank fire began to hit the area.

Meanwhile, back at the intersection, the French had arrived. Truck after truck came trundling down the road to our intersection where I signaled them to turn left. Jerry headed off in front of the lead truck and headed down the road several hundred metres before stopping. After he halted, a French officer informed him they had a breakdown and the tow truck was trying to catch up to the rear.

So we had to wait. We couldn't abandon these two trucks outside the city at night. The last few trucks were blocking the intersection, but there wasn't much other traffic in this neighbourhood. I was more worried about more shooting. With the rear of the vehicles loaded with French troops, stray rounds could be a real hazard.

I strolled up and down the convoy impatiently waiting for the last two to catch up. Meanwhile, I was being brought up to date over my headset by Daryl on the trouble down by the river. 79 still thought we were under sniper fire and were in serious trouble, stalled at the intersection. Because the drizzle had soaked the radios, our transmissions were becoming garbled. Our Vietnam-era radios didn't stand up too well to inclement weather.

I was worried. As I paced up and down the column, French troops watched me from their dry seats in the back of the trucks. The problem was that our convoy was blocking the only route back to Lukavica. The Serb jailers would soon arrive at our traffic jam and be unable to pass.

The Serbs had stopped the bus once they cleared the city. It was here that 73 and 73A caught up with them. The guards were very angry and began to beat the hostages. Sensing a disaster developing, Kevin and Jeff pulled up alongside and, with hands on their weapons, glared at the Serbs. One of the RCMP officers boarded the bus and demanded the Serbs to relax. He decided to stay on the bus for the remainder of the journey back to the prison camp to protect the civilians. So, with the two carriers close by, the little convoy headed towards Lukavica and our unintended roadblock.

We informed Kevin by radio that the road was blocked and he couldn't get through. They stopped the bus and tried to explain to the Serbs, but the guards only became excited and began to become violent again. They all had AKs and our RCMP officer had nothing. Kevin thought about putting a couple of our guys aboard the bus, but that would have only provoked the Serbs who would rightly guess they were now under guard. Kevin got on the radio and told us to get the road clear before we had a disaster on our hands.

Jerry was faced with a dilemma. The road here was narrow, and you couldn't drive on the shoulders for fear of mines. We certainly couldn't let trucks filled with troops pull off the road. If he left without me, I could wait for the latecomers but would be alone for the trip. By day that would have been risky, but by night terminal.

Finally, we couldn't wait any longer. Jerry pulled out and led the convoy away at a slow pace. I had Daryl wheel our carrier around and we headed off into the hills to try to find the lost vehicles. Kevin got the bus going again and they followed the convoy back to the camp.

We hadn't gone far in our search when I spotted the two strays. Someone was taking potshots at our headlights by now, so we grabbed the Frenchmen and turned around. I called Jerry to tell him we were on our way. As we caught up to the convoy, we passed 73 and 73A parked on the side of the road with the now-empty bus. In the darkness, I could make out some large barn-type buildings. These must have housed the prisoners. I waved to Jeff as we went by.

After we all made it back to the PTT later, we had a hot wash up about the day's events. All of us were very critical at the way the operations staff had been using us. No one was planning any of this. The hostage rescue was poorly planned, the POW exchange should not have been done at night, and it required the full platoon, not just two dets. The RCMP should never have been allowed to cross that bridge without some armed security and a radio. The convoy should not have been routed the way it was, on the same route as the exchange mission. All in all, it had been a badly planned day. If we were going to survive this tour, we were going to have to straighten a few things out.

To add to our concerns, Colonel Jones out at the airport was upset because we didn't clear any of our missions through him. He thought we still reported to his HQ. The Ops staff at the PTT believed we worked for them and would task us as they saw fit. We were caught in the middle.

Captain Ready and Warrant Sullivan were a little upset about everything but made it clear that they thought we had done an outstanding job. The only response we got from Ops was to tell us we didn't know what we were talking about, the TDF didn't have any tanks in the city. The Muslims couldn't have been shooting at 73 and 73A with a tank, we must have made a mistake. Jeff and Kevin wanted to go down and "explain things" to the staff weasels, but since we wanted to stay at the PTT, it wouldn't have helped our case. A few days later, a T55 tank was spotted on a hill several hundred metres from our building. It was well within Muslim lines and pointing out towards the Serbs. Even the Ops staff had to acknowledge it was unlikely to be a Serbian trick.

The next morning we all rose wondering what a new day would bring. My first task was to escort some staff types down to the airport for a meeting. I was going alone on this one and was to meet the officer down in Ops at 1030 hours. The run to the airport was pretty routine and we began doing it as single dets. Due to the sniper threat, our jeeps were grounded, so the only method of reaching the airport was with an APC. Since the French and our platoon had the only armoured vehicles at the PTT, we got the job. Soon, the French would start a regular taxi service but, for the moment, it was still one of our tasks.

At 1015 hours, I went down to the Ops hallway to find my passenger. Daryl and Glen had headed for the vehicle to prep it. I was dressed as I normally was for a patrol: battered blue beret, dusty combats, flak jacket, C7 and kukri. As I walked down the hallway, I noticed everyone else was in well-turned-out uniforms and was squeaky clean. In comparison, I looked like I had just dragged myself in from a desert. Everybody was rushing around, and being a fairly big guy to begin with, I used up a lot of space. I began to feel like the proverbial bull in the china shop. I stuck my head into Ops and saw my passenger, a Canadian captain. He said he would be with me in a minute, so I stayed where I was in the hallway, getting in the way.

Suddenly a door opened behind me and I was nearly knocked over by the crowd spilling out. I swung around and found myself face to face with General MacKenzie. He appeared to be trying to escape a group of staff officers hounding him with questions or protests.

Suddenly, he stopped in mid-stride and stared at me. Not recognizing me, he extended his hand and introduced himself.

"Lew MacKenzie," he said warmly.

I was caught a bit off guard and stuttered out, "Sergeant Davis, sir, from the RCR recce platoon upstairs," as I shook his hand.

While I spoke, I was well aware of the cloud of staff officers who were staring at me like I was some kind of bug, obviously upset that the General was bothering with an obvious nobody in the grand scheme of things. They knew better than to interrupt, though.

"Best job in the Forces," continued General MacKenzie, suddenly happy and reminiscent of his days in Cyprus commanding a recce platoon. I smiled back at him and suddenly felt a bit of a connection with our commander. The General was quickly snapped out of his reverie by the crush of staff officers at his heels and, with a final grin for me, turned and strode off down the hall with the hounds snapping at his heels.

Before I could reflect on my first meeting with our commander, my passenger showed up beside me ready to go. I led off down the hallway wondering about the man I had just met. Up until this point in my career I had no use for generals. The way the Forces were being run, I had no respect for the men at the top. Now I figured I was going to have to make an exception to that rule. I liked this MacKenzie. So far he seemed to be running things with common sense, and some balls. He wasn't afraid to call things as he saw them. I suddenly felt a little better about our chances in Sarajevo.

———————

The next day we didn't have any missions, but the day was not without incident. The Warrant came around in the morning and told me it was my turn to go on UN leave. A Hercules was flying out of the airfield the next day for Germany. I could be on it if I chose to. I didn't even think about it; I turned it down. I was starting to realize that these days we were spending in Sarajevo were probably going to be the high point in my career. There was no way I was leaving.

Jerry agreed to go in my place. Two other guys were going as well, Daryl included. My vehicle would be left without a driver. However, Greg Alkerton from 71A was available, so he filled in as gunner while Glen took over driving. This left the platoon a bit shorthanded, but we were told that we had to fill our slots or risk losing our leave altogether.

With Jerry gone I became the group commander for 73 and 73A. Although I was not ambitious whatsoever, I still welcomed the challenge. Responsibility was on my shoulders and I would make the calls. I was okay with that.

In nearby Beaver Camp, November company's home in an old JNA base, tragedy had hit that morning. The first and least serious event was Corporal Jerry Hebert being hit in the knee by rifle fire. The second incident was much worse. Corporal Dennis Reid had stepped on an anti-personnel mine and lost his foot. He had jumped from a fence onto an area everyone had thought cleared and landed on a mine. On detonating, it had tossed him through the air. Once down, he found his foot had gone the other way. The guys nearest him, careless of the threat, rushed to him and gave first aid. Soon, Dennis was on his way to the Bosnian hospital in downtown Sarajevo. We had no surgery of our own capable of dealing with a traumatic amputation, so he was taken to the doctors in town. Once again, our lack of medical coverage was to curse us.

We knew he would need evacuation and, fortunately, a Canadian Hercules had just landed at the airport. Sergeant Marty Spriggs, a good friend of mine, was out at the airport and responsible for organizing operations there. He found the pilot of the plane and explained the situation. Reid was in surgery and we wanted the plane to wait for him to be brought to the airport for evacuation as soon as he was finished. The pilot, responsible for his aircraft, refused to wait. He didn't like the idea of sitting there in Sarajevo during a major offensive.

Marty couldn't believe it. This pilot wouldn't wait for a wounded Canadian soldier. Marty reported to the colonel, but Jones had no authority to order the plane to wait. So off went our plane as soon as it was unloaded. Frustrated and worried, everyone was becoming concerned about getting Reid out. A French pilot who had witnessed the whole affair approached Marty afterwards.

"I hear you have a wounded man," he said.

Marty looked at him and explained.

"I will wait for him, no matter how long it takes," said the Frenchman. Marty couldn't believe it. Our great Canadian ran and here was a foreign pilot willing to wait. Marty could have hugged him.

It turned out that Corporal Reid wasn't out of surgery until well after nightfall. At 2200 hours Marty was informed that Reid would remain at the hospital overnight. The French pilot was informed and flew his plane out without complaint. Reid was evacuated the next day.

I have always wanted to find that French pilot and give him a big hug myself. I also swore if I ever found that Canadian pilot I would beat the crap out of him. It was important to get Reid out, but it was also important for all of us to know, if we got seriously hurt, we would be evacuated to a decent hospital out of the city. The fact that we now couldn't trust the Canadian Air Force to get us out didn't give us a warm fuzzy feeling. I didn't like branding every pilot a coward like the one on this particular day, but now the onus was on them to prove themselves to us.

Medical treatment in the local hospital didn't reassure us either. This place was not anyone's ideal of a modern surgical centre. All of us would rather have decent Canadian, British or American doctors doing the work.

While all this was going on, a sniper was harrassing Serb troops on the ridge to the south. The sniper was holed up in a building across the street from us. Eventually, the Serbs tired of this annoyance and mortared the Olympic village. One lucky hit landed in a TDF ammo bunker in the basement of a two-storey building. The place exploded into a huge fireball and flames roared several hundred metres into the sky.

In Recce, we crowded around the windows to watch the inferno. The flames whipped higher and higher and engulfed the whole building. The local Fire Brigade showed up, but Serb snipers drove them off. The fire raged for more than twenty minutes, ever gaining in intensity, when suddenly a hard driving rain began to fall. Within minutes the flames began to sputter. In another ten minutes, the flames were gone and huge billows of black smoke replaced the inferno.

Sarajevo certainly wasn't a boring town.

———————

On 10 July we had another interesting day. There were no missions for us, but other events kept our attention.

In Beaver Camp, November company was going about its daily business. Suddenly mortars began to fall right on the camp. Everyone ran for shelter. Two soldiers, whom I refuse to identify, watched as the CQ staff rushed out of the stores tent and headed for a bunker. These two, seeing a good opportunity presenting itself, couldn't resist and sprinted for the CQ tent. Inside were all the stockpiles of beer for the company. With mortars reigning down, they each grabbed a case and sprinted back out into the fray. Moments after leaving the tent, a mortar made a direct hit, destroying the tent . . . and the beer, and the evidence.

Out at the airfield, they were getting hit as well. Mortars rained down all over the area, hitting one of the hangars and damaging several vehicles. Luckily, in both places, no one was hurt.

Soon after it was over, Colonel Jones lost it. He raged to the press at the airfield that he would withdraw the battalion from Bosnia and tell the world what was going on here!

In Recce, we heard this and laughed. A mere light colonel had no authority to make that kind of decision. Shortly afterwards, he realized his error and announced he would cease shipments of aid to the population. General MacKenzie was out of the country at the moment for a conference in Rome. Colonel Petrounev was in charge and he quickly overruled Jones on that one.

Finally, Jones had to settle for asking to meet with the leaders of each faction to plead for a safe zone for his UN troops. The end result was a total embarrassment for the Canadians in Bosnia and around the world. The first lesson we all learned here in the former Yugoslavia was that if you make a threat, you had better be prepared to carry it out.

As a result of this situation, Recce and November company were now faced with living amongst the belligerents without any defensive capability. The airport was well defended, but inside the city, Beaver Camp and the PTT were surrounded. Also, now any time one of us said to a local, "Don't do that or we will have to shoot," we wouldn't be taken seriously.

It was only a few mortars and no one was hurt. I figured at the time that if we had pulled out of Sarajevo over those few mortar rounds and run with our tails between our legs, I was quitting the Forces in shame.

Soon after, things got worse at the airport. The locals began lobbing RPG rockets at Canadian vehicles and bunkers regularly. The snipers stepped up their activity as well. Everyone at the airport was now basically under siege.

The Van Doos and French troops manning the airfield had to start digging everything in. Chicken wire was being strung up everywhere to detonate rockets away from the bunkers. MacKenzie got permission from UN HQ to have some mortars brought in. The condition placed on them by New York was that they could only fire illumination rounds. The General agreed and then turned to his Ops people and had them ship in crates of high explosive and white phosphorus rounds on the sly.

As well, we had our TOW vehicles dug in around the airport. These vehicles were state of the art, with thermal imagers and enclosed turrets. The problem was, we weren't allowed to have any missiles for the launchers. Once again, MacKenzie had some missiles brought in without informing New York.

Our snipers were also beginning to have an effect. The Van Doos had found one old Sergeant Major who was qualified and he became their sniper. The French, on the other hand, had quite a few. One French sniper was doing so well, he was getting a reputation in the city. I won't say how many kills he had, but he was eventually flown out to prevent any retaliations.

Things were developing into almost a state of all-out war within Sarajevo. Neither the Bosnians nor the Serbs could openly attack us for fear of international condemnation, so they began hitting us and then blaming the other side for the attack. This had the effect of creating negative press for their opposition in the international press.

At November company's position, things took an even more drastic turn. The TDF were sneaking mortars in and setting them up just outside the Canadian camp. They would then fire at the Serbs, hoping they wouldn't retaliate for fear of hitting the UN positions. Major Devlin's protests to the local TDF commander only brought denials, so exceptional measures had to be taken.

After night fell, small teams of Canadian troops would leave their UN kit behind, camouflage their faces and creep out into the night. They would patrol the neighbourhoods, searching for any TDF mortars being moved in. It was highly dangerous and "illegal" work. Obviously, the Rules of Engagement were blurred slightly here. Anything covert was totally against the Chapter Six rules. In New York, no doubt some bureaucrat would have a cow, but he was sleeping all cozy in bed at night. In Sarajevo, desperate times . . .

On 12 July I escorted a representative from the UNHCR down into the old city. He had to get across the canal to an old office they had on the Serb side. This time I took my vehicle right across the bridge while 73A covered us from the friendly side. I didn't want a repeat of the POW fiasco.

We were about 800 metres from the site of the exchange and everything seemed quiet. I noticed on the bridge beside us a historical marker commemorating the spot where Archduke Ferdinand had been gunned down in June 1914. It was on this spot that World War One began.

I stayed close to the UN rep as he did his business and then we mounted up and headed back. On the way out, we came to an intersection being manned by Sergeant Sam Pengally of November company and his men. A former member of Recce and my first group commander, he was manning a checkpoint for the aid convoys.

Sam was crouching on the ground behind his carrier, taking cover, because a Serb sniper was raking the area of the intersection with automatic fire. I had passed this way on our trip in and there had been no problem, so when Sam held up his hand, I thought he was waving. I waved back and we reached the intersection and turned into the fire. I didn't see Sam waving at me to stop because I was watching a civilian running beside the carrier on the opposite side. He was using us to block him from the fire as he crossed the intersection. I never heard the bullets over the noise of the APC and thankfully, none of us were hit.

Several hours later, one of the Van Doos recce dets was at the intersection when two women were hit by fire. The Sergeant in charge had his driver roll the vehicle out into the intersection to give cover while he crawled over to the women. He checked them both. One was dead and the other wounded. He dragged the wounded woman into the back of his carrier and got her to safety. All the while the sniper was trying to get him as well. Afterwards, the survivor was quoted in the local press as blaming the Canadian for not rescuing the dead woman as well and blamed him for her death.

I later heard from Sam about the shooting we had obliviously driven through. I told Greg and Glen and they just laughed. Oops.

Later that day we were deployed to provide local security for a TOW det. These guys had moved their vehicle up onto an over-ramp to give them a good shot into the village of Dobrinja. November company was attempting to move an aid convoy into the suburb to assist the civilians trapped by the fighting. The TOW det was tasked to cover them. A TOW det is vulnerable to local fire and, when concentrating on a target, cannot secure its surroundings. Therefore, my group was providing local security for them.

Beneath the overpass was a TDF checkpoint. It was manned by a couple of troops with AKs. After we had been in place about an hour, a car drove up and a TDF officer got out. He went to talk with his men and then walked out from under the bridge and fired a burst into the air from his AK. The rounds passed close to the TOW det but did no harm. We swung our machine gun around to threaten the TDF troops and immediately the officer got in his car and drove off. Since no one was hurt, I couldn't fire back under our rules of engagement, so I dismounted and headed for the TDF checkpoint.

I acted quite angry and impressed upon the soldiers present that I would not tolerate that type of activity again. My limited Serbo-Croat must have been sufficient because they got the message. They were very apologetic and more than a little worried by the sight of Greg manning the .50 cal and waving. I went back to the carrier, and we had no more problems with the TDF.

Elswhere in the city that day, a New Zealander lost an eye and both feet when his jeep hit a mine. The casualties were beginning to mount.

Around this time, November company was having to learn to drive the big aid trucks. Originally, they had been driven by a group of Dutch civilian volunteers. These had all quit, however, after a convoy was ambushed. They hadn't minded the ambush so much, it was the fact the two Van Doos carriers protecting them took off and abandoned them. Troops from November company had to go out and rescue the drivers under fire. They found them hiding under their trucks and cursing the Van Doos. Afterwards, the drivers refused to drive anymore and went home. We couldn't blame them.

C h a p t e r   8

STAND-OFF

THE NEXT DAY, 13 July, was a day I will long remember, and regret. In the morning, Eric's 71 group and my group were tasked to take Colonel Gray down to the presidency and then out to the former Olympic Stadium north of the old city. The HQ here had been trying to get a flight of French helicopters attached to our force but needed someplace secure to keep them. Because the airport was so unsafe at night, they wanted to see if they could keep them in the stadium for protection. We drove down to the Presidency to locate a government official who would take us into the stadium. I dismounted and took up a position to guard the entrance to the building.

While we waited in front of the Presidency, a teenage girl approached me and addressed me in accented English. She was very pale and didn't look too healthy.

"Excuse me, but I am very sick. I need special medicine or I will die. Can you help me?" she pleaded.

I looked at her. She was so sad. I told her as sympathetically as I could to stay where she was. I went and found Colonel Gray and told him about the girl. His initial reaction surprised me.

"Who the hell do I look like, the Red Cross? You sort it out!"

I was a little stunned, but I guess it was to be expected. I had heard that when he arrived in Sarajevo, the Colonel had been full of hope and energy. Now after weeks of watching these people kill each other and destroy his many attempts to help them because of petty jealousies, he was growing tired. I didn't blame him at all.

Then his expression softened a bit and some of the old compassion returned.

"Tell her to go to the PTT and see the UNHCR people there. They might be able to do something." Then he turned away. I could see him choking back down any sympathy that might have welled up. He was a man who was holding on very tight.

Soon, we had our Bosnian representative and we were off to the stadium. Colonel Gray had told me that the place was liable to get hairy, so be careful. Eric was leading and had the Bosnian rep with him. We passed a burnt-out school bus and Eric radioed back that we were now in no-man's-land and not to stop for anything.

As we turned into the stadium, we were faced with crossing a huge, wide-open parking lot. It had the occasional wrecked car in it but otherwise offered no cover. I told Glen to gun it and we raced across the open ground. I pulled off one headset earpiece and could hear machine gun fire but couldn't see any impacts, so I ignored it.

As we approached the stadium building there were two huge access tunnels leading under the stands. Eric and Wayne headed for one and we headed for the other. Faubert was manning the gun in 73 with Jerry gone. I signalled them to follow me.

As we reached the tunnels, Glen spun the vehicle around and we backed in under cover. Faubert and Horse backed in with us. We shut down and had a listen. There was some shooting outside, but no hits inside the entrance. I dismounted and followed Colonel Gray through the interior of the stadium to Eric's track. There we linked up with the Bosnian rep and went to have a look at the stadium. As we entered the inner area under the stands, the first thing we saw was a group of TDF soldiers standing around a large mortar. Immediately, Colonel Gray lost it. There was no way we could put helicopters in there if the TDF were using it as a fire base. We checked out the rest of the stadium. Being made of concrete, it was in pretty good shape. While we watched, a volley of mortars crashed down both inside and outside the stadium. I could see Colonel Gray wasn't impressed. He and the government rep went off to view the rest of the stadium, while I stayed with the vehicles.

After about twenty minutes they returned. I looked at Eric and he shrugged. It was up to the negotiators now. We mounted back up and with mortars crashing down on the stadium's northwest wall, we raced across the parking lot once again.

Our patrol got back to the PTT in time for lunch, only to find it was borscht again. After eating, we were told we had another mission. A hot one. The platoon was going into one of the most heavily contested zones in the city, the area between the TDF lines in the Olympic village and the Serb-held areas in Dobrinja. This area was a large open field across which both sides regularly fought pitched firefights. The reason for going in? An artillery impact had shattered the water mains into the suburb and people were at risk of dying of dehydration. In the middle of the field, beside a paved road, water bubbled out of the shell crater and drained away. The Bosnians trapped in Dobrinja could see this water welling up one hundred metres away, but they couldn't reach it. Some Bosnian city engineers had volunteered to go out and try to repair the line to save their comrades. They needed protection to do it. That was our mandate in Recce, so we prepared to go out again. Later, due to the extensive negotiations required to get us in, the mission was postponed until the next day.

The day wasn't over though. For the past few afternoons, local kids and teenagers had been coming around the PTT building and hanging out. Sometimes the Dutch signallers would go out and talk to the young ladies. Our guys would see this and ask to go outside. So far we, the NCOs, had refused. It was far too dangerous. The guys were angry, but what could they do?

That evening there were some kids hanging around on a patio at the base of the building. The guys had thrown them some candy until I told them to stop. I didn't want every kid in the city coming to hang out beneath our windows. Also on the patio was an attractive teenage girl. She spoke some English and was having a conversation with some of our guys who were hanging out the window.

Suddenly, out of the corner of his eye, one of the troops saw something race past. He immediately looked and recognized it as a mortar bomb. In the moment before it detonated, he realized it was heading right for the kids. Before he could shout a warning, the bomb exploded. The impact threw our guys back out of the window and onto the floor. Immediately, more rounds followed and the building rocked.

I had been lying in my cot when the first round hit. I rolled out of my cot and onto the floor, trying to get well below the windows. There was lots of yelling going on and the Warrant was shouting for everyone to get to the basement. I grabbed my rifle and vest and headed down. Outside, the rounds continued to hit.

Our drill in this event was to get to the basement and all go to a certain corner for a head count. The count turned up one short. I am not going to mention any names because it wouldn't be right, but one of the guys who had been blasted out of the window had made the mistake of going back to have a look before he was hauled away. On the way downstairs, he had broken away and headed outside to help the kids. Warrant Sullivan immediately rushed outside to find our man.

What he found shocked him to the core. There were little pieces of children everywhere. Arms, legs and blood covered the patio. The teenage girl had died instantly. The other kids were badly wounded. Brit medics showed up and tried to sort out the mess. Our missing man was there, trying to help. Warrant Sullivan, no longer worried about our stray soldier, jumped in to help out as well. They got the kids on stretchers and tried to match the arms and legs with the proper child. It was horrible.

Later they returned to us in the basement. It was an emotional moment. Many of the guys in the platoon had young kids of their own. It was easy to imagine their own children being out there, or how the parents were going to feel when their children didn't come home that night.

While the guys remained alone with their thoughts, I told Captain Ready I was going out to check on Corporal Whitten, who was in our comms APC in the parking lot. I didn't want to dwell on the tragedy and preferred to keep busy. So, I sprinted out into the parking area towards the vehicles. I could see that some rounds had landed in the parking lot and several trucks were badly damaged. When I reached our vehicles, I saw they were all intact. I hammered on the door and Whitten opened it up. I quickly crawled inside and shut the door. Whitten was fine . . . until I told him what happened.

Later that night, the platoon area was pretty subdued. Some of the guys blamed themselves for talking to the kids and throwing them candy, but we all knew—we hadn't launched those bombs.

The next morning, a report came in from the observers that no

Serb mortars had fired that they were aware of. The trajectory was calculated and it was determined that the Bosnians had mortared their own children. For public relations purposes. Sure enough, the morning news in the city reported that the UN and their Serb allies had killed these children.

We couldn't believe it. I can't speak for the others, but that morning I would have happily killed any TDF troops I saw. I was growing tired of the whole mess. These people didn't care. They were animals.

Still, it was my job. We were still a platoon with a job to do. I tucked all my ill feelings away and tried to be my normal, carefree self. It wasn't the last time the Bosnians murdered their own people in well-staged attacks for PR reasons. At the ordinary soldier level, we had no authority to stop it, so we just had to turn away. Soldier on.

The mission to the Dobrinja water main was a go, so we had our breakfast and headed down to the carriers. The whole platoon was in on this one. It was only a short drive to the other side of the Olympic village and we were out in no-man's-land a few minutes later.

First, we split up and fanned out over the area between the two sides. There were some paved roads and we used these to get in. We all faced out from the broken water main with our vehicles separated by no less than a hundred metres. Before anyone dismounted, we had to be sure we weren't going to be attacked. The engineers were in a little station wagon and stuck close to 79, parked by the break. We were most concerned about the Serbs at this point because in less than three days, all opposition in Dobrinja would cease if water service was not restored. Everyone would be either dead or weak from dehydration. It was definitely not to the Serbs' advantage to get the water turned on.

We couldn't disregard a TDF attack either, because it would be a perfect excuse to wipe us out and blame it on the Serbs. So we waited and watched. After about forty minutes, nothing had happened, so we closed in and let the engineers get to work. The platoon parked their tracks to shield the civvies as best they could. I dismounted with a radio to walk the area. They might very well become spooked if we all stayed buttoned up in our vehicles. With my C7 held close, I walked around the area trying to look casual. Captain Ready was dismounted as well. Together, we put on a show of our professional nonchalance.

While I was standing there, I couldn't help but think about how many guns were trained on us at that very moment. I guessed ten or fifteen at least, with another hundred waiting. I wasn't sure what was preventing them from firing, but hoped that whatever it was, the spell would last.

I had an inner laugh when I thought about how my headstone would read, "Killed while defending a water main." What a reason to die! Oh well, you take your pay, you do your job.

When the job was done, we all quickly mounted up. We had one more task to do. The civilians wanted to recover a body that was beside the road on the way back. It was lying in the open, which was bad for local morale. This person deserved a decent funeral. Captain Ready agreed and came up on the air to announce a "Bernie recovery operation" would take place on the way out. The engineers drove up beside the body, jumped out and threw it in the back of the wagon. Wanting to be away from the area as soon as possible, they jumped in the car again and tore away in a cloud of burning rubber. My group was up in front, clearing the way. 73 group was behind the car, trying to cover their withdrawal, but they were going too fast for the APCs to keep up. This turned out to be fortunate because the excited engineers took a corner too fast and the tailgate of the wagon swung open. Predictably, the corpse came tumbling out. I don't know who it was, but someone got on the air and immediately reported, "Bernie escape attempt!"

It was very sick and totally in poor taste, yet we all had a good laugh. In these places, if you lose your sense of humour, you lose your mind.

Later that morning, I had a mission to do. The press had heard that General MacKenzie would address them about the mortar incident and were camped out on the main steps of the PTT. Christine Amanapour was there for CNN, the BBC was there, some guys from CBC and about every other news service in the world. Someone saw me coming towards the entrance of the building and shouted, "Here he comes!" Every journalist in the place jumped up and rushed the doorway. As I emerged, they all thrust their cameras and microphones in my face. I just stood still and stared at them. Because I was at the top of several steps, I towered above them.

I don't suppose I looked very pleasant because they immediately parted like the Red Sea to silently let me through. I strolled off towards the carriers without looking back. As I went I over-heard two well-known correspondents talking.

The famous BBC reporter was saying to the CBC representa-tive, ". . . You know what is different about this war from most of the others?" he asked.

The CBC guy shook his head.

"No war whores," the BBC guy finished.

As I walked out of earshot, I couldn't help but dislike any and all reporters. They were like leeches, just hanging around waiting to suck the life out of you. Still, they were here in Sarajevo, dodg-ing bullets with the rest of us, and probably working for some equally misguided bosses back in their home countries.

Most of these characters lived down at the Holiday Inn, near the centre of town. Originally, we were supposed to stay there until the manager decided he wanted to charge each man $75 a day. Now it was the home of the reporters. Ten storeys tall and bright yellow, it looked like something out of a Monty Python film. Most of the south wall had been blasted away by tank fire. It probably made the most attractive target in town for bored Serb gunners in the hills.

I had to go in there once. The UN had rented some space in the basement to store supplies. I was supposed to pick up a package at the hotel, so I drove down with my two vehicles. I had heard they didn't allow weapons inside the main foyer, but was curious, so I wandered in the front door. The interior looked pretty good. They were obviously trying to keep up appearances. The concierge spot-ted me immediately and hustled me over to a stairwell and out of sight. In the basement, I found Master Corporal Caroline Pagee, who used to work out in our building back in Polom.

I explained my problem and she led me to a storage room. As I walked in, the first thing I noticed was some supply goof fooling around with a grenade. He was slumped in a chair and kept pulling the pin out of the grenade and then putting it back in. I grabbed my package from Caroline and made my exit. That was the last place I wanted to be, with some psyched out loser and a live grenade.

Instead of causing another fuss, I decided to leave by the underground parking entrance. I strolled up the ramp and out into the sunlight. As soon as I reached the top of the ramp, I heard yelling. Looking to my left, I saw my two vehicles. The guys were waving at me to come over. Faubert signalled to hurry, so I jogged over. The vehicles were sitting in the shade of a large building about fifty metres away.

As I approached, Greg called out that someone had just been shot by a sniper. The casualty had been standing close to where I had emerged from the garage.

My luck had held out again.

———————

On 15 July, I was tasked to collect eighteen Ukrainian soldiers who were arriving at the airport and take them to the PTT. It had been decided that the Canadians would be replaced at the end of the month by a battalion of Ukrainians and one of Egyptians. This crew was to be the Ukraine advance party.

Horse was pretty excited because his ancestors lived in the Ukraine before being driven out of their homeland. He couldn't wait to greet his fellow countrymen.

As we arrived at the aiport, Marty wandered over to say that we were getting thirty-eight Ukrainians, not the original eighteen, and they all had luggage. I realized my two APCs wouldn't cut it and called back to Recce for two more dets and a truck for the kit. A few minutes later, Eric and Wayne were on the way.

As 71 was driving along the the road leading to the front gate of the airfield, a sniper tried to hit the lead vehicle's driver. A 7.62 round struck the APC two centimetres below Corporal Whitten's face. The bullet had hit the steel guard over the headlights and broken apart. One piece struck Whitten in the forehead. It only broke the skin and drew a little blood. Rather than wait for another, more accurate round, Whitten accelerated into the airfield and pulled up next to my two dets on the runway. As he dismounted, he told everyone what happened.

Eric got on the horn and reported that Whitten had been hit in the head by a 7.62 round. It was over an open frequency and immediately everyone in the Battle Group thought Whitten was dead. Captain Ready got on the horn and called for details.

"71, this is Sunray, confirm callsign Whitten has been shot, over."

Eric responded. "71, yes, but he is OK. I'll have him report to Starlight [the medics] when we get back to your location, over."

Of course, this message confused everyone. Not too many people get shot in the head and then continue working. We had work to do though, and left it at that.

As the Ukrainians showed up, they threw their kit in the truck and then scrambled into the carriers. The big surprise came when a full Ukrainian general strode up. An English-speaking Ukrainian officer explained that the general would like a staff car to take him to the HQ.

I had a hard time not laughing.

"Tell the general that this is it," I said, pointing at the M113.

When the general was told, he shrugged and headed for the back of an APC. All the troops inside saw him coming and scurried out. They crowded into the other, already overburdened vehicles. Soon we were loaded up and on our way.

Before we left the airport, we were told that the Van Doos sniper had nailed a local the previous day and to watch out for retributions by the locals. We laughed—too late for that advice, as Whitten had already discovered. So, as we rolled out of the airport, we kept all our weapons trained on the houses of Dobrinja waiting for another attack. Staring down the wrong end of four .50 cals probably discouraged the locals and they left us alone.

That night we invited the Ukrainians up to our apartments and had a little party. These guys all had paratrooper uniforms and striped t-shirts underneath. I had always wanted one of these shirts and traded a recce platoon t-shirt for one. The Ukrainians brought in a couple of bottles of vodka and we all celebrated into the night. I tried out my minuscule knowledge of Russian on them, but had no luck. Fortunately, their company 2IC spoke some English and we all got along well. The OC claimed to have fought in Afghanistan and we pretty much believed him. You have to take all military boasts with a grain of salt. Every American who ever retired from the U.S. Army was in Special Forces. Every Brit was in the Falklands. You nodded and made the appropriate comments, but who knew?

Some of the several hundred bottles of Croatian beer we had brought down had gone skunky, so we traded it to the Ukrainians for some vodka. They didn't drink beer at home and had no idea there weren't supposed to be things floating in it. Some of our guys thought that we might make our guests sick, until they saw some Ukrainians go downstairs and return with IV bags of surgical alcohol to drink. We figured any bacteria in the beer wouldn't stand a chance against this stuff, so no one worried.

The next morning there were some heavy heads. Horse had tried a few gulps from the IV bags and felt like death. No one made it to breakfast, but at lunch we were greeted with some kind of stew . . . sort of. I asked the Swedish cook what it was. He gave me some name I couldn't pronounce.

"But what is it?" I asked again. The cook looked at it for a moment before he answered.

"It tastes like shit, but it won't kill you," he said.

If that was the cook's advice, I wasn't reassured, so I passed.

On 17 July, we were tasked to provide VIP security for a meeting between all the factions and Sir Douglas Hurd, the British Foreign Secretary. Once again, we had almost no prep time. Our dets met him at the airport and provided an escort as he was brought down to the PTT.

He was travelling in a French VAB, and the locals loved to try to shoot out the tires on these things, so we were along as well. We spent the day moving the Foreign Secretary around and dodging well-staged incidents the locals put on for his benefit. At the Bosnian Presidency the TDF mortared their own people again as Hurd arrived. He had just dismounted from Kevin's track when several mortars slammed into the square across the road, killing several civilians. It had been staged by the Muslims to impress Hurd. They told him the Serbs did this to them everyday, when in fact they had killed their own people again for political reasons. Animals.

My group was tasked to pick up the Serb leader, Dr. Karadzic, and take him to the airport for a meeting with the Bosnian leader, President Izetbegovic, and Hurd. Because we would pass through Muslim lines, there was a distinct danger of an ambush. The meeting was not a secret and we anticipated trouble. The LOS with us tried to assure the Serbs that they could trust us to protect their leader. The JNA weren't too happy about handing over their leader to us, but it was the only way to get him to the meeting.

While we were mounting up the President, some small-arms fire cracked overhead, but it was poorly aimed. Once everyone was in place, we set off. The VIP was in my second vehicle, 72. I led with 72A, with Glen driving and Greg at the .50 cal. Somewhat strangely, we reached the airfield without incident.

There was a bit of confusion when we got there. Izetbegovic had refused to meet with the Serb President, but Douglas Hurd showed up under 71 and 73's protection. They had their meeting and 71 took Dr. Karadzic back to Lukavica while the remainder of Recce secured the Foreign Secretary's plane. The French did a runway sweep and, when all seemed ready, Sir Douglas boarded his aircraft. The plane took off immediately and, as it climbed out of the mountain valley, a missile radar lock set off alarms in the plane, but no missile was fired. Just a warning for a nosy politician, I guess. Sir Douglas had accomplished little and it was probably a subtle way of discouraging him from returning.

As we returned to the PTT that night, we were informed that the general wanted a sniper det on the roof. Someone had been harrassing our people from a position several hundred metres away to the north. Sooner or later, he was going to hit someone. Our snipers were quite happy to comply and began constructing a sniper OP.

I was personally more than a little happy about this development. I hadn't admitted to anybody that, a few nights before, I had gone up on the roof for some fresh air and had been gazing out at the sunset when an insect buzzed past my ear. I wasn't really paying attention because I was deep in thought about something. When I was buzzed a second time I took notice. These insects were really moving! The next "insect" passed on my right side and ricocheted off the building behind me. It suddenly occurred to me that I was being shot at and I dropped below the parapet.

I was confused because I hadn't heard the shot or the crack normally found in supersonic rounds. Either this guy was pretty far away and the bullets had slowed to under the speed of sound or he was using high-tech subsonic ammunition. Either way, he had barely missed me with three shots. I felt pretty stupid about it and decided to keep it to myself. Now I discovered he had been shooting at other people as well. Fortunately for us, he was a terrible shot. Still, he had picked up a weapon and joined the game, so if Jeff or Wayne nailed him, it wouldn't bother me at all.

No names mentioned, but a case of beer was offered to the first sniper to make a kill. While we were lugging sandbags around to set up the sniper OP, a TDF soldier was shot in the leg in the street outside. There goes the neighbourhood.

Out at the airport something interesting had happened. Some RPG rockets had slammed into the bunkers around the airport and mortars had landed about the buildings. A large-calibre machine gun then began hammering at Colonel Jones's HQ building. Many of the bullets penetrated the walls and one round struck the RSM. Once again the inexplicable Canadian luck was with him and the bullet hit his sidearm at his hip. The pistol was destroyed, but the RSM was fine. The airport had quite a bad time after Hurd's aircraft left. Attacks went on all day and the RSM's close call was only one of many.

The violence of our surroundings was hard on all of us. What amazed me, though, was how many of our senior people, mostly near the end of their careers, had no stomach for a bit of shooting. Certain Sergeant-Majors, Warrants and Officers had the troops build them deep bunkers and refused to come out of them. Instead of setting an example for their men, they hid in their little holes. Fortunately, these characters were in the extreme minority. It was only their senior ranks that made them so visible. As for us poor slobs, we had to go out every day and take our chances.

Another morale lifter came from our Minister of National Defence. We would receive photocopied news articles from Canada so we knew what was going on at home. I was flipping through the latest stories when I found an article that covered several decrees by our Grand Poobah, Marcel Masse. From his desk came a proclamation that all military bases in New Brunswick were no longer permitted to purchase maple syrup from local suppliers. In the future, all maple syrup would be purchased from Quebec producers.

I was speechless. It was astounding to me that while we were dodging all manner of horrible deaths in Sarajevo, all he was worried about was Quebec's maple syrup producers. Oh well. No sense getting our hopes up.

I also saw an article that explained how the Royal Canadian Legion had requested that the soldiers in Sarajevo receive veteran status when they returned home. The Department of Veterans Affairs shot it down before it gained any momentum. The last thing the government wanted was any more veterans running around. They were too expensive. The government couldn't wait until our present aging veterans died off so they could close the accounts.

Fortunately, these big issues didn't make an iota of difference here in Sarajevo. I was still a part of a really great group of guys and we had an important job to do. That was the only real issue.

On the morning of 20 July, Warrant Sullivan shook me awake at
0730. He told me I had to be at the Van Doos HQ at the airport
in twenty minutes. My group had a task. I jumped up and kicked
my guys out of bed. Glen was going as my driver as usual and
Greg was still filling in as my gunner. In the other vehicle, it was
only Horse and Faubert.

We raced down to our carriers and took off, pulling into the
airport with two minutes to spare. I grabbed my map and rifle
and headed into the HQ building. The first thing I noticed was
the damage the machine gun fire had done all over the walls.
There was no time to admire the decorating though, as I was
rushed into a conference room to find eight other people waiting.

Major Collins was giving the brief. He was a tanker who had
replaced Colonel Gray as head Liaison Officer. Also in the room
was Major Devlin, the impressive OC from November company,
a Captain Juneau from the Van Doos, Captain Duff, a fellow
rugby player and Royal from Baden, and two engineers I didn't
recognize. Also present was a very attractive interpreter. Her
name was Jana and she was a university student who lived across
the street from the PTT. I had seen her a few times and admired
her long blond hair and sparkling smile.

The briefing started immediately. I forgot my notebook in the
rush and had to write my orders on the back of my map. I still have
the map and those orders to this day. Major Collins gave a short
introduction, and then Captain Duff took over to present the details.

The mission was a reconnaissance. The LOs wanted to establish a new aid route in the city. This was to be their most ambitious attempt yet. They wanted to open a route between the TDF
positions just east of the PTT, across into the Serb lines in the
south of the old city. The river was inside TDF lines at the crossing point chosen and the two opposing sides were about two
hundred metres apart, separated by an open area.

The mission would be broken down into two teams. The main
body would enter no-man's-land from the TDF side. This group
would consist of three jeeps with the LOs and the Engineers on
board. Major Devlin would go in his command track to have a
look at the route, since it was his company that would eventually
have to run the route. My two dets would provide security for
this group. I was named security commander for the mission.

Captain Juneau would proceed to the Serb side with only his driver to prepare for our arrival. Once we reached the TDF front, the LOS would liaise with the local TDF commander, and when all was ready, we would cross.

The deep purpose in all this wasn't to deliver food. We could easily accomplish that from existing routes. The plan was to establish a crossing point as we had in Croatia. Once it was open, a phone line would go in and the two sides could begin discussing problems instead of opening fire.

During the briefing, a mortar fire mission walked itself across the airport. The entire building was shaking as bombs impacted no more then twenty metres from the outside walls. On several occasions, Captain Duff had to stop his briefing when the noise became too loud to shout over. Between the shaking building and the deafening roar of the explosions outside, I was finding it hard to concentrate. I was a little worried about Glen and the guys out in the carriers, but they were big boys; they would look after themselves.

Captain Duff finished his briefing by saying that all parties had been warned off about this and there shouldn't be any surprises. As we filed out of the office and headed for the door, the mortar barrage lifted. Convenient, I thought.

As we filed out of the building I could hear Captain Duff asking Jana if she would rather ride in an APC than in a jeep. She agreed and Captain Duff sent her over to me. I was formally introduced and said I would be glad to have her as a passenger. As I walked over to the carrier and opened the combat door for her, I could see Horse and Faubert were a little disappointed I was taking her in my vehicle. I dug out my helmet and told her she had better wear it. She pulled it on and it sagged down nearly to her nose. She stood in the rear hatch with me as we pulled out of the airport.

The four jeeps were leading as we turned out onto the main road into the city. I shoved Jana down inside the carrier because this was the section where snipers always had a go at us. She would present too good a target with her long, blond hair blowing in the wind. Once we passed the PTT, we continued on for about another kilometre, before turning right into a side street. We crossed over the river, which at this point ran beside the main street.

The road we had entered ran between large, five-storey apartment blocks and several smaller buildings. Two hundred metres up the street the buildings ended, and the road was barricaded by large concrete blocks. Beyond the buildings and the barricades, the road continued straight for another two hundred metres, then turned sharply to the left. Beyond the turn was a small hillside covered with ruined houses. This was the Serb front line. Between the blocks and the abandoned homes lay two hundred metres of open ground: no-man's-land.

The jeeps pulled up near the barricade and halted. I told Glen to pass them and then park to protect the jeeps from view by the Serbs. Glen wheeled the big APC into a position between the lead jeep and the barricade. The Serbs would have a flank shot on the APC, but that was better than the unprotected jeeps. Faubert and Horse had stopped one hundred metres back to cover us. Our drills were improving.

I dismounted and walked over to Captain Duff and Major Collins, who were conferring over the hood of the lead jeep.

"Major Collins, I would like to move these jeeps back behind my rear callsign until we are ready to go, if you don't mind," I asked.

Before he could answer, we heard a shout from behind us. Turning, we saw a middle-aged man striding purposefully towards us. He was dressed in a dark blue coverall and wore a chrome revolver in an open holster on his hip.

Here we go, I thought.

Jana dismounted and came over to our group. As the commander arrived, he began speaking quickly and authoritatively. He was talking much too fast for me to follow, but it was easy to see he wasn't happy about something. The way the local media pumped out totally ridiculous stories about the UN, who knew what had him upset. Some truly believed we had killed those children. Other elements had issued death warrants against MacKenzie for "war crimes." The TDF commander was talking away, with Jana trying to keep up with the flow.

"He says that no one told him you were coming," Jana translated. The "Gunslinger" continued to rattle on and Jana tried to do her best. Finally, Major Collins interrupted and instructed Jana to tell the commander that this mission had been approved by his government and he had been told everyone was informed of our arrival. After hearing the translation, the Gunslinger suggested they should go into his headquarters and discuss the situation. Major Collins agreed and off they went, the Gunslinger, Collins, Duff and Jana. I had to sort out our situation in the street but kept a close eye on where they went. Beside 72 was a two-storey office building set off a small parking lot. It was into this building that the Gunslinger led our LO team.

I quickly set about squaring away our vehicles. I had all the jeep drivers move their vehicles back towards my other APC. Major Devlin's APC had stopped close to 72 on the other side of the street, so the jeeps pulled in behind his carrier. I left Greg and Glen where they were so they could both block the street and cover the rest of the party behind us.

I was starting to become a little concerned, because groups of TDF soldiers began arriving in large numbers. They appeared casual but at the same time took up positions where they could cover both our vehicles. As I was pondering whether or not we were being set up, Major Devlin walked over.

"What's going on, Sergeant Davis?" he asked.

"Sir, the local commander said he wasn't told we were coming," I answered. "He's taken the LOs to his HQ, in that building," I said, pointing it out, "and now it appears we are being surrounded."

Major Devlin gazed around at the growing numbers of TDF troops.

"Did Major Collins take a radio?" he asked.

"Yes sir, Captain Duff has a 126 set," I responded.

"Hmmm . . . ," Major Devlin appeared to be as concerned as I was.

The Gunslinger had removed our leaders and probably now had them under guard and out of our reach. I guessed the TDF commander now believed the UN troops outside to be leaderless and vulnerable. Unlike non-professional armies typical in the region though, our soldiers were quite capable of thinking for themselves in the absence of their officers. Also, we had Major Devlin, a very competent infantry officer, out in the street. My only concern was for getting the officers out of the HQ building in the event of trouble.

Major Devlin headed back to his carrier to call the airport and inform them of our situation. As he climbed into his track, the Gunslinger reappeared from the HQ building. He headed straight for my vehicle. I waited for him beside my carrier. In tow beside him was a TDF soldier with an AKS. When he arrived beside me, the soldier with him began to speak in poor English.

"My commander would like to look in your vehicles," he said, a little nervously.

I thought for a moment. This guy had no authority to inspect our equipment, but he is obviously agitated about something. We had nothing to hide, so if I didn't let him look in, he would prob-ably imagine all sorts of things. Better to let him have a look, and keep everyone from getting excited.

"Okay, tell your commander he can look inside, but touch nothing," I said forcefully. This guy might have been afraid of the Gunslinger, but I certainly wasn't. I turned and pulled open the small combat door on the back of the carrier.

The TDF commander strode to the back of the vehicle and peered in. I pushed past him and climbed inside, in case he wanted to know about anything in particular. He had a good look and then spoke sharply to his soldier. The soldier then turned to me.

"You cannot now close this door. If you try, I have been ordered to shoot you," said the soldier.

Things were not looking up. I watched as the Gunslinger headed for 72. Before I could get on the radio, Horse called up and said there was a guy there saying he had to open his door and keep it open. I thought quickly.

"72, this is 72A, open your door and leave it open for now, out," I said. I had to think this one out.

I looked at the guard by our back hatch. He was staring back at me. I figured that the Gunslinger now had all the cards. He had our LO party as hostages and, if UN troops outside tried any-thing, his guards would just fill our vehicles with automatic fire. We were backed into a corner.

Well, someone had to do something to get the initiative back and, since I was security commander, I guessed that was me. I turned to Glen and said in my best Hollywood voice, "Cover me." I then turned and climbed out of our rear combat door. The guard backed up as I got out and brought his weapon up to a ready position. I turned and closed the combat door.

The guard immediately started shouting at me in Serbo-Croat. The gist was, he was going to shoot me if I didn't open the door. He stuck his AK barrel in my chest to emphasize the point. I had my c7 in my hand, but kept it by my side. Instead—and I still can't believe I did this—I gave him my best Clint Eastwood stare. I dared him to shoot. I looked him right in the eyes and could see he was terrified. I really didn't think he had the guts to shoot. Unlike the civilians he had probably terrified, I wasn't a blubbering fool begging for my life.

After a couple of seconds, I pushed his barrel aside and told him I wanted to see his commander. The guard took off shouting for his boss, who was up at Major Devlin's carrier telling them to open their combat door. I think the Gunslinger got a shock when the door swung open and he was staring into the eyes of Warrant Officer Joe Parsons. Joe could be knee deep in crocodiles and still look bored, so I'm sure the Gunslinger was a little unnerved.

Before anything else could happen, his attention was caught by his guard running up the street calling for him. As he turned and approached, I could see the guard was telling him what I had done, and the Gunslinger's eyes showed his displeasure clearly. I was walking calmly toward him with my rifle at my side while he listened to his man report. Before he could say anything, I demanded to see my officers in his HQ.

This threw the Gunslinger off a bit. He blustered a bit but eventually told me to go and look for them in the HQ building. So I wandered casually over to Major Devlin's track and told him I was going in to talk to Major Collins. Major Devlin nodded and I then turned and walked over to 72. When I reached their position, I could see a guy with an RPG anti-tank rocket launcher standing nearby and at least twenty other troops with rifles. Faubert and Horse were both relaxed and sitting in their hatches. Faubert's arm was laid on the .50 cal.

"Things are going bad. I shut the door on my carrier, but leave yours open for the moment. I'm going to find Collins and Duff. Stay relaxed and if I don't come out in fifteen minutes, you're in charge."

Faubert and Horse both smiled.

With a deep breath, I marched across the small parking lot and towards the front door. There was a guard there, but I have found in these situations that if you look like you are doing something important, people usually get out of your way.

As I approached the guard I asked in Serbo-Croat, "Where are the Canadian officers?"

The guard pointed to the stairs inside the doorway, and I brushed by him before he could say anything. Inside, I found a stairway on the left wall overlooking a trashed lobby. I turned and climbed the stairs. At the top, I found a short hallway leading to an office. I strode up the hall and stopped in the doorway. I was pretty tensed up, not knowing what I would find.

Inside was a thirtyish woman in a skimpy mini-skirt and far too much makeup. She looked up to see me and her smile faded. I guess I must have looked pretty intimidating. She pointed through the doorway across the room and I strode over and stepped through the half-open doorway. There, sitting around a table, were Collins, Duff and Jana. The two officers were a little surprised to see me, but Jana brightened considerably with my arrival.

"Hello, everyone," I said. I looked at Major Collins and reported. "Sir, the local commander has tried to order us to open our vehicles. In the spirit of goodwill, I complied. Now, he has a guard at each door with orders to shoot if we attempt to close them."

"I see," he responded.

Captain Duff spoke up: "Negotiations aren't going well. I don't know if this will come off."

As he finished speaking, the Gunslinger strode in. He stood beside me and I got a good look at him. He was extremely agitated. He was bouncing on the balls of his feet and his fists were clenching and unclenching. I also got a smell of his breath in the close quarters. This guy was drunk!

I could see that he was about ready to explode. I needed a bit of distance to react, so I backed out of the room. Perhaps, without my presence, he would settle down. I moved into the outer office and took a position where I could see what was going on inside. The woman in the outer office smiled at me provocatively. Definitely a prostitute, I figured.

Not interested in the slightest, I searched the room for anything I could use. The most important item I noticed was a loaded sub-machine gun resting on a shelf beside the door. This was a weapon unique to Yugoslavia and was fairly rare. It was .22 calibre and was fed by a 150-round drum on top. Excellent for close quarters, I thought. The C7 was great, but the 5.56 round would go through three people before slowing down. That little beauty could come in handy if things went bad.

Now I was in a dilemma. I needed to stay in the HQ and protect the LO party, but if things went bad, no one outside would know the location of the hostages. My personal radio was out of range. I had to get back to my guys and make a plan.

I stuck my head back in the meeting room and announced I was heading back outside. I stared right at Captain Duff and I hoped he got the message. With a reassuring smile for Jana, I turned and headed back out.

As I emerged back into the sunlight, I headed for 72.

"What's happening?" I asked as I arrived.

Horse filled me in. "There is a dude back there with an RPG. There must be thirty other guys standing around, watching us."

From behind the .50 cal, Faubert piped up, "We closed the back hatch, too. The guy argued, but . . ." Faubert just smiled. With a big handlebar moustache and a hand on that .50, I could see why no local would argue too much.

Then over the air, I heard Major Collins's voice. The speaker was on in the carrier and I could hear it clearly. He announced that negotiations had failed and we were going to call off the mission. I figured that it was all over and started walking back to my track. When I got there, Greg shouted at me,

"They've got the officers," he yelled. "They're not letting them leave!"

I must have sagged. Before I could even process the information I heard the sound of a heavy vehicle. I turned around and saw a large truck with a big steel trailer pulling across the entrance to the street. It left a small space that was soon filled by a small car. Well, so much for leaving.

We needed a new plan now. I told Greg to quietly prepare some M72s, but to keep them out of sight. I told Glen to have a smoke grenade handy and told them I was going over to talk to Major Devlin. Before talking to him though, I headed over to 72. I was worried about their morale. I needn't have bothered. As I walked up, Horse was grinning from ear to ear.

"It's starting to look grim," I said. "Horse, what have you got?"

Horse reached down and pulled out a huge homemade Bowie knife in one hand and a grenade in the other. "I've got this little guy," he said, referring to the grenade, "and Uncle Buck!"

From the huge grin on his face, I could see he wasn't worried in the slightest about the turn of events. I almost laughed. Here we were surrounded by people who hated our guts, they had us boxed in and outnumbered four to one and Horse couldn't have given a damn. I looked at Faubert and he just smiled and patted the .50.

"Well, play it cool for the moment until I can figure a way out of this mess," I said and headed for Major Devlin's track.

Major Devlin and I had a short discussion about the situation. He had already called November company and ordered a platoon to stand-to for a rescue. I explained to him the location of our LO party. We both agreed the odds didn't look good for us.

About this time, Captain Juneau came up on the air from the Serb side of the line. He explained that the Serbs had been watching the whole situation develop. They were prepared to cover us with two tanks if we wanted to make a run for their lines. I looked at Major Devlin with a tired expression.

Great. Just what we needed.

I could see it now. We would attempt a break out and most of us would be killed in the attempt. The few survivors (assuming there were any) would make it to Serb lines. The next day in the world press, the story would say how heroic Serbs tried to save some UN peacekeepers murdered by the evil Muslims. The Bosnians would trumpet about their proof of UN and Serb collusion. The PR value of wiping us out would be tremendous for both sides.

I told the Major I would have a look around and see if I could figure a way out. He agreed and got back on the radio to keep everyone outside informed of the situation. The RCR platoon had mounted up and moved to a position a few hundred metres away. I assumed that Major Devlin would give them detailed instructions of how to find the LOs. I was more worried about what the rest of us would do. The street was narrow and there were no exits large enough to take an APC. I strolled down to the concrete barricades. As I approached them, a young TDF soldier signalled to me. He pointed up the hill and made a motion with his rifle of shooting. I took his warning to mean that there were Serb snipers up there. I smiled and pointed to my UN beret and walked on. Well, at least one of the TDF is worried about us.

As I reached the barricades, I had a good look around. I stared up at the abandoned houses on the Serb side. I knew at that moment, some Serb sniper was watching my face closely through his scope. I smiled at my unseen observer and turned to stroll back. What I had noticed was that there was a three-metre gap between the last concrete block and the nearest building on the western sidewalk. A gap that an APC could fit through, no problem.

I went back to my carrier. As I climbed in, Greg told me to look to our front. There, five metres ahead, was a TDF soldier with an RPG pointed right at us. Other troops were arriving by the minute. I looked around and estimated there to be about seventy-five to a hundred TDF troops surrounding us. They were all alert and had their weapons ready. About twenty metres up the street, a machine gunner had us in his sights from behind a bush. Things were looking worse by the minute.

I had a funny feeling the TDF had monitored the broadcast from Juneau with the Serbs. The TDF had a lot of the same old radios we had and no shortage of English speakers to listen to them. By UN rules we weren't allowed to scramble our messages, so we had to call in clear. Juneau tried to call back again later with more information about Serb plans, but Major Devlin told him to stay off the air.

I explained my plan to Greg and Glen. First, we would have to wait until they made the first move. UN rules. After the first shot was fired, I was going to shoot the guy with the RPG. Then Greg would open up with the .50 and hose down the whole area. I would start tossing smoke and fragmentation grenades all over the place. The idea was to cause as much confusion as possible. Once the others were all loaded in the APCs we would bust out toward Serb lines. With luck, the platoon from November would attack from the other end at the same time and we should be able to make it.

"Until then, laugh, smoke and joke. Put them off their guard. Make them relax," I instructed.

I then went to Major Devlin and explained my plan. His part would be to load the engineers in with him and head for the gap in the barricade. The jeeps would be left behind. He agreed and got on the air and, guardedly over the open airwaves, explained the plan to all concerned.

I was a little surprised he took my advice. He was a good officer and I was waiting for him to take charge. I think he realized that our only hope was coordination with the rescue force. He would command all the elements in the event a battle started. He was content to let me do my job for the moment. I felt quite proud that he trusted me that much.

I went over and explained the plan to Horse and Faubert. I could see in their eyes, they knew we didn't stand much of a chance with all the firepower pointed our way. Yet their morale didn't flinch. Horse was still grinning from ear to ear.

"I'll take some of the bastards with me anyway," he announced. He said it just loud enough that the TDF troops standing around may have heard. As long as they knew we weren't surrendering. Ever.

At that moment I was as proud as I had ever been in my life. I was working with the absolute best. My back was covered. I loved these guys.

As I walked back to my carrier, I had to face the facts. My vehicle might make it, but the chances for the other two were slim. The officers and the interpreter in the HQ weren't going to make it either. I discussed it with my crew. If it looked like no one else was going to make it to the gap in the barricades, then we would stay and fight. Greg and Glen agreed. We would turn into the fight instead of heading for Serb lines. Horse and Faubert would do the same for us.

I climbed back up into my carrier and began preparing my grenades. I laid a row of them out along the upper deck of the APC. I laid out some spare mags as well. Having a good look around, I noticed that behind us the TDF had already begun to relax a bit. Five or six troops were standing close together about five metres behind the carrier. The RPG gunner was still in front of us, but the RPG now rested with one end on the ground.

So, the RPG gunner gets a burst first. Then a grenade into the group behind me, followed by a full mag. Greg had opened up his M72s and they lay beside him. He would immediately fire one into the building above us and then rock and roll with the .50. Daryl would start us moving. That was the plan. Smoke, confusion, speed, violence.

Now we just had to wait.

The way this town worked, even a stray shot could create a misunderstanding and start a battle. Even more likely, the Serb sniper up on the hill would shoot one of us or a Muslim and, in the ensuing confusion, a fight would start between us and the

TDF. That way the Serbs would ensure the world knew that Bosnian Muslims had killed a UN patrol. Juneau could even say that the Serbs tried to help us. Either way, I wasn't going to wait until it was too late. I told the guys that at the moment the first shot was fired, we go. No turning back.

It was at this moment I knew, for sure, I could pull the trigger. I wouldn't even give it a second thought. My philosophy has always been that war is a game. If you pick up a weapon, you join the game. If you don't have a weapon, you are a spectator and are safe. Therefore, anyone standing outside my vehicle with a weapon was a player. If they didn't want a fight, they could lay down their weapons and go home, no questions asked. If they stayed, well, game on.

I wasn't frightened either. I knew we would probably die if the shooting started, but I wasn't worried about it at the time. My mind was going a mile a minute, planning, assessing and observing. I didn't have time to worry.

Suddenly, a single mortar bomb crashed down in the next street over. I could see the smoke ten metres away. I knew instinctively that it was the Serbs registering us as a target. Now the tube would be brought over a few degrees and the next round would land right beside our carrier.

Fortunately, the TDF didn't turn on us when the mortar went off; they knew we had nothing to do with it. Still, it served to heighten the tension again.

We were now truly in a Mexican stand-off. We weren't laying down our weapons and were obviously prepared to fight. The TDF had a drunken commander with a grudge who wouldn't let them back down either.

It was about this time that I saw a UN white flash go by on the street behind us. There was only one person that could be. Because of all the death threats, General MacKenzie was using a little French armoured car to get him around. Basically an armoured rally car, this thing could hit 120 kilometres an hour. Before anyone could get him in their sights, he was gone!

MacKenzie was on the job. He was obviously headed down to the Presidency to sort out this mess. Sure enough, Major Collins emerged shortly afterwards and was allowed to get in a jeep and head for the Presidency.

Soon afterwards, he returned with a Bosnian government

representative and a local TV crew. The Gunslinger was insisting that we were shipping arms to the Serbs and demanded that the government rep look in our vehicles. Major Collins agreed and each of our vehicles were opened up. The big issue was our M72s. This is a green fibreglass tube that houses a 66 mm rocket. They are made in the U.S. and are very common in western armies. The problem was, the Russians had copied the design and produced a similiar looking version called the RPG–18. The Gunslinger thought we were shipping RPG–18s to the Serbs. Even after we showed him the English printing all over the M72, he still refused to back down. He insisted that we were peacekeepers and didn't need these kind of weapons. We must be giving the Serbs American weapons. Major Collins quietly explained, with only a hint of sarcasm, that we were combat soldiers whose lives were threatened daily. We were quite capable of fighting if the need arose.

The Gunslinger took the point. Soon, Captain Duff and Jana were released and the truck was moved. We all quickly mounted up and got the heck out of Dodge City. I breathed one big sigh of relief as we got back out on the main drag and were headed for the PTT once again. Once back there, I heard the version of events that were going on outside our little stand-off.

Apparently, all the Van Doos had wanted to mount up and charge to our rescue. The reserve platoon from November company had been just itching to get in there and mix it up. Basically, the Canadians were about to start their own little war. It was lucky for the TDF that they had finally backed down. I wouldn't have wanted to be up against us.

As the excitement wound down later in the day, I went to sit on my bunk. The adrenaline high was wearing off and I began to have the shakes. I got really cold and curled up on my cot. Suddenly, the fear hit me. I nearly felt like throwing up. A little while later, everyone was going down to supper and I forced myself to follow them. I only poked at my meal. I really didn't feel like eating.

I excused myself and decided to walk around a bit. As I walked through OPS, I ran into Jana. She thanked me for protecting her. Before I showed up in that office, she told me, she had been very worried. She thought the drunken commander would kill them all. When I showed up, she said, she suddenly felt much safer knowing I was around. I suddenly felt much better as well. That is, until I realized that I probably couldn't have saved her. Like the little Serb girl in Okacani, I would have failed her, too.

At 2200 hours that night, the Bosnian media reported that a heroic local commander had interrupted a shipment of arms to the Serbs by UN forces. Hooray for the good guys. I also heard that General MacKenzie knew a videotape had been shot of the incident. It was in the BBC's hands. He had told the Bosnian President that ten minutes after the first shot was fired, he would have that video all over CNN and he would tell the world who was responsible.

Since then I have always believed that the General saved our lives that day. I will always be in his debt. He is a great man and a better soldier. He is a genuine Canadian hero.

During the next couple of days there was another attempt to open the new aid route. It was also unsuccessful. We began taking more and more incoming fire as the various factions began to lose faith in our ability to live up to their incorrect expectations. General MacKenzie was told he would be replaced. There were reasons given, but we all knew it was because he pulled no punches and the media loved him—a dangerous combination in a politically sensitive position.

On 23 July, I was told another Hercules was leaving the airport the next day, headed for Germany. I could be on it for my leave, if I wanted. I didn't have to think too long this time. The Canadian Battle Group was scheduled to leave by the end of the month, so I would only miss a couple of days and another long ride. Jerry was coming back in on the same flight, so he could take over the group. I figured, "What the hell," and accepted.

I had had enough of Sarajevo. Being shot at nearly every day and not being able to fire back was wearing on my nerves. Seeing murder and injustice surrounding me and being unable to change it was frustrating. The sad part was that, as I fell asleep that night, I knew my military career had just peaked and I was on the downside starting tomorrow.

The next morning at about 1030 hours I boarded a Virginia National Guard Hercules and headed for Germany. I didn't look out the window as we took off. I had already fallen asleep.

PARTING SHOT

" **... 79** THIS IS 72.... 72A *has just exploded.... They just disappeared. They must have hit a mine. I think they're all dead...."*

After two wonderful weeks off, in which I tried to forget about life in Yugo, I found myself standing on the runway in Lahr, looking at an extremely doubtful DC–9 belonging to Air Slovenia. This was their only serviceable plane and they had won a contract to fly UN troops from Germany to Croatia, no doubt because they bid the lowest. They must have been saving all their money for insurance for when it crashed.

We took off and headed south over the mountains. While we were passing over the Alpine peaks the engines suddenly shut down. I looked around to see if anyone else had noticed. If they did, they were, like me, trying to keep calm. The plane started dropping towards the mountains. I could see the sharp, rocky hills growing closer and closer. Suddenly, the nose tipped down and the pilot went into a shallow dive. The Alps were getting a lot closer by the second and I am sure we were no more than a thousand metres from the highest summits when I heard the engines rumble back to life. The pilot pushed the throttles hard and we started to climb slowly away from certain death.

Only minutes later, we surged over a final peak and immediately dove down into a green mountain valley on the Slovenian side of the Alps. The plane banked steeply and we pulled out just in time to touch down on a single runway airfield lying somewhere north of Ljubljana.

As we got off the plane, I began to feel that two mysterious forces were at war for my soul. One spirit was trying to kill me and the other was working his ass off to protect me. Everywhere I went, I seemed to be getting in trouble.

Next, a bus arrived to take us to Zagreb. I swear the bus driver was the same guy who piloted the plane. I'm sure the pilot jumped down from the plane and switched uniforms. Hmmm.

After a bus change in Zagreb, we arrived in Camp Polom at about 2230. Warrant Sullivan was waiting with a truck. He whisked us down to the Recce clubhouse where Pete Ainsworth, Dion Henn and I had ten minutes to grab the kit we needed and get back on the truck. We were off to the enclave and a new mission. The rest of the platoon was already down there patrolling. The Warrant filled me in on the way down.

The enclave was now being patrolled by a Nepalese battalion and a Jordanian battalion. The Nepalese were from a palace guard unit. They didn't have very many hill people and were mostly flatlanders. As a palace unit they had very few soldiering skills outside drill and ceremonial duties. A couple of nights ago, a group of Nepalese troops had been pinned in a ditch by machine gun fire from the south bank of the Sava. Since they had no experience, no armoured vehicles and only a few light machine guns, the troops had to spend the night chewing mud while trying not to get hit.

The next day the Nepalese commander had appealed to the returning Canadians and Argentinians for some support, so three Argy Marder fighting vehicles had been dispatched to the Nepalese HQ. These were kept there as a ready-fire force for emergencies. To assist in patrolling the Nepalese zone, our Recce platoon had been seconded to them. We were responsible for patrolling the sector and backing up a Nepalese platoon guarding the bridge over the Sava.

The situation in the enclave had either improved or deteriorated, depending on your point of view. All the Serb heavy equipment had been withdrawn across the bridge into Bosnia and now only Serb "police" were allowed to carry weapons. The Croats were supposed to have withdrawn five kilometres back from the enclave on all sides, but we could still see their units five hundred metres from the bridge. There was even more fighting in the area now because Croat troops operating in Bosnia had cut off the Serbs in northern Bosnia. This meant that the Serbs in the enclave and below the river were now surrounded. The Croat front line was only a few kilometres south of the bridge at that point.

On the boundaries of the enclave, fighting took place almost daily, with our guys sometimes watching the tank battles from the bridge. Because Serb troops couldn't carry weapons inside the enclave, the Serbs had erected a big tent to store weapons. In the morning, the Serb husbands would kiss their wives and kids at the front door and then walk across the bridge to work. Here they would pick up their rifles and head off to the front to fight for the day. The night shift would walk home shortly afterwards, leaving their weapons at the bridge.

We sat by and watched all this because, technically, it was within the rules. We also witnessed a large number of refugees flowing into the enclave as the Croats squeezed the Serb lines south of the river. I felt sorry for the Serbs. The international community was slamming them as the aggressors, but in a lot of places they were on the run, sometimes because the UN had disarmed them. The Croats probably wouldn't be threatening the enclave if we hadn't convinced the Serbs to get rid of their equipment with promises of protection. The Serbs knew what was probably in store for them if the Croats won.

After arriving at the Nepalese camp, I found Recce living under a couple of tents. I grabbed a beer and listened to the stories of the pull-out from Sarajevo. Apparently, the last Canadian vehicle was Jeff's 73A. General MacKenzie had reached up to shake his hand as they pulled out. After hearing all the stories, I was glad I had flown out. The trip back to Croatia was as boring as the trip down. I was bagged and, after a short while, went to ground.

The next three weeks were a monotonous round of patrolling and sitting at checkpoints. There was still shooting going on, but it was nothing compared to Sarajevo. We had only about a month and a half left in the tour and figured it would be a breeze after Sarajevo. Daryl was back, but Glen had gone on leave in the second week of September. I had moved into the gunner's hatch for a couple of days, but on the morning of 15 September I decided to change back to my normal rear hatch. I locked the gunner's hatch shut and swivelled the .50 cal around so I could reach it from my position. Our group headed off for an eight-hour stint at the bridge. Later, as the sun set, we took over the patrol task from 71 group and our two vehicles headed off in separate directions to check out local villages.

We had been recieving reports that the Croats were massing forces in a large wooded area on the eastern edge of the enclave. Late in the evening, Serb police units had reported hearing tanks in these woods. At midnight, Jerry received a radio order to go and check out these woods. We were several kilometres apart at that point and Jerry suggested we meet at the entrance to a dirt track that passed through the centre of the wood. I agreed, and Daryl and I headed for the rendezvous.

We, in 72A, arrived moments before 72 and turned down the trail. Jerry's carrier caught up quickly and we both headed down the dirt track with my vehicle about fifty metres in front. I told Daryl to take it slow and watch for surface-laid mines. If the Croats were in here, they would undoubtedly have laid out some mines to keep out unwelcome UN trespassers. We weren't too worried about mines because we could see our engineers had been down this road before us. The trail had been backbladed, which meant that the route was clear of buried mines.

As we inched along at about five kilometres an hour, Daryl watched the trail closely. I was standing in the back, swinging the spotlight across the woods. Normally, we liked to move as fast as we could, but this time I just felt that we should be extra cautious.

After we had travelled about fifteen hundred metres, Daryl slammed on the brakes. Before I could ask, he let me know over the intercom that he thought he had seen a mine. He backed up a little bit and had a good look. It turned out to be just a rock. Relaxing a bit, we proceeded. I was guessing that if the Croats were in these woods, we would reach their positions soon as we were approaching a junction in the trail. I scanned the spotlight to the right and then back to the left. At about the same moment, Daryl spotted a patch of loose dirt on the trail, but the tracks continued on the other side and he figured it was okay.

Behind us, 72 was following about twenty-five metres back. Suddenly, the night disappeared in a huge blue-white flash. The

earth roared and 72A disappeared in a huge explosion. Debris
was flung high in the air and a huge cloud of dust roiled down
the trail towards Jerry's vehicle. The concussion was terrible and
seemed to have been amplified in the narrow trail. As the echoes
died away, the moment of shock wore off. Debris was still falling
from the night sky as Jerry and Greg searched for any sign of life
in front of them. They could see nothing.

Jerry quickly got on the radio and called the Recce command
post. He was still in a bit of a state of shock but reported the situation to 69er. He knew we had hit a mine and thought we must
be dead; the whole vehicle seemed to have disappeared. There
was silence on the other end. Carl Fletcher was manning the
radio and he had a few beers in him. He wasn't sure what to say.
Just as everyone was starting to believe the platoon had incurred
its first KIAS (killed in actions), another voice came on the air.

" . . . ah . . . 72, 69er, this is 72A. We're okay, over."

––––––––––

Daryl had driven on, over the loose dirt. As the tracks rolled over
the spot, a buried TMA–3 anti-tank mine was detonated under the
right track. First, our vehicle was lifted up in the air and tipped
high to the left before it came crashing back down two metres further forward. In the front, Daryl remembers the flash but was
protected from any harm by the engine block between his body
and the blast. In the rear, I had just turned to look to the left when
the mine exploded on the right side. I was thrown high, out of the
vehicle, and came crashing down on the top of it. Everything was
engulfed in thick dark smoke and my ears were ringing. I knew I
was alright, but my first thoughts were for Daryl.

"Daryl, are you okay?" I shouted.

"Yeah . . . I'm alright," came the shaky response.

I wasn't convinced. "Are you sure? Check yourself over. You
might be in shock."

"Yeah, I'm sure. You check yourself over," he yelled back.

I did. I felt down my arms to each hand and then, holding my
breath, felt down both legs to my feet. The last thing I checked
was my balls. Everything was where it should be. I breathed a big
sigh of relief.

It was then that I noticed the radio. I could hear 72 announcing our demise over the air. I reached around for the headset, but
it had come off during my flight. It was probably inside, but I

was worried about secondary explosions and wasn't too keen about getting down inside the carrier. With all the grenades, M72s and machine gun ammo down there, I didn't want to survive the first explosion only to get it in the second. Instead, I reached down with one arm and clawed around until I found the headset cord. I pulled it up and found the headset still intact. I took a deep, calming breath and tried to relax before I went on the air. I remembered in that moment that everyone had commented on how calm my voice was over the air during the hostage crisis, so I didn't want to disappoint. I casually reported that we were okay. My throat felt like sandpaper and my adrenaline was pouring into my bloodstream, so I don't know if I really sounded calm, but I tried.

Immediately, Jerry was on the air, "Hey, we thought you were dead . . . good to hear your voice, over."

"72A, no, we're both okay. I think we hit a mine, over."

"No shit, Sherlock, over."

The next few minutes were spent assuring everybody that we weren't in shock and all our body parts were intact. Carl had finally been replaced on the radio by Captain Ready.

"72, this is 69er, how bad is the damage, over?" he asked.

"69er, wait out," I cut in.

It had been several minutes and I figured the chance of secondary explosions was pretty much over, so I crawled inside and amidst the chaos found my flashlight. I leaned over the right side and had a good look.

"Jesus, Daryl, come and have a look at this," I said.

Daryl had climbed out of his hatch and walked to the right side of the carrier. He leaned over the right side.

"Christ!"

The whole upper half of the track was gone. That piece alone weighed about 150 kilograms. It was nowhere to be seen. The first road wheel was damaged and the second was shattered. The feature that caught our attention the most was a crater a metre and a half long and a half a metre deep. It was located just behind our third road wheel and extended to the back of the carrier.

"Shit."

I crawled back to the radio and got on the air to give a report.

"72, 69er, this is 72A. The right track is gone and there is a huge crater under our right rear, over."

"72, 72A, this is 69er. Stay where you are. Don't dismount. I will call for engineer callsigns to come down and get you out," responded Captain Ready. We were obviously thinking the same thing. Whenever you lay anti-tank mines, you usually scatter a few anti-personnel booby traps around to discourage the curious.

It was then that Daryl came over and said he thought that he had heard someone running away just after the explosion. That could very well point to a command-detonated mine and that meant it was an ambush. Probably Serbs hunting the Croat tanks. They had bagged us by mistake.

Regardless, it got me thinking. Both sides will have seen the flash and will probably come to see what had been caught. I yelled back to Jerry and told him about our concerns.

"Not much we can do about it except keep watch," he answered.

Captain Ready called back on the radio to report that the engineers had been having a party back in Polom and no one was sober enough to come down until morning. Since it was just before 0100 hours, we had some time to kill.

So began a long nighttime vigil. On several occasions we heard movement in the woods and once we heard someone cock a weapon. We had pointed our spotlights onto our UN flags and would shout out, "*Uyedinenih Natsiyah*, United Nations!" We hoped they would have a chuckle and go home once their curiosity had been sated.

Figuring we might have to fight a defensive battle from our stranded vehicle, Daryl and I began to root around inside the vehicle for gear.

"Hey, I found a grenade," Daryl would say while I reported my discovery of our night vision equipment. It was during this search that Daryl noticed the hole.

In the right front corner of the passenger compartment, a jagged hole had been ripped in the floor. It was blown inwards and was only centimetres below two M72s that were strapped to the sidepanel. I looked down and discovered the culprit amid the wreckage. It was an end connector from the track. Basically a two-kilogram hunk of metal, it had blown clear through the APC's thin skin. I called up to Daryl to announce my discovery.

"Well, if you liked that, you're gonna love this," he replied.

I stuck my head up out of the hatch. Daryl was pointing at the open gunner's hatch.

"Hey, I thought that was closed," I said. Then I looked closer. In the centre of the hatch was a gouge about ten centimetres long by two centimetres deep. It didn't take very long to put two and two together. If I had been standing in that hatch, the two-kilogram hunk of metal would have hit me just above the right hip, travelled through my torso and exited around my left shoulder. I would be quite dead. Seeing how I had been travelling in that hatch for over a week and had only changed this very morning, I was a little stunned. My tremendous luck had held again. If Jerry or any other commander in the platoon had been leading instead of us, he would be dead now.

I swore to myself at that moment, that for the rest of my life, I would always trust my instincts above all else. Whatever had caused me to go against military SOPs and change hatches only a few hours before the explosion had saved my life.

At about 0500 hours, as the sun was just rising, Sergeant Mike Foster and Captain Ready came walking down the trail. Mike was an engineer and we had worked together before. They had walked down in our tracks and stopped at Jerry's carrier.

Daryl and I looked at each other. We had made it. Around us in the growing light, it appeared we had been ready for a long fight. Grenades were lined up and loaded magazines for the C7s lay on each side of the cargo hatch. We were both tired and dirty, but plenty happy to be alive.

On Mike's advice, we swung open the rear hatch and gingerly stepped down into our vehicle tracks. Then we both hurried back to the relative safety of Jerry's vehicle. A few minutes later, Sergeant Mike Ralph joined us with a couple of troops. They went forward and swept around our vehicle to look for any other mines. None were found, so the rest of us headed up and had a good look at the damage.

The vehicle was ruined. Underneath, the entire belly plate was warped inwards and the suspension was shot. We looked around and still couldn't find the missing three metres of track. It had just disappeared.

I climbed inside the vehicle and hauled out my video camera. I shot a bunch of footage of the vehicle and then got Greg to hold the camera. I stood behind the vehicle and pointed out the damage and made a few wisecracks. When I finished, I stepped away from the edge of the crater.

Moments later, Mike Foster looked and noticed a second mine slightly protruding from the edge of the crater, exactly where I had been standing moments before. Mike carefully dug it out and disarmed it.

Well, now I had even stood on a live mine and survived. Years later a newly trained engineer had recognized me in a hallway in Petawawa. He approached me with a grin.

"Hey, you're the guy. The one who stood on the mine. Yeah, they showed us the film in training!"

So, I had achieved immortality by proving you can stand on a TMA-3 without detonating it. Frankly, it was not the type of recognition I needed.

Later, as we were preparing to pull my vehicle out, Jerry accidently set off a smoke grenade inside his carrier and just about set it on fire. In trying to pour water on it, he inhaled so much smoke he nearly asphyxiated himself. This day just kept getting better and better.

When it was time to pull the wreck out, we hooked it up to 72. Greg would drive. Mike Foster and Mike Ralph were worried that there was another mine. There was a good chance it would go off when we attempted to pull the track out, so Mike made everyone move back a hundred metres. All except Greg. But Greg couldn't see to back up, so someone had to stay with him in the APC to guide him. I figured I had the luck, so I volunteered. I think Greg was much happier to have someone with him. When the time came, we hunched our shoulders and Greg stomped on the accelerator. The battered 72A came away without any more calamities. We dragged it to the road and it was hauled aboard a flatbed. Daryl and I felt sort of sorry to see it go. As much as I hated the damn thing, it had served us well.

Later that day, back in the Recce tents, we put away quite a few beers and retold the story far too many times. Warrant Sullivan and most of the others were amazed when we related the story of switching hatches. Everyone agreed that if it had been anyone else, we would have had a death in the platoon. Jerry was just glad we had made it to the head of the trail ahead of his vehicle or he would have been leading. That was our normal patrol SOP.

In the afternoon, I think it was around 1400 hours, I was lying in my cot writing a letter when I heard an explosion. We later learned that Mike Foster and Mike Ralph had gone back to clear the trail by daylight. Foster had been walking in front, supervising two troops sweeping the trail with a mine detector, while Ralph followed a hundred metres back in a pick-up. The TMA–3s are all plastic and couldn't be detected with the magnetic sweeper, so when the lead group walked right over several, Mike Ralph didn't have a chance. His truck ran over a stack of mines and set them off. He died instantly.

Some of our guys went to help get him out to a hospital, but it was too late. Mike Foster and his crew were shaken up, but okay.

Mike Ralph had saved my life a few hours earlier. He was a brave man. I only wished some of my luck had rubbed off on him. It was not to be. He left a wife and two daughters behind. I am sorry for their loss.

We had a service at Camp Polom two days later and all the contingents sent guards. As I was leaving the service afterwards, a Norwegian I'd never met walked up to me.

"You're Davis, aren't you?" he said in accented English. I nodded. Then he reached out and touched my sleeve.

"I hope it rubs off," he stated with a warm smile and walked away. Thus was born my temporary nickname of "the luckiest man in NATO."

Our time in Croatia was just about up. The last hurrah was to be a medals ceremony held in a field near Daruvar. During the rehearsal, we had to cancel the march past because there were air scatterable mines on the chosen parade square. During the practice, someone fired a couple of 7.62 rounds over our heads, but I don't think anyone noticed. Finally, we were supposed to sing "O Canada" as they lowered the flag. On the RSM's cue we began to sing. The Van Doos, of course, sang in French. November company tried to out-shout Alpha company and consequently the Van Doos began to shout. It became a screaming contest and a total sham. The RSM tried to stop us, but he couldn't be heard over six hundred screaming voices. I was laughing so hard, I just about cried. What a disaster!

At the ceremony the next day, I was presented with my UN medal by French Major-General Philippe Morillon. He was an amazing officer who went on to prove his worth in the stand-off in Srebenica where, with a half-a-dozen Canadian troops, he defied the Serb army.

Recce's tour of duty was pretty much finished up. The lead

Patricia elements had arrived and were prepared to take over. We took them out on a few patrols to show them the routes and generally briefed them on the situation. We were told that there was a second Canadian Battalion coming to Yugo and the Airborne had just been committed to action in Somalia. Maybe my career wasn't going to slump after all!

On 7 October, I flew home to Germany.

The front gate at the milk factory in Mareru, Rwanda. Two Airborne security troops control access to the compound. Local children were always about hoping for candy or other presents. JAMES DAVIS

The 2 Field Ambulance hospital complex in Mareru, Rwanda. The hospital tents extend some distance to the right; in the distance are the uninhabited hills of the military preserve. JAMES DAVIS

Inset: Paratrooper Corporal Adam Thibodeau (R) lending a hand in the triage ward in Mareru, Rwanda. Paratroopers often volunteered as a method of brushing up on their first aid skills. UNKNOWN

Above: Author visiting Dian Fossey's grave in the Virunga Mountains of Rwanda. The bulge in his shirt is a hidden 9 mm pistol used to protect medical staff. JASON FAFORD

Left: A young mountain gorilla at rest in the jungle. These creatures were always gentle, intelligent and often playful. Less than 2 metres away, the gorilla displays no concern at the proximity of humans. JAMES DAVIS

Above: 3 Commando troops on Physical Training (PT) in Rwanda. All off-duty troops did PT daily and this often consisted of mountain hikes. Here the troops take a break before descending. Note that all personnel are armed. JAMES DAVIS

Right: Corporal Jeff Harrison (L) and author take a break. The large white building in the centre distance is the milk factory at Mareru. JAMES DOCHERTY

The disbandment parade of the Canadian Airborne Regiment, March 1995. Preceded by a mass parachute drop, it was a dark day in the history of the Canadian Forces. Despite its rogue reputation, the unit's epitaph is recorded as "Obedient to orders until the end." Author is second from the right. LORNA DAVIS

RWANDA

IT WAS JUST AFTER 0400 *hours in the morning. The bus pulled up outside 3 Commando's building on the Airborne parade square. Thirty of us, all wearing civvies, climbed aboard. We weren't allowed to wear any clothing that would associate us with the Airborne. No military kit either. Completely clean. No casual observer would know who we were.*

A man in his mid-thirties, dressed in black, boarded the bus and called our names. Satisfied we were all there, he told the bus driver to follow him. The man then climbed into a big Chevy Suburban and drove away.

Two hours later, the bus followed the truck through a high security gate. Inside the compound, the bus was led to a large parking lot. Here the Suburban stopped. The man in black got out and walked back to the bus. Before he could speak, the bus driver began asking him a questions.

"What is this place?"

"Nothing," replied the man in black.

"But, what is it, what goes on here?" the driver asked again.

"Oh, it's just a place . . ." said the man in black. He waved to us and we got up and followed him off the bus.

*The driver tried to ask us a few questions, but we all
ignored him. What did he expect? You pick up a bunch of
paratroopers in the middle of the night and take them to
a high security compound in the middle of nowhere and
no one is in uniform. . . .*

Our bases in Germany were closing. My wife, Karla, and I had
no interest in staying around and watching the base dwindle into
nothing, so we took an immediate posting to Petawawa, Ontario.
I had decided that I would never again serve in a mechanized
unit. It was my intention to never ride in another M113 again if I
could manage it. I hated them after Yugo.

I knew that I had two choices, 2RCR in Gagetown or 1RCR in
Petawawa. Knowing 2RCR had APCs and 1RCR didn't, I wanted
Petawawa. I really wanted to join the Airborne Regiment and get
to Somalia, but I wasn't jump qualified yet. So I decided on 1RCR
to begin with. The Airborne would come next.

In Recce, we were disbanded as soon as we got off the aircraft
in Lahr. We had a couple of parties, a hockey game and that was
about it. We each recieved a handmade, numbered broadsword
as a parting gift. They were engraved with the words "Recce in
Yugoslavia." Because we put away so much beer during our six
months in Yugo, our canteen profits covered the cost of the
swords nicely. Today, it hangs on the wall in my living room.
After saying goodbye to all my comrades-in-arms from Recce,
Karla and I flew back to Canada.

I reported to work on 6 January 1993. I was assigned to the
Duke of Edinburgh's company of the first battalion. My first day
back to work, we packed up and deployed for a two-week winter
exercise. I hadn't been out on one of these since the Remembrance Day Massacre back in the 1980s.

Each soldier had a locker in the company area for his kit. I had
arrived in a sweat suit that morning and began to dress in front of
my locker. Almost immediately, a crowd began to form to watch
me dress. I was the first Yugo veteran to arrive at the battalion
and as such was a curiosity. Even more intriguing to the young
soldiers in the company was all my high-speed kit from Germany.

First came my Brit naval engineers' mesh vest, then my Helly-
Hansen long underwear. As I pulled out each item from my
locker, one of my audience would ask what it was. When I pulled

out my Gore-Tex body suit they all oohed and aahed. They nearly lost it, though, when I pulled out my rucksack.

I had decided there was no way I was going to carry that useless, spine-crushing issue rucksack, so I had gone out and bought up an Airborne rucksack frame and a new rucksack main pouch. I had, over the holidays, constructed a Canadian version of a U.S. Alice pack complete with extra pockets and custom straps. When the troops saw that, they all got excited.

"You can't carry that! No way! You're in for a surprise if you think you can use that thing!"

I just smiled and put it down next to my webb gear. I had strapped my kukri to the outside and they all drew in to check out the big knife.

"What's that? You can't carry that! You're not allowed!"

Again I smiled. I could care less what these guys thought. Either join me or get out of the way.

With that auspicious beginning, I headed off for my first winter training in years. The average rucksack weighed more than thirty kilos with all the gear the troops were carrying. I would be surprised if my ruck weighed fifteen. The first night, as we all pulled out our sleeping gear, it was another show-and-tell parade when I pulled out my snooze kit. I had a big, warm fur-pile hooded shirt and a featherweight polypropylene sleeping bag. This little number rolled up into something the size of a loaf of bread and was as warm as a normal sleeping bag. Also, it was still warm when wet, unlike our issue down sleeping bags which when soaked were terribly cold and heavy.

By the end of the exercise, no one had said a word about my kit, except to ask about this and that item. Even my rucksack attracted very little attention.

As the days went by, my morale plummeted. I had forgotten what soldiering back in Canada was like. In both Germany and Yugo I had been dealing one-to-one with majors and colonels. I didn't bother much with lieutenants or 2nd lieutenants. Basically, I received a mission and got on with it however I best saw fit. Now back in Canada, as a junior sergeant, I was lucky to be able to go to the bathroom by myself. All decisions had to be passed through my platoon 2IC, then to the Platoon Commander—a young 2nd Louie. It would sometimes take a day or more for the message to find everyone involved, be considered and come back down. I felt totally frustrated at the level of supervision imposed on me.

The next blow was my pay. In Germany, we received extra pay bonuses for serving overseas and to equalize our salaries with the local cost of living. We also received allowances for living off-base and had subsidized fuel for our vehicles. In Yugo, I was getting an extra $1,300 a month, tax free, on top of everything else. Now back in Canada, all that was gone and my pay had been reduced by nearly half.

There had been some soldiers posted back to IRCR ahead of me, but these were guys who didn't go to Yugo. Mostly fat, out of shape or injured types, they had not set a good impression for the rest of us who followed. No one initially believed I had been posted in from Germany because I wasn't a fat slob.

A peacetime battalion is also prone to office politics. There is always the "in" clique. These are the big egos in a unit who have the senior officers' and RSMs' ears. Since we were coming back from Germany and Yugo with far better training and operational experience than Canada-bound troops, the CO and RSM now turned to the new veterans for advice. Suddenly the in-crowd was being challenged for their cushy jobs. It created a sense of hostility and professional jealousy in the unit. As more vets returned, the situation got worse. Most of us couldn't have cared less. We just wanted to be treated with a bit of respect and be left alone to do our jobs.

All these new realities combined, I wasn't too happy at my new job. I also started seeing more of the officers who had never seen a shot fired in anger dictating to the veterans all the mistakes we had made overseas.

In one instance, a presentation was given by Captain Brian Gray, a friend of mine and a former platoon commander in Germany and Yugo. He showed the senior NCOs and officers of IRCR some slides of Yugo and explained how operations had been conducted. Amongst other things, he explained how you had to swallow down your customary glass of slivovicz before every meeting with local forces.

After Captain Gray finished his presentation, the CO got up and lectured everyone about how he would never let a single one of his officers drink while conducting negotiations. Brian, myself and a couple of other vets in the room looked at each other and smiled. We knew it was a load of shit. His battalion would never have accomplished a thing.

After the briefing, there was a workshop where we had to prepare answers as a group to peacekeeping scenarios. A veteran was placed in each group. The first question was, "You are escorting an aid convoy and are delayed. You must spend the night on your own. What do you do?"

The general consensus was to find a large field and marshal all the vehicles there in a defensive formation until dawn. When all the Yugo vets were asked, we all replied that you never left the road. You stayed right where you were. No one could accept that answer, so we all shrugged.

The next question was, "You are escorting a convoy through Bosnia and one of your vehicles hits a little girl. What actions do you take?"

The MPs in the groups started explaining how they would initiate an investigation and the medics would give first aid and move the victim to the local hospital. The senior officers all wanted to contact the local authorities to discuss the accident and so on.

Then they asked the vets. We all responded that you give the kid a quick bit of first aid and then get the hell out of town before the locals find out. The assembled audience was shocked.

"You're not serious?" they asked in disbelief.

"You're damn right we're serious! If the locals find out what you did they'll start a fight. You either hand over the guilty driver to the mob for torture and death or you all die."

They still couldn't grasp it.

"Look, a lot of people die there. One more little girl won't make a big difference. Help her as much as you can, but . . ."

I couldn't blame these guys for their attitude. They were Canadians who still thought like Canadians do. The world is a bad place sometimes and to survive out there you don't have to become bad yourself, but you must accept the way life is.

It isn't Sesame Street out there.

When you go to work in the morning and find a little girls' scalp, with long blonde pigtails and a red bow, lying in a pool of blood in the middle of the street, you have to broaden your horizons a little bit.

A couple of days later, a local news crew showed up at the unit and wanted to interview a Yugo vet. I was put forward. These guys were looking for an angle about how terrible it was and how the government shouldn't have sent us there, which was the general consensus at the time. I thoroughly disappointed them. I told them that I missed it and wished I was back there right now. In a war zone, soldiers are doing their real jobs; that's where a soldier belongs!

They cut short the interview and left in a huff.

My opinion about soldiering had pretty much clarified at that point. Operations are the only time when we really do our jobs. We should be doing more of them, not less. Training exercises are okay, because they prepare you for operations. Garrison time, though, is a total waste. I couldn't stand hanging around, Monday to Friday, collecting my pay and accomplishing nothing. If it wasn't for a long conversation I had with a tremendous officer, just prior to leaving Germany, I might have quit right there.

Captain Bruce Pennington, a very professional and intelligent officer who didn't get to Yugo for several more years, said to me, "Well, you've got all this experience now, it's your obligation to pass that knowledge on."

I had always admired Bruce and considered him a friend. He warned me that people would be slow to change, but it had to be done. It was this advice that always got me through when it seemed I had hit a wall at work.

Instead of complaining, I spent my time training troops in recce skills. I was helped greatly in this by the arrival of Warrant Officer Mark Ford. A grizzly bear of a man and a long time recce patrolman, he and I immediately saw eye to eye. Mark tolerated my eccentricities and employed me to my best potential. It was because of him that I began to enjoy coming to work again.

By the next winter, my time was waning at IRCR. I spent a year and a half there before finally getting my jump course. In doing so, I was introduced to another ex-recce malcontent like myself, Sergeant Warren Ashton. Warren and I became good friends and, after surviving the jump school, we were both posted to the Airborne Regiment in June of 1994.

The Canadian Airborne Regiment. I was finally there. All those years ago, in the recruiter's office in Toronto, when I had proclaimed my desire to be a paratrooper. Now, I had finally made it.

Almost.

You weren't ever officially a member of the Regiment until you had completed the Airborne Indoctrination course. Afterwards, you would be presented with a serialized Airborne coin, the only official recognition of service in the Regiment. Then, and only then, were you a full-fledged member of the Regiment. It didn't matter if you were a private soldier or a captain. Everyone did the course. Failure didn't necessarily mean expulsion from the Regiment, but you were certainly held in low regard and would probably quit voluntarily.

Unlike other postings, you couldn't just show up and become one of the boys. Even our service in Yugo didn't count for anything. These guys had all been through Somalia and weren't impressed. The fundamental was that you were now a "jumper."

Everyone else was a "Green beanie-wearing Leg!" The past didn't count for squat, now only your performance mattered.

I was in heaven. Finally, a unit that didn't build careers on the parade square and sucking up during coffee breaks.

I had quite a few old friends in 3 Commando who had made the transition a few years before. One of them was a scrappy little character named Tim Barratt. A corporal, he had no respect for anyone, regardless of rank, who didn't measure up. He reminded me regularly that I was just a "Fucking New Guy" (FNG), and had a long way to go. Rather than be offended at the arrogance of a junior rank calling down a sergeant, I was happy as hell. Here, I had to prove myself. Once I did, then I would be accepted as an equal. Forever. I dug right in and accepted the challenge.

Warren and I were to be spared the Indoc course for awhile. As we arrived, the Commando was down in Meaford training the militia. We drew our kit and headed down to join our new unit. 3 Commando had the job of running a shortened version of battleschool for reserves. A handful of Airborne NCOs and troopers would be assigned twenty to thirty volunteers each and had only a few weeks to whip them into shape. It was fun, but not particularly exciting.

The old hands would always be going on about the last time they had been down working with Special Forces or the Rangers. They would tell war stories about Somalia and there would be great bouts of drinking and arguing over details. Warren and I were left out of these conversations, but we were always welcome to listen in, as long as we bought rounds.

The OC of the Commando of this time was a Major Horn. He was a very hard character and generally not well liked by the troops. That is not to say he wasn't well respected. Every soldier there knew he was a tough bastard and despite the complaining, they wouldn't have wanted it any other way. An Airborne OC didn't have to be a buddy with his troops, as long as he shared their hardships. In the time I knew Major Horn, I never saw him cut a corner for himself or for his men. He did look out for their welfare, as long as it didn't make them soft. As far as I am concerned, he was perfect for the job. He won my loyalty, and that is no easy task.

The Commando Sergeant-Major was Jimmy Vienneau. A tough little NCO, he suited his role perfectly. He reminded me a lot of Hodgins, who was by now an RSM at the Airborne school in Edmonton. Full of colourful phrases, he was a good balance for Major Horn. Together, they made a good team. Not that everything was rosy and there were no problems, but these two always kept things running smoothly by force of will.

At this time the Airborne was under a cloud from the killing of Shidane Arone in Somalia. Warren and I knew it going in, but we figured it would be sorted out eventually. From all we had seen, this was the most professional outfit either one of us had come across. Every man here had to strive constantly to achieve. There was no coasting. You always had to be fitter, to learn a new skill, to be ready to go even farther. Compared to the RCR battalions, the Airborne Regiment was in its own class.

The Regiment at this time was the size of a large battalion, roughly five hundred soldiers. It consisted of five Commando sub-units. 1 Commando was French and was recruited from the Van Doos battalions. 2 Commando was recruited out of the Patricias. 3 Commando was manned by RCRs. There was also Combat Support Commando and Service Commando. These latter two were manned by qualified members from across the Regiment and the Forces.

Unique to the Airborne was the Pathfinder platoon. This was basically Airborne Recce, but with many different roles from traditional recce platoons. Before I could get to Pathfinders, I would have to earn my way in a Commando and then pass one of the harshest courses in the Forces, the Pathfinder course. Since it sounded like a hell of a challenge, that is where I set my sights.

We spent the first three weeks of July teaching the reserves and feeling out our new surroundings. During the middle of August, a platoon from the Commando was hauled out of Meaford to prepare for a mission in Africa. The UN was going to get involved in Rwanda, and as the resident experts on Africa, the Airborne was tasked to send a platoon along to guard the Headquarters. General Romeo Dallaire was the commander on the ground and he wanted some paratroopers with him in theatre. The Belgian Paras had recently departed after the slaughter of their men at the hands of the Rwandans and the Canadian Commander needed some suitable replacements. I was jealous of the guys going, but I hadn't even passed Indoc yet and couldn't expect a tour.

The rest of us had to fill in the slack left by the departing troops and finished up the school in the last week of July. Everyone headed back to Petawawa and after some torturous physical training to remind us to keep fit, we all left on two weeks' summer leave.

I was having a snooze at my parents' house in Barrie a couple of days later, when I heard my mother call me. She shouted down that there was a Sergeant-Major somebody on the phone for me. I rushed upstairs and took the call. It was CSM Vienneau. He told me to get back to Pet ASAP. I was going to Africa.

I said my goodbyes to my wife and family and raced back to Petawawa. I reported in wearing jeans and a leather jacket. When I reached the Commando office, I met the Sergeant-Major. He told me they had been ordered to prepare a second platoon for Rwanda and I was up for a job as a section commander. He asked me if I wanted the job. Naturally, I jumped at the chance.

Another operation!

Warren walked into the office. He was going as well, along with a third sergeant I had known years before in Germany, Kenny Nunn. The rest of the command staff would be Captain Dave Simkin and Warrant Officer Stu Hartnell. Of the five of us, all except Ken had just arrived at the Regiment. Fortunately, our troops consisted of a few veterans and we ended up with a good mix.

The job was a security mission. The Canadian government had decided to send a military hospital over in addition to their UN commitment of support troops to the headquarters. This mission was to be strictly Canadian and not under the UN mandate. To us, that meant no blue berets. I still had a lot of ill will towards the UN and was quite happy to go under a maroon beret.

After watching the UN make a mess of Yugoslavia and Somalia,

I didn't want to serve in a blue beret again. I know that they have the best intentions, but soldiers are not health care workers or policemen. If the UN wants to send soldiers into a war zone, they must expect them to fight. As we discovered in Yugo, the implied message of sending armed troops into an embattled country is that, if you don't comply with UN rules, the UN will enforce them. Since the UN will only allow a minimum of light arms and tiny quantities of ammunition, it instead becomes a big bluff. That makes for great-looking policy back in New York, but it seriously jeopardizes the soldiers on the ground. No thanks. I'll go anywhere, no matter how dangerous, as long as I go as a soldier and not a UN peacekeeper.

Five hectic days later, I was standing in an empty mess hall in Petawawa at 0400 hours, preparing to leave. Warren, Ken and I were taking twelve troopers and flying out to Rwanda later in the morning. Captain Simkin was already in theatre with Major Horn, scouting things out. Warrant Hartnell was staying behind to bring the rest of the platoon and all our kit with the main lift. The fifteen of us were to get over there, link up with the officers and secure the area for the arrival of the hospital a few days later.

I had the most time in rank at this point and was technically the senior man. That left me in charge. There were fifteen Combat Engineers going with us and their senior rank was a warrant officer named Hartinger, but he wasn't necessarily in overall command. In the Combat Arms, sometimes an individual with lesser rank can be placed in command if he has the necessary expertise in a certain field. This Warrant was happy handling heavy machinery, but he didn't feel comfortable handling security functions or commanding Airborne troops. So, I was the man.

We were processed through a "sausage machine" to finish our administrative details prior to boarding the bus for the airfield. We had our pictures taken for identity cards, received diplomatic passports, signed for our copies of the Rules of Engagement and collected our first bottle of Mefloquin anti-malaria pills.

At the end of the line was the Regimental Commander, Lt Colonel Kenward.

The CO was another tough-as-nails Airborne officer. He tolerated only the best and at forty-four was one of the fittest men in the regiment. He called the NCOs together and told us the reputation of the regiment was on the line. We were under a microscope and had to do everything we could to both promote the maroon beret and ensure we brought no more shame to the regiment. We promised to do our best and then boarded the bus.

So began my second operation.

We were flying out of CFB Trenton airfield and the bus trip took three hours. When we arrived, we were met by our TAMS people. These are supply technicians who specialize in moving kit by air. Tactical Air Movements by full name, they were both a great help in preparing loads for shipment and a pain in the ass when it came to anything combat oriented. The long, long list of safety regulations lugged around by these people put them at the top of my Safety Nazi list.

On this occasion, they had objected to our bringing live ammunition on the same aircraft as troops. It didn't matter that we were on our way to a place where, several weeks earlier, a group of tough Belgian paratroopers had been slaughtered. It was still against the rules.

Fortunately, we were not flying on Canadian aircraft. For this job, something larger was required. Enter the biggest group of drunken, misfit, air mercenaries since the CIA ran Air America in Vietnam.

Sitting out on the tarmac were two huge Russian-built IL-76s covered in a snazzy white and blue paint job. These were to be our ride to central Africa. With the name "Atlant" painted brightly on the hulls, they were recently decommissioned Soviet Air Force transports bought up buy cunning eastern investors. Manned by former military crews, they now plied their trade around the globe, hauling supplies in and out of risky little dirtholes.

These guys didn't give a damn about safety and had the TAMS people just slide a couple of pallets of ammunition and explosives onto their back ramps. Before boarding, one of the TAMS guys hauled us aside and said he wouldn't fly with these clowns and neither should we. We shrugged. Not much chance of that.

So we grabbed our kit and headed out to the big Russian planes. The engineers were going on one plane and we were riding on the other. Inside our aircraft, we found two big six-wheeled military trucks called a Medium Logistic Vehicles Wheeled (MLVWS) and a large pallet of ammunition and explosives.

Puttering around the load were a half a dozen Russian crew.

Some still wore their military-issue coveralls in Afghan camouflage. Others wore a mixed bag of military kit and civilian gear.

We picked out the pilot right away and Kenny immediately
nicknamed him "Buck Rogers." Impeccably turned out in a tai-
lored orange jumpsuit, he had that rich and useless look about
him. Not a hair was out of place on his blond head and he
almost looked like a California surfer, except that he would be a
Vladivostok surfer.

We introduced ourselves and found Buck spoke passable English. He was decent enough, as mercenaries go, but he let everyone know he was The Pilot. Kenny asked him how much these
planes could lift and Buck said he wasn't sure.

"We are five thousand pounds over the maximum acceptable
weight now, so we shall see, yes?" he replied with a grin.

With that ambitious beginning, we all tossed our kit into the
back of one of the trucks and found a seat for take-off. The seats
consisted of fold-down wooden benches running along both sides
of the fuselage. I squeezed in near the front and waited for the
adventure to begin. The planes fired up and pulled away with little fanfare. Once we were out on the runway, the engines roared
and we began to pick up speed. It seemed we were racing along
on the ground for miles. I was figuring we would reach Lake
Ontario any moment when, finally, the nose lifted and a few seconds later we struggled our way skywards.

Soldiers are generally uncomfortable when they are not in control of their own destiny. Sitting in the back of the plane, we had
no way to influence the outcome of the flight. Most of us would
rather be facing a dangerous situation on the ground than be
cooped up in the aircraft.

The crew didn't care what we did, so the troops found themselves comfortable niches and promptly went to sleep. We were
only in the air a few hours because we had to put down in Gan-
der, Newfoundland, to fuel up before heading across the Atlantic.
I give Buck Rogers full credit as a pilot; he landed that thing like
it was a Cessna.

We were going to be on the ground for an hour and a half, so
some of the guys headed off to the terminal for a beer. Back on
board the plane, the crew had opened the starboard door to get
in and out. A couple of the guys wanted to have a smoke and
told Buck Rogers they were going some distance behind the plane

to light up. Buck told them to just smoke on the plane and immediately pulled out some Camels and lit up. Our guys were a little shocked. Little more than five metres away, outside the open hatch, the fuel pod was refuelling the plane with jet fuel.

Safety? Hah! Ken lit up.

Eventually, I became bored with waiting to explode and headed into the terminal with Warren. I grabbed a Guinness in the airport bar and stuffed down a sandwich from a vending machine. When an hour had passed, I rounded up the troops and we headed back out to our respective planes. After another incredibly long run, we managed to struggle off the ground again under the combined weight of the cargo and full tanks of fuel. Next stop, Oostend, Belgium.

Buck Rogers landed us at around 0200. We were immediately whisked downtown to a hotel and given rooms at Atlant's expense. No one went to bed though. Most had slept all the way across the Atlantic, so everyone headed downtown for some refreshments, including Buck Rogers and the Pirates of the Air.

Warren and I couldn't be bothered changing and wandered into the night in our combats. We found a little bar and sampled the beer. The owner of the place had been in the military and treated us well. Buck came in later, but the owner ignored him until he left. None of my business why.

We were on our way again at about noon the next day. We had all slept in until 1000 and then were whisked in a double-decker bus to a restaurant for lunch. The owner of the hotel also owned the restaurant and there was obviously some wheeling and dealing behind the scenes. We didn't care, the lunch was free and the bar well stocked.

Finally, we were airborne again and on our way to Cairo for the next stop. By now, no one bothered to take a bench seat for take-offs or landings. Guys just climbed into whatever corner they could find and went to sleep. Feet stuck out of the cabs of the trucks and from underneath the wheels. Actually, the benches were dangerous because the trucks weren't too well strapped down and tended to shift during take-off.

Come to think of it, I don't think there was a single safe thing about that entire plane. The crew seemed to live in a progressive hangover, when they weren't outright drunk. There were a couple of spare tires for the landing gear stacked in the front of the cargo bay. These were worn down to the belts and those on the plane's wheels weren't any better. I watched out of the starboard door window as we crossed the Mediterranean and into North Africa. When we crashed in the desert, I wanted at least to know what country we were in.

We landed in Cairo at about 2100. A customs official met us at our plane, took all our passports and left in a Mercedes. I figured that was the last we'd see of those and settled down to wait on the tarmac outside the plane. Nearly an hour later, a bus pulled up and took us to the terminal, a two-minute walk away. We were led into the terminal by a customs official who brought us to a large area, jam-packed with a thousand locals. Then he left us. We had no idea what was going on and just stood there waiting for someone to come and get us. We certainly couldn't go anywhere without our passports.

At least I wasn't worried about our weapons and kit. The airport was covered in sub-machine-gun-toting police and army units. I figured if someone wanted it that bad, fifteen of us wouldn't have stopped them anyway.

While we stood around, totally bewildered, the Canadian Military Attaché from our embassy showed up. We figured, "Great, now we're getting somewhere." The attaché welcomed us to Egypt and wished us good luck and then disappeared in the crowd. So much for any help.

A couple of hours later two garishly painted nine-passenger vans showed up to take the forty of us to our hotel. Buck Rogers said he and his crew would wait for the next lift, so the thirty of us squeezed into the two vans for what we hoped was a short ride to the hotel.

No such luck. Our hotel was clear across Cairo and it took an hour to reach. The entire way, our driver maintained a steady sightseeing explanation of the wonders of Cairo. The fact that it was pitch dark and no one cared didn't put him off a bit. He even had a microphone and a PA system inside the van. Of course, you couldn't hear much over the wailing stereo anyway. The Egyptians would have loved Spinal Tap's amplifiers. Any speaker that goes up to eleven would be perfect for these guys.

Finally, we arrived at the hotel and our driver ran around to whip open the side door and put out his hand to collect his tips for his magnificent tour of the city. He was lucky none of the boys dropped him where he stood. Completely miffed, he jumped back in his van and, with speakers roaring, raced away into the night. Good riddance.

The hotel had been expecting us and had supper waiting. As they brought out the meals, there was quite a delay in the service. Some guys got there early and got served; others had to wait an hour. One of the troops wasn't feeling too good and only managed a few bites before telling the waiter he didn't intend to finish his plate. The waiter shrugged, picked up the plate and walked to the next table. He put the plate down in front of another Canadian. Once again, another international incident was avoided only by the arrival of the first rounds of beer.

No one wanted to sleep and we all went down into the local bars for some nightlife. We got drunk while watching belly dancers and generally annoying the local crowd. We danced and I played a drum while trying to sing "Wasn't that a Party?" by the Irish Rovers when the locals called for a song from Canada.

Early the next morning, it was on to a regular-sized bus for the trip back to the airport. When we got there, we nearly started yet another international incident when we tried to pass through security with our weapons bolts in our pockets. We routinely took them out of our weapons so, if they are stolen, they can't be used. Of course, airport people don't like it when you try to board a plane with weapons parts in your pockets. I didn't think it would help to explain how we had enough ammunition and explosives on the plane already to start a small war.

Eventually we boarded but were not given permission to take off until 1730. Airborne again, we headed south, paralleling the Nile. I was using my wrist compass to track our movement, once again in case we ended up in the desert somewhere. We all had a good laugh after I mentioned to the troops that, with all the gear we had on board, we could probably land in most small African countries and overthrow the local government. Fifteen paratroopers, some combat engineers, three trucks, a couple of tons of ammo and explosives . . . no problem. The air crew were mercenaries anyway; they would land us wherever we wanted if there was enough money in it. We laughed about it, but you could see the wheels turning behind a few eyes. If the next stop was anything like Cairo, we might just as well overthrow the government. Maybe that way we'd get some decent service.

We landed in Addis Ababa at around 2100 hours to refuel. Buck Rogers announced that it was too late to proceed to Kigali that night. We would have to wait until morning. There were reports of fighting around the airport there and he didn't want to land during a battle in the dark.

We didn't care. It had already been nearly three days since we left Canada. Another night wouldn't hurt. Buck told us that there was no money in his budget for hotels for the night, so we were on our own. He ordered some of his crew to stay behind and headed for the terminal to get a cab down to a hotel. I told the troops that if they wanted to fork over the cash, they should go and find a hotel. Personally, I was fine with sleeping on the plane.

We all went into the terminal to check in with customs and found Buck Rogers upsetting the local staff. He just didn't seem to be a people person, or maybe it was his nationality. Ethiopia had been a pawn of both superpowers for years and the fighting had nearly destroyed the country.

We all figured on another horrible mess and fully expected another Cairo. As it turned out, these were the kindest and most helpful people we had yet met on our trip. Not only did they process our passports in moments once I got Buck Rogers out of their hair, they even located hotels and cabs for all our guys. About half the troops headed downtown with the order to be back by 0730 hours or they were staying behind.

Ken had discovered a bar upstairs and Warren and I went up to have a beer. This place closed down after a while, so we all went back to the planes. Here we found the two Russians left behind to watch the planes well into a bottle of vodka. They were quite happy to share and for the next several hours we all passed around a couple of bottles and tried to communicate in a variety of languages. Our guys didn't have the stomach for power-drinking and eventually went to ground.

The Russians kept at it for a while, tossing their empties out the open hatch and onto the tarmac where they smashed. Some-time during the wee hours, one of the Russians leaned out of the hatch and vomited all over the side of the aircraft and the ladder. Just as we were all drifting back to sleep after that performance, there was a great crash and Warren and I leapt to our feet. We thought a Russian had fallen out of the plane. Since it was good three metres to the concrete below, we figured the drunken slob had killed himself. When we reached the front of the plane, we discoverd him passed out in the narrow corridor leading down to the navigation console. He had fallen over some garbage and ended up wedged in the passage. We figured he was as safe there as anywhere and left him.

Meanwhile downtown, the troops had found themselves a great little location. They had delicious steaks and goulash soup for supper and were waited on by a half a dozen servers, catering to their every wish. Surrounding them was a large group of the local ladies, all dressed up to the nines. These were beautiful women, tall and elegant with fine features and well-proportioned figures. The boys had a great time dancing, drinking and having gorgeous women hang all over them. They didn't want to leave. The moral of the story: If you ever find yourself stuck in Addis Ababa overnight, head downtown and spring for a hotel. It is far more pleasant then spending the night listening to a drunken Russian mercenary throw up all over the plane and then pass out in the cockpit.

The next morning, the troops pulled up to the airport and sauntered out to the plane having had the best time of the whole trip. They arrived to find the area around our plane covered in broken glass, the plane stinking of vomit and a very angry Buck Rogers. Apparently, Buck didn't approve of his crew throwing up all over his ship and the barely conscious crewmen received a good earful.

Everyone had made it back on time and we took off for Kigali around 0800. The flight only took an hour and a half from Ethiopia and we were descending into Rwanda before most of the revellers had sobered up. We touched down in Kigali and were waved over to a parking area by U.S. troops who were running the airfield. Once down, Buck wanted us and our kit off the plane pronto. He didn't want his valuable bird damaged by any stray rounds. We were unceremoniously dumped on the tarmac and the Russians were gone minutes later. So ended our great air adventure.

The city of Kigali was set on a small range of hills. Being almost at the equator, it was warm, but not too hot. The sky was a little cloudy as we arrived and there was a gentle breeze. The airport was being run by American troops who had established a perimeter and set up an HQ. We could see Hummers racing about and soldiers laying out wire around the terminal. At the moment, there were no sounds of fighting.

A Canadian captain showed up with a twenty-passenger bus and a Bedford truck. He was a medical officer from the field hospital. When we hit the ground the troops had started to pull out their weapons and break down some ammo boxes to load up. When the captain saw this he freaked.

"You can't unpack your weapons," he blurted, "the CO has ordered no weapons!"

I looked at him like he had two heads. What the hell did we just spend three rotten days in flying deathtraps for if the CO didn't want us to have any weapons? You don't fly combat troops ten thousand kilometres to provide security and then tell them to use harsh language!

I kept cool though. I nodded and smiled at the officer and said, "No problem."

Warren and Ken looked at me now as if *I* had two heads. Satisfied, the officer left. Once he was out of sight, I turned around and told the troops to unpack the weapons and ammo and load up their magazines.

In the Forces, medical people can attain just about any rank right up to general. However, every private soldier knows that they have no authority in the chain of command. This was a war zone and I was under no legal requirement to obey a medical officer. There was no sense in getting the officer all upset. Now that he was gone, we got on with loading our kit. Driving the bus was a corporal who would now be our guide up to the Zaire border. I explained the situation to him and then we started loading the trucks.

The Engineer's aircraft had been loaded with another MLVW and a military pickup truck called a Five-Quarter. This made our convoy three MLVWs, a Five-Quarter, one Bedford and a bus. Hell of a combat unit. Not my most promising command to date. Still, with fifteen paratroopers on board, they might as well have been tanks.

We were warned by the bus driver that there were checkpoints all along our route. This presented a dilemma. Technically, we didn't work for the UN. This was strictly a Canadian venture. Worse, we were on our way to establish a hospital, yet we didn't have one single piece of medical equipment. What we did have in abundance was ammunition and explosives. If the trucks were searched, what would we say? No one back in Pet had mentioned this point.

The only answer was to bluff our way past. This much ammo would be a tempting prize in a poor African country and we weren't about to just hand it over to the locals. We were all too aware of what had happened to the Belgian paratroopers only a few weeks before.

During the initial UN involvement in Rwanda, there had been troops from Bangladesh and Belgium here to protect the UN staff. In the first Hutu uprising, rebel Hutus had surrounded a platoon of Belgian Paras. The Paras could have easily fought the amateur Hutu militiamen, but the Belgian officer in charge ordered his men to lay down their weapons to avoid an incident. The Hutus bound the Belgians, then tortured and killed them one by one. The last the Belgian headquarters heard was a radio message from the platoon commander saying they were coming for him next.

Last to die was the platoon master sergeant. He had taken a hostage and held out for several hours awaiting rescue, but the UN commanders in the city were afraid of the consequences of an armed rescue. With the city already in chaos, an armed assault on Hutu HQ would only escalate the fighting. So the master sergeant was finally overpowered and murdered as well.

The remaining Paras knew what was happening but were prevented from going to the aid of their fellow soldiers by the UN commanders. They could have rescued their comrades but obeyed their officers and remained in their compounds. When the Paras returned home to Belgium, they built a fire at the airport and burned their UN berets in front of the international press.

With that incident in mind, there was no way our convoy was laying down its weapons for anybody. Stuff the Rules of Engagement. To hell with the CO. Better tried by twelve then buried by six.

On the way over, we had read the Rules of Engagement. Basically, they were a collection of rules for different courses of action. They outlined when we could use force and how much, who we could protect and who we couldn't. At the end was a disclaimer that stated that everything in parenthesis was still under review. If you looked in the book, everything pertaining to the use of force was in parenthesis. That way, no matter what we did, if it looked bad in the press, the government would be safe in saying we hadn't followed approved procedures and could hang us out to dry.

Great.

After loading all our mags, we packed the remaining ammo in several different trucks and then threw our kit on top. Then we laid a couple of tarps over our controversial cargo. Finally, I placed a couple of paratroopers on each vehicle, sitting on top of the cargo with their weapons handy. I instructed everybody to smile and wave; be as charming and friendly as possible. If anything went wrong, no one was surrendering. We would fight our way out of the immediate area and then plan our next move when it was over.

My best guess was that if we had to do any fighting, we would move into the mountains and hole up until reinforcements arrived. The French Foreign Legion's 2nd Parachute Regiment was in country and they had no Rules of Engagement. If you got in the Legion's way, doom on you. I'm sure that we could convince them to come to our aid.

I wasn't alone in all this planning. Ken and Warren were both involved in all the decisions. We also listened to the opinions of Warrant Hartinger. Out of the four of us, though, I was the only one who had been on an operation in a while and I was taking everything pretty seriously. I had seen what happened first hand when Canadians relaxed and let down their guard overseas.

When the plan was as clear as we could make it, we mounted up and headed out. The bus was leading and I rode in the front seat, opposite the driver. In with us were all the engineers. Behind our bus, the trucks maintained about a one-hundred-metre distance and had orders not to close up if we were stopped. I didn't want our whole convoy in the sights of any one weapon. If something happened at the front, it would give the others time to react.

I briefed the driver on our cover story for when we were stopped. As far as anyone would know, we were UN and were on our way to set up a hospital. We were carrying medical supplies and equipment.

Strangely, we encountered no checkpoints in the city. We had cleared the city limits before we found the first one. We bluffed our way by and continued on into the mountains. The trip took about four hours. All along the route we passed a continuous stream of refugees. I tried not to pay too much attention to them. The last thing I needed was any emotional involvement in their plight. But it became harder and harder to ignore them. At one point, we were crawling up a long hill and I had a good look at a group of seven or eight children. The oldest was a girl of about eight. The children with her were mostly three or four years old. One was a baby who was being carried by a four year old. There were no adults around. They were alone. How do you not feel for them? How do you handle being a mom at eight?

We couldn't stop and help them because another kilometre down the road were more abandoned children. Fifteen paratroopers and some engineers couldn't save all those refugees. What would we give them, bullets?

Our convoy continued on.

Finally, at mid-afternoon, we reached the "Milk Factory." This was to be our new home. We were met by Captain Simkin who, with the CO and the RSM, had been there since the previous day. We moved inside the compound and dropped our kit. Our trip was finally over.

The Milk Factory was a large warehouse-sized building located in the village of Mareru. We were about twenty kilometres from the Zaire border and near the top of a range of mountains running along the western border of Rwanda. The main road from Goma, Zaire, ran right past our front door on its way to Kigali, in the heart of the country. The plan was to render assistance to returning refugees after they had struggled up from the lowlands around Lake Kivu. Here they would rest, be fed and given water, healed if necessary and sent on their way again. A good plan.

The compound itself consisted of two sections: the factory itself and, next to it, a three-hectare residential site for the factory's management. The whole complex was surrounded by fencing, reinforced at intervals by mortar and stone pillars. It was big, but we felt we could manage the security with a platoon.

The factory had been built by the French government with aid dollars. It was intended to improve the locals' diet by increasing their protein intake. Local farmers would bring in their milk, it would be heat pasteurized and sealed in long-term storage containers for distribution throughout the country. The whole plan hit a snag when it was discovered the vast majority of the populace was either lactose intolerant or unable to stomach the high-protein diet. The plant was closed and had sat idle for five years. Until we arrived, that is.

The residential area consisted of two buildings. The first was a luxurious private bungalow with kitchen, bathroom, living room with fireplace and several bedrooms. It would have belonged to the chief administrator of the factory. It wouldn't be much by North American standards, but here it was a palace. The other building was a single-storey "C" block of eight smaller apartments. Each of these had a kitchen, bathroom, living room with fireplace and two bedrooms. Fairly nice and still way above local standards. We weren't sure why the homes had fireplaces, being only a few hundred kilometres from the equator, but who were we to complain?

The area surrounding the compound was beautiful. Across the road to the south, a huge cliff climbed out of the trees and rolling, steep-sided hills stretched into the distance. This was one of the few areas of jungle left in the country and it was marked on our maps as a military reserve. The jungle extended south for fifty kilometres, paralleling Lake Kivu.

To the north lay the Virunga mountains. A chain of jungle-covered volcanoes, they were the home to the late Dian Fossey's mountain gorillas. The highest peak, Karisimbi, was only fifteen kilometres away and dominated the northern sky. It rose 2,200 metres above us and topped out at 4,500 metres above sea level.

The countryside was almost completely deforested except for these two areas. Every square metre of ground is cultivated. Even slopes as steep as eighty degrees have potatoes growing on them. People are everywhere, as even after the fighting and slaughter, Rwanda remains one of the most densely populated countries in Africa.

As confusing as it may sound at first, the situation in Rwanda was pretty straightforward. When the colonial Belgian and French masters left Rwanda in the early 1960s, they left behind a divided populace. The two major tribes, Hutu and Tutsis, were at odds over the country's future. The minority Tutsis, descended from Watutsi warriors, had been given preferential treatment by the Belgians. Although only comprising fourteen percent of the population, they controlled most of the government. The Tutsis were hard workers and the Belgians had rewarded them with education and employment in the colonial government. When the Belgians left, they left the Tutsis in charge.

Almost immediately, the Hutu majority rose up and overthrew the Tutsis and chased many of them out of the country. Some ended up in Uganda, which borders Rwanda on the north. Here they joined the national army and fought in Uganda's ongoing civil wars. Eventually, the Tutsis formed their own force in Uganda and began cross-border raids back into Rwanda.

The Hutu government tired of this nuisance and was negotiating to accept the exiled Tutsis back into the country. This was the state of affairs in early 1994. Then everything changed. A rogue Hutu element in the government opposed any reconciliation with the Tutsis. This group had the president's plane shot down en route to a peace negotiation. Immediately, the rogue elements seized power and began a systematic elimination of all Tutsis or Hutus sympathetic to the country as a whole.

The situation really got out of hand when large numbers of teenagers with nothing else to do in a dirt-poor agrarian country decided to form their own gangs and start killing Tutsis themselves. These groups, known as the Interhamwe, would roll into a village and grab a Hutu family. They would threaten to kill the father's entire family if he didn't take a machete and slaughter every Tutsi in the village. This he had to do. With no law to turn to in the now non-existent government, the Tutsis were on the verge of extinction.

Enter a man named Paul Kugame. As a young boy he had followed his family into exile in Uganda. As a grown man, he was an experienced soldier who had been educated at a U.S. military school. With his band of Tutsi guerrillas in Uganda, he realized something had to be done to save his brethren back home. Although badly outnumbered, they attacked. The Hutu army, a poorly led and disorganized force at best, fell back rapidly before the Tutsi guerrillas. As they went, they caused panic amongst the Hutu populace who were told the Tutsis would murder them all. So, the refugee crisis was born as roughly fifty thousand government soldiers and Interhamwe groups drove hundreds of thousands of Hutu villagers from their country and into refugee camps in Burundi and eastern Zaire.

When the Tutsi army, known now as the Rwandan Peoples Army (RPA), consolidated their hold on the country, the killing stopped. The RPA were a tremendously disciplined force and there were no official reprisals. It would have been impossible to prevent all acts of retribution, but as a whole the country became peaceful again very quickly.

During the whole mess, the UN had been more or less present. It was during the initial Hutu revolt that the Belgian Paras had been slaughtered by the Hutu army. After a total withdrawal during the fighting, now the UN was returning. It wasn't to help the now-peaceful Rwanda to rebuild and heal its wounds though. The UN and a hundred aid agencies descended on the Hutu refugee camps in Zaire, ignoring the shattered country struggling to recover.

The retreating Hutu army and their hapless tide of now-homeless Hutu civilians crossed the border into Zaire and immediately plunked themselves down on the shores of Lake Kivu in the area of a small town named Goma.

Now the situation becomes complicated, as we were to soon discover at the hospital. When the Hutu hordes settled down in the now-growing refugee camps, the Hutu army and the Interhamwe soon took control again. As the International Red Cross, CARE, UNICEF and an endless stream of aid groups arrived and set up shop, they unwittingly played right into the hands of the Hutu troops. The army and the Interhamwe had been beaten, they had many wounded, and they were weak from hunger and dysentery. As the aid agencies arrived and began dispensing food, water and medical aid, the military ensured the bulk of the aid went to their men first. The vast majority of the refugees received nothing.

What was worse, they were now trapped on a barren and lifeless volcanic plain. Around them in the hills and further into Zaire there was plenty of food and water to be found in the forest, but they couldn't leave. The army and the Interhamwe knew that if the refugees dispersed and the crisis was over, their new supply of food and medicine would leave with them. Those who tried to head back into Rwanda or move deeper into Zaire had their hamstrings cut by the Interhamwe.

Trapped in the camps with no food, medicine or clean water, the refugees began to die. Because of the essentially impermeable basaltic rock beneath them, their urine and feces lay stagnant on the ground. Soon cholera broke out and the refugees began dying in large numbers. Still, the military refused to release their grip on the refugees.

It was into this situation that we had arrived. Many Hutus, who had somehow avoided the camps, were heading home as we arrived, but those numbers began to dwindle in the first few days. Soon, they almost stopped.

As the situation began to clarify in our minds, our overwhelming concern was the presence of more than thirty thousand Hutu troops recuperating twenty kilometres away. When they were ready to go on the offensive again, we sat right on the only road to the capital. Memories of Sarajevo and the enclave began springing to mind.

The hospital staff and the rest of our troops arrived a couple of days later. We had been cleaning and doing twenty-four-hour security patrols while we waited for them to arrive. Once our full platoon was on the ground, we moved into the block of apartments with the engineers. The luxury residence was to be the home of the doctors. All the other senior people moved into the offices in the factory's administrative area. The rest of the medical people and support staff set up their cots amongst the machinery.

In the apartment complex, there was one apartment we couldn't occupy. We called it "The Blood Room." A family of Tutsis had been murdered there. In the living room, dried bits of flesh and blood covered the walls and a distinct handprint and face profile made a red streak to the floor.

In one of the bedrooms we found a closet riddled with holes. Inside the closet a young girl had hidden until the Hutus tossed in a grenade. There were no bodies left when we arrived. The locals, Hutu and Tutsi alike, had buried them in a mass grave behind the building, along with some other casualties of the "ethnic cleansing." We just avoided the whole apartment.

The clean-up went quickly. The troops had built up a pile of garbage next to the factory and Warrant Hartnell decided to burn it. Unknown to all of us, the heap had been littered with various types of ammunition which began to cook off soon after the fire started. Everyone ran for shelter.

We soon noticed that only ten metres away were a dozen drums of gas, diesel fuel and naphtha. Master Corporal Trent Hollihan, my section 2IC, jumped in a Five-Quarter and drove it between the fire and the drums before bailing out and running for cover. Brave man.

While we all stood back and watched the fire and the

pyrotechnics from a safe distance, Warrant Hartigan showed up on the scene. Hearing the bullets cracking in the air and not aware of what was going on, he ran shouting into the factory to evacuate the area. We all had a bit of a chuckle and the fire burned down after an hour or so.

One of the MLVWs was supposed to belong to the security platoon, but it was quickly commandeered to haul equipment from the airport. The platoon still had work to do, including securing a portable water purification unit set up by the Engineers twenty kilometres to the east. With no vehicle, we were stuck. Enter Corporal Dave Bona. A typical scrounger, he had been on a run to the airport when he noticed a compound full of UN vehicles abandoned by the withdrawing Belgian and Bangledeshi units. These were guarded by UN troops, but most of the vehicles were smashed or stripped of parts.

Inside the compound were Russian-built BTR–70 armoured APCs, a few trucks and several jeeps. Dave asked the guard on duty about the vehicles and was told no one really owned them; they were UN property and were awaiting repair. After chatting for a while, Dave asked if he could have one of the jeeps. The guy told him if he could get one running, he could have it. After enough tinkering, Dave drove away with a beat-up, right-hand-drive Toyota Land Cruiser and trailer. The vehicle was immediately claimed as the platoon's official transport and it was dubbed "The Anti-Christ" after a troublesome jeep in the movie *The Gods Must Be Crazy*.

The hospital staff arrived about a week after us but could not get the hospital operating for several weeks. Their equipment was landed in Uganda, instead of Kigali, and no one could find trucks to haul it down to our location. Finally, a firm was located and the equipment arrived. The medics attacked the gear and got the hospital up and running a couple of days later. The problem was that, by then, the flow of refugees had almost stopped and they ended up treating mostly locals.

The hospital was a huge tented arrangement similiar to the old M*A*S*H television series. Except this unit didn't have surgeons, only general practitioners. Named the 2 Field Ambulance, it was cobbled together from medical units from across eastern Canada but was primarily staffed by personnel from CFB Peta-wawa. It was an immense, self-contained facility consisting of triage, three wards, obstetrics, a pharmacy and treatment rooms, all under one tented roof. It was designed to process up to fifteen hundred people a day and could keep up to three hundred patients in its beds. Our medical people are some of the best in the world and they were sure to be a great help to the refugees . . . when they came.

The problem was, twenty kilometres down the road in the refugee camps around Goma, very few people were moving. They were still dying in large numbers but the Hutu militia were preventing them from leaving. Instead of the refugees returning to their homes in Rwanda, a flood of relief agencies raced past our gates headed for the camps. Already, four other hospitals were going up in the area and scores of aid groups established stations in Gisenye and Goma. With an uncertain future back in Rwanda, the militia threatening to kill and maim anyone trying to leave and foreign food and medicine flooding into the camps, those refugees well enough to travel were not in a hurry to leave.

So, we sat up on the mountain feeding "magic water" (clean water with oral rehydration salts added) to the locals, while waiting for the refugees. From a security standpoint everything was going fine. The locals were decent, lawful people and we had no trouble whatsoever with theft. We did play a bit of a game with some of the local kids. They would watch our patrols pass and then hop the wire and race for our refuse pit to grab some old ration crackers or something. Then our guys would jump out of the grass where they had been hiding and chase the little kids out of the compound. When we caught the kids we would give them a stern lecture and take them back outside. Occasionally, other kids would shout and give away their friends over the wire and we would reward them with candies. In this way, we encouraged them to stay out of the compound.

The locals were very friendly and we felt fairly comfortable among them. Soon, the hospital began hiring locals to work in the hospital and clean the buildings, similiar to our system in Yugo. They were issued ID cards and earned a good local wage. Some of the best workers were the kids. Not that we used child labourers; we usually hired the kids because of their language skills. Before the schools all closed, the kids were taught French and English. The hospital hired some of these students, some as young as ten or twelve, to work as interpreters for the hospital.

Our security duties included manning the front gate of the compound during hospital hours, conducting roving patrols twenty-four hours a day and guarding the water purification site as it went out each day to a local lake.

Everything was going well until we received reports that the Hutu military in the camps might try a counter-offensive aimed at seizing areas in western Rwanda. The proposed plan was to establish a Hutu stronghold on the eastern shores of Lake Kivu. This meant a drive at least as far as our camp on the heights. Immediately, we began looking at emergency plans. I had already drawn up an escape and evasion map for my section and this was distributed to the platoon. I took the Anti-Christ and, with Captain Simkin and the CO, Lt Colonel Anderson, we scouted routes north to the Ugandan border, to the north on the far side of the Virunga mountains. After selecting a suitable escape route, we dropped off the CO and Captain Simkin and I headed down to Gisenye to have a look around.

There were four Canadian signallers manning a communications van in the town. They were located in a battle-scarred hotel on the shores of the lake. It would have been a pretty scenic place except for the dead cow in the swimming pool and about two hundred bodies rotting in the sun on the shores of the lake. Captain Simkin and I worked out an arrangement with these guys for early warning in event of an attack by the nearby Hutu forces. They would also give us the occasional update on activity near the border. From the sandy beach in front of the hotel, you could look across the large bay into Zaire.

These guys would have a ringside seat in the event of a Hutu push. For their own escape, they commandeered a Zodiac launch and an outboard motor from the hotel. They would grab a radio and head out into the lake before calling for evac by UN helicopters if life got a bit too interesting on shore.

We felt sorry for these signallers, but they were only one of many teams scattered around Rwanda providing communications for the UN forces in the country. Unfortunately for these guys, they got one of the hot spots. We wished them luck and headed back to Mareru.

Our plan for evacuation was fairly simple. If the battle threatened our position, we would abandon the hospital and mount all the medical personnel up in trucks. Escorted by two sections of our security platoon, they would head for either Kigali or the Ugandan border, depending on the situation. The remaining section of paratroopers, with a few engineers, would destroy any ammunition or sensitive equipment that we couldn't take with us.

That was the game plan. I wasn't totally satisfied with it. I felt we needed a dismounted escape route as well, avoiding the main roads altogether. I felt this way for two reasons.

First, in event of any fighting, the hospital would no doubt be flooded by casualties and the CO, being a doctor, would probably delay our departure to aid the wounded. If, at the crucial moment, the CO decided to have the hospital stay put and continue treating the wounded, it would put our security platoon in a difficult position. Medical personnel could probably surrender to the advancing Hutus and go on to treat their wounded as well. Presenting no threat, they might be spared. If, as the hospital was overrun, the Hutu began slaughtering the medics, our platoon would be hard pressed to do anything about it. Although the compound was a great site for a hospital, it was hardly defensible.

Either way, the medical staff might be overlooked by the Hutu, but our paratroopers certainly wouldn't be. We would certainly be disarmed and detained. Considering what happened to the Belgians before us, I already planned to consider such an order illegal and would have refused.

Herein lay our problem. NDHQ back in Ottawa had placed a medical officer in charge of our mission. Technically, he had no authority over his combat troops in matters of security or defence. Also, the senior Combat Arms officer was a captain and he could not legally order the CO to do anything either. So we were in a Catch-22. If the CO made an error in judgment at a critical moment, we in the defence platoon were hamstrung. Either we stay with the medics and face almost certain death by torture or we abandon them to their fate and head for the hills. In which case, if they were slaughtered, we could never return home because we would have failed to protect our charges. We would have been disgraced.

My second big concern was a result of the French Foreign Legion's activities to our south through the jungle. The Legion had established a large pocket of Rwandan territory that was under their strict control. They were not permitting the RPA access, and already there had been skirmishes. Inside the pocket

were the remnants of the Hutu government that had master-
minded the war. Perhaps inadvertently—it's hard to tell with the
Legion—they were protecting these people with their safe zone.
The RPA was going nuts, but the Legion wouldn't budge.

It was this government in exile that was announcing its intent
to establish a Hutu enclave east of the lake. If they were to march
north for a link-up with forces advancing eastward from Goma,
they would meet in the area of our hospital. The RPA, intent on
maintaining civil control, seemed to patrol only the main roads
and villages. That left the military preserve across the road as a
perfect approach route to the main road between Goma and
Kigali. A flanking manoeuvre heading north out of the Legion-
held safe zone would cut off the RPA units at the border in
Gisenyi and allow the Hutu forces sallying out of Goma to seize
the border without fear of Tutsi reinforcement from Kigali.

Now, I'm not a great general trained at Sandhurst or West
Point in strategic manoeuvre, but then again, neither were the
Hutus in charge. It seemed like a very reasonable plan to me and
I always trusted my instincts. Because I had learned the hard way
in Croatia and Sarajevo to not underestimate seemingly scattered
and poorly armed local forces, I took these threats seriously. My
concerns were compounded by the lack of experience in the platoon. Many of the soldiers in the platoon had been in Somalia or
Yugo, but the platoon's leadership was short on operational
knowledge. Captain Simkin had served in Yugo, but his tour had
been extremely quiet compared to mine. Warrant Hartnell had
not had a tour at this point and saw everything as 3RCR had
done prior to heading to Yugo two years earlier. I was not critical
of their ability to command, but personally I felt that they were
not taking the situation seriously enough. Both were falling into
the same trap we had years before. Neither Ken nor Warren had
done a tour, other then Cyprus, so I had no support from that
quarter. My suggestions fell on unsympathetic ears.

Now I was quite willing to accept that nothing would come of
the Hutu threats but, if they did . . . fail to plan, plan to fail.

Therefore, I sat my section down and explained the situation
to them as I saw it. I explained that I was in an ethical Catch-22
of my own because of these concerns. My first loyalty was
always to the soldiers who served under me and, as such, if the
situation went from bad to worse, I would make my own tactical

decisions if the platoon was caught unprepared. I issued them escape maps and told them that under no circumstances, even on order of the platoon commander, would we lay down our weapons. I would accept responsibility for the decision if and when we survived.

On the other hand, as an NCO, I was obligated by loyalty and professionalism to support the orders of my commanders. If I sided with the welfare of my soldiers over the wishes of these commanders, I was not worthy of my rank and position of respect as an NCO.

The troops listened and I felt they understood. I told them the only way out of the dilemma was for us to obey all orders that kept us armed and fighting. I was quite willing for us to fight and die in defence of the hospital, if that was what was required. The moment we were ordered to lay down our arms, I drew the line. If we did fight and a few survived, our section plan was to lead whatever survivors we could north over the mountains into Uganda and head for either of two rendezvous.

I caused a lot of ill feeling in those first few weeks between myself and the platoon commander. My "rogue" attitude was somewhat of a challenge to his authority. I never wanted it to happen that way, but I had made that promise to myself back in Yugo to do things my way regardless, and I was sticking to it. The situation wasn't helped when the other paratroopers in the platoon saw my section's escape maps and wanted their own. Finally, Warrant Hartnell hauled the three sergeants in and tore a strip off us. I knew it was coming and accepted the blame. My initial preparations were complete at that point anyway, and afterwards I worked hard to re-establish the confidence of the captain and the warrant. They were both good men who had earned their rank. I felt sorry for causing so much trouble, but it was necessary as I saw it.

One major difficulty was that none of the commanders had ever worked together before. Captain Simkin had just been posted in from 2RCR in Gagetown, New Brunswick. Warrant Hartnell had just shown up from the RCR Battleschool. Ken had been with the Airborne for a couple of years and Warren and I had just arrived from 1RCR. With no prior knowledge of each other, we had to have time to adjust to our personal command styles and personalities. Neither the warrant nor the captain knew me from Adam, and they were understandably having a bit of difficulty with a young sergeant who did things his own way. Warren knew me a bit, but not well. Ken I remembered vaguely from Germany, but we had never worked together. We sorted it out eventually, and I count each of them as my close friends to this day.

One of my first duties was to organize a VIP security detachment. On 11 August, Major-General Romeo Dallaire, the Canadian commander of the UN mission in Rwanda, and Lt-General Gordon Reay, Commander of the Canadian Army, were going to fly into our compound by helicopter and then proceed to a meeting with local leaders and the RPA commanders in Gisenyi. This meeting would take place at the hotel where the signals detachment was located and was, as I already knew, in direct line of sight of the Hutu forces across the bay in Zaire.

I had little time for proper preparation because none of us was aware of the visit until the evening of 10 August. With only the one night and a couple of hours in the morning to prepare, I was under the gun. Fortunately, Captain Simkin allowed me to choose my team from across the platoon. I also had access to whatever equipment we had, which wasn't much for close protection work.

I got to work immediately and began by selecting my team. I decided on a five-man protection element and a three-vehicle mounted element. My first choice for personnel was Master Corporal Roy Van Den Berg. Roy had served in Recce platoon with me in Germany before departing to the Airborne in 1991. He is an extremely intelligent man and an excellent soldier. A qualified sniper and master of several languages, he was my first choice as second-in-command. Roy would be responsible for the mounted element. For my security escort, I selected four troops from my own section. Anyone in our platoon was good enough, but I knew these guys the best. Tim Barratt got General Dallaire and Corporal George Arnt was assigned General Reay. I also picked my two machine gunners to fill out the team. Corporals Fafard and Aprile were both good men and they would provide extra firepower with their C9 light machine guns if we met any serious trouble.

For Tim and George, we selected shotguns both for their stopping power and for their psychological effect. They both carried 9 mm Browning pistols in shoulder holsters as well. Roy, the drivers and I carried c7s.

For vehicles I got the Anti-Christ, the CO's Land Cruiser (also a "liberated" item) and a Five-Quarter. The rest of the equipment was collected from around the platoon. I had brought a couple of small, short-range radios with single earbuds from Canada and we made good use of these as well. We spent the night getting the equipment and vehicles ready.

In the morning, before the generals arrived, we spent our time rehearsing. The plan was an obvious shoot and scoot, but I still felt almost totally unprepared as the time arrived for the helicopter to land. I hadn't scouted the route. There was no one from the team in Gisenyi checking the meeting site. I didn't know if the generals were bringing a huge entourage that would want to ride along. How long was the meeting to last? Where was the pick-up point? I just felt that there was so much left to do. Once again, Canadian belief in the goodwill of warring factions had prevented these generals from considering their security before arranging these meetings.

I had done a threat assessment as best I could the night before. Once again, Canada's lack of any battlefield intelligence collection capability hampered my efforts. I didn't know if there had been any specific threats against the UN Commander. I didn't know the exact status of the Hutu forces in and around Goma. I didn't know if there were any factions inside Rwanda that could be opposed to the UN's presence. I therefore had to suspect everything. Our biggest worries would be the trip down to Gisenyi and the meeting itself.

While I was still pondering the imponderables, the helicopter flew into sight. A white Twin Huey, it stood out like a sore thumb. This war had started by shooting down an aircraft with VIPs aboard. Great.

As it landed beside the factory, my team rushed into place. Tim and George took up their stations next to the generals and my gunners watched the fences. Of course, every local within kilometres was streaming to the wire to look at the helicopter. Another concern.

The generals had brought two aides-de-camp with them as well as a big Nigerian sergeant as a personal escort. I didn't know anything about this guy, so I just let him do his thing and didn't involve him in my actions.

The CO was there to meet the generals along with the RSM, the

Deputy Commanding Officer (DCO), the senior doctor, a Public
Relations team with a big video camera and a couple of other
interested officers from the camp. The whole procession headed
into the factory for a briefing from the CO and his staff.

After the meeting was over, the generals took a quick walk
around the camp. While they were inside the hospital, I broke off
and went over to the helicopter. I found the pilot fiddling with
something and we had a chat about timings, frequencies and
emergency plans. I felt a bit better after talking with him and then
went in search of one of the aides. These guys would know the
routine better then the generals. After tracking one of them down,
I got a shock. The helicopter was to pick up the generals on the
beach in front of the hotel! Even the pilot hadn't been told yet. I
tried to explain the security problems involved in this, but I was
talking to a self-important officer with more important things on
his mind than safety. That was my concern, according to him.

I had the vehicles brought up. They had been idling nearby so
that we didn't have any surprises in the event one wouldn't start.
When the generals left the hospital, there was a moment of confusion when it came time to mount up in the vehicles. With two
VIPs, the CO, RSM, Captain Simkin, nine security men, two aides
and camera team, not everyone could get on board. I sorted it
out with a VIP and several guards in each Land Cruiser and the
remainder in the Five-Quarter. I rode in the front Land Cruiser;
Roy brought up the rear in the truck.

We got down to the hotel with no difficulty and led the VIPs
through the hotel. Once inside the building, it became a race for
my team to juggle the crowd inside, sweep the outside of the
building, check the beach and watch the Rwandans at the meeting. Roy took Fafard and Aprile and searched the landing zone
on the beach while Tim, George and I swept the rooms around
the meeting. During the meeting, I placed Tim and George on the
entrances, while I checked, checked, checked.

The meeting went well, and after it was over, I held the generals inside the building until the helicopter arrived. Once it was
down, my team surrounded it and, after a short wait to ensure
there was no immediate attack, brought the generals out. Once
he was on board, I could hear General Dallaire thanking the CO
for his efforts—I assumed that included us—and then the door
slid shut. The helicopter's blades wound up to speed and the

machine lifted off and pulled out over the bay. I watched with held breath as it completed its turn over the water and headed east, gaining altitude.

When it was out of sight, I gathered in my team and thanked everybody for a job well done. The generals were away safe and that had been our mission. A soldier always feels good when a mission went well. We headed back to Mareru and a few bottles of warm local beer.

As I sat in front of the fire later that night listening to Fafard's CD of *The Last of the Mohicans* soundtrack, I couldn't help feeling a little exasperated with our senior officers. I remembered well the pictures of General Schwarzkopf dismounting from his helicopter in the Gulf surrounded by ex-Delta Force security men. Even on a huge American base, his security was tight. Our generals and their staffs, in the middle of a small African war, couldn't spare a second thought to security. That meeting should have taken a week to set up. Instead it was off the cuff.

The problem in this isn't the inconvenience to the generals, but the risk to the security men. Without adequate preparation, the guys doing security are tipping the balance in favour of an ambusher. When, or if, an attack takes place, the security people will try to save the VIP, but they will be the ones to pay the price whatever the result. With time to prepare, dangerous situations can sometimes be avoided. In this case, if the generals were killed in an ambush, our Airborne security team would have been blamed for the failure. No one would care that none of the security issues had been dealt with. My guys would have fought and died because no one wanted to take the time to prepare.

Our life in the camp began falling into a routine. We broke down our work into a three-day routine. Day one was twenty-four hours of camp security, patrolling, manning the CP and handling the front gate. Day two was security down at the water purification site. Day three was our day off. Each day a section would have a new task. It worked pretty well. It was boring, but so is most security work.

Down in Kigali, the other Airborne platoon had arrived to work for UN headquarters. The Canadian press was always about and a reporter had hoped for a good sound bite when he asked a female nurse how she felt about Airborne troops being back in Africa working with more poor black Africans. After the

Somalia incidents, he was no doubt hoping for a complaint about the presence of Airborne troops. Instead, the nurse replied, "I wouldn't want anyone else protecting us!"

The Airborne platoon there was tasked with both security duties and patrolling the countryside, carrying out a variety of missions. They looked for signs of refugee movement on the Burundi and Tanzanian borders, they visited the dispersed signals detachments and on one occasion they relieved a French Foreign Legion garrison at a jungle village.

A signals det was to set up shop in the village and the Legion was pulling out of the country. The Airborne troops, including Sergeant Mark Godfrey, relieved the French and were shocked to discover a large pit filled with dead and dying prisoners. If the Legion considered a local a criminal, he was thrown into the pit and left to die. Mark and his troops had to separate the living from the dead and get the survivors some medical attention.

In another instance, Mark travelled through a remote section of jungle with Corporals Evans and Okerlund. They were tasked to reach the river marking the border with Tanzania and report on activities there. As they reached the river, they surprised a group of traditional natives fishing on the far bank. The sight of three white soldiers appearing out of the jungle must have surprised them, and they took off into the bush. After several hours of prompting, Evans and Okerlund coaxed the locals from the jungle and with hand signals and body language learned from them about military activity in the area.

For any of the clowns back in Canada who believed the big, tough Airborne troops needed sensitivity training, they should have been in the jungle that day. Two hardened Airborne troops made simple forest folk trust them and communicate with them. After exchanging some simple gifts, Mark led his two diplomats out of the jungle. Mission accomplished.

Back in Mareru, I had decided that more knowledge of the surrounding area was in order. I asked for some volunteers and, with webb gear and weapons, we headed out the front gate. I wanted to see if I could find any sign of military activity in the hills to our south. Captain Simkin and Warrant Hartnell had no problem with our "sightseeing" excursion, so off we went.

Immediately, the thin mountain air took effect. We were some 3,000 metres higher then we were in Petawawa and had to climb another three hundred metres in elevation to reach the top of the range. As we travelled, we stopped often, both to catch our breath and to admire the view. We were travelling through secondary jungle, and when we couldn't find trails, we needed machetes to move. The vines and bushes were too thick to plow through and we quickly discovered a variety of stinging plants and vines.

After reaching the crest we could see the jungle gradually turning to more of a primary forest, but there was still a considerable amount of undergrowth. As we walked along a narrow trail, I watched the ground closely for signs of activity.

We came to a small clearing and immediately my sixth sense started sending warnings. Something was wrong there. Behind me, Dave Bona, Scott McCready and Jeff Harrison had halted as well. They were wondering what was wrong in front. Slowly, I walked into the clearing. The others followed me, all alert now. I just couldn't put my finger on what was wrong. I looked around the sides of the clearing and then down to my feet. There I found the answer.

There were millions of tiny black spiders all over the ground. As I looked around me now, I could see the ground was moving with their frenzied activity. That was what had set off the alarm bells! The ground was moving. Seething in fact. We all watched these critters swarming across the grass, bushes and tree trunks. A huge nest must have just opened up. These babies were heading out into the world and we were there to witness it.

They didn't seem too interested in us at the moment. A few were trying to crawl up our boots but we just shook them off. No arachnaphobics here. After watching the spectacle for a while, we pushed on down to an old watercourse and deeper into the forest.

I was hoping to run into some Twa. These were the third, "invisible" tribe of Rwanda. The Twa were pygmies and stayed mostly up in the mountains. I had only seen a couple so far, and that was down on the roadways in the villages. I would like to have met some of these forest people both for the adventure of it and the value of any knowledge they might have of military activity in these mountains. As hunters and gatherers, they would know the hills inside and out.

I would travel into the mountains whenever I got the chance. It was good to just get away from the camp and get some exercise. Our wanderings also gave us an insight into the conditions the local people lived under away from the main road. I had also learned in Yugo that the best warnings of impending danger can be gathered from the local populace. If you can learn enough about them to sense their moods, you can get a feel for when trouble is coming. I also patrolled out towards Karisimba a couple of times. If things went bad, that was the direction in which we would withdraw, and I wanted to have a sense of the ground.

It was during these first couple of weeks waiting for the hospital to be up and running that we had our second conflict with the CO. When we had arrived at the compound, the apartment block was a disaster. The locals had been through it and the rooms were disgusting. There were feces and urine all over and garbage rotting in heaps. The factory was reasonably clean, so the CO decided his people would live there and the Airborne platoon could live in the shithole with the Engineers.

No problem. As combat troops, we are experts at cleaning and scrubbing, so we dug in and cleaned out the apartments. We scrubbed floors, washed walls, cleaned bathrooms. Someone joked that it was lucky our wives couldn't see us or we'd be in for it at home. Finally, the place was clean. Spotlessly clean. There had been a lot of furniture in the apartments, but most was broken or missing parts that the locals had stolen for firewood. The guys rebuilt the furniture and bought other items from the locals with their own money.

Being competitive personalities, it became a matter of section pride to have the best apartment. The walls were decorated and shelving built. Interior walls were added and everything was kept extremely clean. Every morning, we scrubbed the rooms from end to end. Three section hung a handpainted sign over their front door announcing "The Barking Fish Tavern." Everyone was happy with their quarters.

Enter Lt Colonel Anderson. Seeing how nice these buildings had become, he announced that the senior officers would be taking over the apartment block and the Engineers and our platoon would relocate to the warehouse area in the factory. Naturally, we all freaked. We told the platoon commander to let it be known that there would be as much urine and feces on the floor as when we arrived if he moved us. Also, we would smash all the furniture.

This "rumour" was leaked to the CO and he reconsidered. Instead, we could keep the apartments, but all the furniture would be handed over to the officers for a lounge in the factory. One doctor actually showed up and tried to walk away with a chair. Warrant Hartnell told him to bugger off. The furniture was either the personal property of the individuals who had bought it or the property of the person who took it out of the garbage heap and repaired it.

Finally, the CO decided to just commandeer the apartment we were using as a command post. The vacated space would be turned into VIP quarters. We couldn't complain about that. If there were VIPs coming, we wanted them to be comfortable, and the apartments were the obvious choice. So, all the sections donated a bit of furniture and we prepared a nice little VIP area.

It turned out for the best because in the next few weeks we hosted Morley Safer of "Sixty Minutes" fame and a pleasant elderly couple from England who were helping the gorilla researchers get the program restarted in the wake of the fighting.

For a new CP we turned to the Blood Room. Over two days we scraped off the flesh and bleached the blood stains. Someone located some maroon paint and we painted over the walls. The bullet holes ended up as a nice touch in the decor.

About the same time, someone decided the mass grave behind our apartments had to be moved. Because it was located slightly uphill from where the hospital would be situated, the incessant rains would create a health hazard from the shallow grave. Warrant Hartnell took a group of medics and a couple of Airborne volunteers and began to dig up the corpses. They expected to find only a half a dozen bodies, those of the murdered family and a few others. What they discovered instead was quite a few more.

There were women with babies still in slings on their backs, children with machete wounds, all just piled on top of each other. As the digging progressed they found over thirty heads but could not match up the number of bodies. It was disgusting and sad.

The bodies were moved to a new grave at the far end of the compound. The locals were upset at first about our disturbing their dead until they learned our Padre would bless the new grave. Deeply religious people, they thanked us for giving their dead a proper burial and some respect. A huge white cross was erected over the grave and the locals were content.

We had our first trouble with the locals shortly afterwards. The water purification site was located at a small lake twenty kilometres east of Mareru. The water was processed by a large machine named the ROWPU (Reverse Osmosis Water Purification Unit), which was worth more than a hundred thousand dollars. It could clean hundreds of gallons of water an hour and was the pride of our engineers. The unit, mounted on the back of a truck, would be hauled each morning down to the lake. The site used initially was just off the main road on a river feeding the lake but was soon moved down to the lake itself. Here, the ROWPU would be set up in the middle of an RPA base.

The RPA was a pretty professional army. They impressed me a lot more than the Croats or the Serbs had, back in Yugo. Their weapons were clean, they did regular fitness training and they were never drunk on duty. They still suffered from an inability to organize anything, but as fighters they were impressive. Whenever the ROWPU deployed, a security team of four paratroopers and a medic went along. The Airborne security team would set up a complicated HF radio antenna which still gave them only marginally reliable communications with Mareru. The medic was on hand to deal with any emergencies until help could arrive.

On one occasion, a female medic was sent with the ROWPU team. Her presence inside the RPA base caused a bit of a stir among the off-duty soldiers. Eventually, a group of RPA troops wandered down to have a better look. Thinking they were a little too curious, one of the Airborne guards decided to intervene.

Corporal Felice Aprile told the Rwandans to get lost; the girl was not available. To the Rwandan soldiers, women were not soldiers and they thought she must have been a prostitute working for the Canadian troops. Knowing that they outnumbered the Canadians about a hundred-to-one, the Rwandans insisted on taking the female medic for their pleasure. Aprile just stood there.

"If you want her, you'll have to get through us first," he stated in no uncertain terms. The other Airborne troops were standing casually behind him. The RPA didn't want to make an issue of it and backed off. Aprile reported it to me later and we decided to not send any more female troops down to the ROWPU site.

By the end of August the hospital was up and running at full capacity. Unfortunately, it was still only treating the locals. The refugees weren't moving and not much was being accomplished. The staff was kept busy because the locals were all suffering from worms, AIDS, numerous tropical infections and festering wounds.

Also, the women here would have an average of ten children. There were many pregnant women coming to the hospital to have an actual doctor administer their deliveries. Some of the babies were premature and would have died except that the engineers improvised an incubator to help them survive.

Still, the hospital was not treating the refugees it had been sent to help.

Near the end of April, General Dallaire flew out to Mareru again. This time he was accompanied by General Tousignant, his replacement. As part of the handover of duties, they had come to discuss moving our hospital to a new location. With many refugees still dying elswhere, to them, moving the hospital seemed like a good idea.

I guess this must have totally frustrated our CO. We were only going to be in the country for three months and had sat idle several weeks already while waiting for all the equipment to arrive. Moving now would put us back several more weeks. I'm sure he just wanted to get on with the job. Certainly, there were refugees in need elsewhere, but who knew when the masses in Goma would start moving again? The hospital could end up moving right back if the situation changed. So, it was important to impress our visitors when they arrived.

The hospital, being capable of handling thousands a day, needed more patients. All available trucks combed the roads and local villages and brought as many people as possible to the hospital gates. By the time the generals flew in, the hospital was full and there were several hundred people lined up outside.

Dallaire and Tousignant were suitably impressed and agreed to leave the hospital where it was, to continue its good work. Instead, a British hospital, forty kilometres to the east in Ruhengari, would move.

To the Airborne guys, this whole display was amusing. I think most of us would have welcomed the move. Mareru was boring. There were still some fighting in the south near Bukavu and we wanted to get down there. It was not to be though.

As a result of the movement of the Brit hospital, the CO was tasked to maintain a small clinic in Ruhengari until a civvy organization, Doctors Without Borders, could take over the site. So now each day, three truckloads of medics, doctors, supplies and Airborne security troops were off to Ruhengari to run a clinic.

Ruhengari was a small town located on the main road to Kigali. It was famous for being the jumping-off point for all expeditions up into the Virungas to study the mountain gorillas. I remembered reading about Dian Fossey buying her supplies here. In the centre of town was an abandoned teaching hospital. The Brits had occupied it and, like anything Brit troops touch, it was filthy. We mucked it out, cleared all the mines and explosives and set up a clinic. Since we only used a small corner of the facility, security wasn't too much of a problem. The former staff of the hospital, including Rwandan doctors and nurses, returned to work and lived at the site to keep it secure at night.

At one corner of the compound there was a fenced-off section with one building. It had only two entrances: one to the street and one into the compound. It was here the clinic was set up. I was the first section commander on site and had to establish a security routine. We established a CP in the residence next door and ran our operation from there. One Airborne soldier would work the main entrance to the clinic, letting in only the number of patients that could be handled. Another paratrooper worked the compound with him, controlling the patients. That way, if there was problem, the man at the gate wouldn't need to leave his post. A third paratrooper controlled access to the clinic from within the compound. Finally, a single soldier patrolled the entire site at irregular intervals. There wasn't too much of a security threat at the clinic, but being so far from help, we wanted the locals to be clear on the level of security at the compound.

One of the issues that had not yet been resolved for us concerned our Rules of Engagement. As an armed soldier, I could protect, by whatever means necessary, my own life and the lives of other Canadian soldiers. What was unclear were our rules governing civilians. For instance, if a patient were in the hospital's care and the RPA wanted to arrest the patient, could we intervene? If a civilian aid worker, say an American, asked us for protection from a local threat, could we do it?

In Yugo, I got tired of having to stand back and watch people being killed without our interfering because those were the rules. Here, if someone wanted to kill a sick woman or child because they were the wrong ethnic group, would we allow it, or were the sick under our care under our protection as well?

These questions were still unresolved in our useless Rules of

Engagement books. My plan was to play it by ear. My biggest concern was a patient dying from some allergic reaction to a drug or something and an irate relative coming to seek vengeance on our medical staff. So, despite our constant exposure to the meek and the infirm, we kept up our guard.

On a couple of occasions, it was fortunate that our security troops were present. In one instance, all the kit had been loaded and the clinic packed up for the day when a woman was brought to the gate who was in the process of giving birth. One of the doctors had her brought in just in time to deliver the baby. He was then left with nothing to cut the umbilical cord until a paratrooper whipped out his Leathermen pocket tool and quickly sterilized it with an alcohol swab. The cord was cut and the mother sent home with a healthy baby.

On another occasion, a woman had shown up with a very ill and weak baby. The child was having difficulty breathing and it was decided to take them both back to the hospital for better treatment. As we left the compound that day, the woman was riding with me in the front of the Five-Quarter. The rest of the troops were riding in the open back of the pickup. Behind us followed the two MLVWs carrying the medical personnel and their supplies. About halfway back, the baby's eyes rolled back and it stopped breathing. The mother began shouting at me and I hauled the truck over.

I had a good look at the child after we stopped and it wasn't breathing. Its lips were turning blue. I ran back to the cab of the nearest MLVW and grabbed a doctor. After having a quick look at the baby, he massaged its chest a bit and got it breathing again. He told me the only way to help it was to get it to the hospital as fast as we could. I jumped in the truck and we tore off in a cloud of dust.

It was a wild ride through the twisting mountain roads. We still had over twenty kilometres to go and the road was full of pedestrian traffic, as it normally was. I kept the pedal to the floor and did what all Rwandans do, held the horn down almost continually. In the back, the boys were holding on for their lives.

Finally, we raced up to the front gates. The guys on duty had heard us coming and had already opened the gates. We wheeled into the compound and I bounced us right up to the triage tent. Tim Barratt jumped out and grabbed the baby from his mother's arms. He ran inside with the child and delivered it to the doctors.

We had made it. The kid had stopped breathing a couple of times on the way, but the mother would shake it until it began breathing again. Now, they were both in the doctor's hands. I apologized to the guys in the back for the rough ride home. They had a chuckle and accepted my apology. We learned later that the child gained strength for a while and then died. It was buried in our hospital graveyard.

As life in Mareru settled down into a routine, the guys looked for new challenges. The Airborne tends to breed men who are always trying to learn some new skill or master some unique knowledge. The presence of a hospital outside our front door was too good an opportunity to pass up. We all dug in and began to build our medical skills.

We already had a good knowledge of first aid techniques and were easily capable of administering ivs. Now the guys learned to suture and apply dressings, how to do casualty assessments and assign priority to wounds. Some of the guys spent their spare time volunteering in the hospital's triage ward and racked up some excellent experience.

One day, some Australian doctors and nurses came down to visit our hospital. They were being given a tour of the wards just as some accident victims were brought in. They watched medics giving ivs, removing burnt flesh from a victim's torso and cleaning the wounds. One individual had nearly lost his arm and it was only hanging by a bit of skin. The medics cut off what was left of the remaining arm, applied a pressure bandage to the wound and got two ivs into the casualty. The doctors on duty were working on another patient, who was in even more dire straits.

The Aussies commented on the professionalism of the young medics. They were doing tasks usually only performed by skilled doctors. Then someone told them that these guys weren't medics, they were Airborne soldiers just helping out. The Aussies were stunned.

As I picked Trent's brain at night for information about the Airborne, I began to learn more and more about not only the Regiment, but about the ethos. The more I heard, the more impressed I became. Everyone was always seeking to improve themselves. Everyone had a specialty, whether it was unarmed combat, demolitions, mountain skills, scuba diving, biathlon or even extra schooling. To sit around and coast was criminal. The Regiment needed every edge it could get. The guys working in the hospital were learning valuable skills that they could bring back to the Regiment and pass on. No matter how much you did, it was never enough.

"Okay, job well done on that. Now go back and learn some more. Let us know when you've got it sorted out."

I was damn glad to have finally found a unit that was made up of professionals and not parade square soldiers. I could see that when I got back to Canada, I was going to have to work pretty damn hard to win the respect of my troops. Of course, I didn't have to wait until I got back to Canada, and I dove right into anything that was going on.

A great opportunity came our way when the local workers looking after the mountain gorillas offered to take us up to see them in exchange for money. These guys, called the "Gorilla Cowboys," lived at the Karisoke Research Centre. They were the men who tracked the gorilla families and protected them from Twa traps. The researchers had all fled during the war and, if the cowboys were to continue to live and work in the hills, they needed funding. We were only too happy to oblige. Soon, groups of twenty Canadian medical personnel with a small security contingent from our platoon began making the long treks up into the misty forests to see the great apes.

On my first trip up, we first visited Dian Fossey's camp and the gorilla cemetery. Fossey was buried there next to Digit, her favourite silverback male who died defending his family. From old *National Geographics* I had read, I remembered the names of many of the gorillas buried there.

Later we went to find the gorillas. There were families that had been exposed to humans regularly and others that were kept separated from human contact. The families we visited showed no concern at our presence and even became playful at times.

My first glimpse of a gorilla was breathtaking. We were in a large open area covered by chest-high jungle plants. A family was feeding nearby and we slowly approached. When the handlers thought we were close enough, they stopped us and we waited. We could hear the gorillas approaching, slowly. Soon, I could hear them all around me, but they were hidden by the branches. Then, suddenly, I saw a head.

It was huge! About three metres straight in front of me, a

silverback rose above the stalks of wild plants and looked at me.
I was speechless. It was like running into a grizzly in the woods,
but different. There was no dull animal gleam in the eyes that
stared back at me. I could see the intelligence in those eyes.

The silverback was big. Nearly two hundred kilos, I guessed. It
watched us for a few minutes and then went back to eating. After
about twenty minutes during which we snatched glimpses of the
rest of the twenty-member family, the cowboys led us away. I
couldn't wait to get back and went again the next day.

This time, though, I wasn't hanging around waiting for them
to come to me. Scott McCready and I immediately crawled off
into the undergrowth the moment we got close to the family. The
cowboys were a little concerned, but they knew the moods of the
family and were watching the silverback closely. Several of the
female medics crawled right up to the silverback and began
grooming it. Scott and I crawled around and interacted with a
number of different individuals. Sometimes they would come up
to you and check you out. In this case, I remembered Dian Fossey's descriptions of the correct behaviour and kept my head
down, avoiding eye contact.

Juvenile males would come up to us and, being curious, inves-
tigate. We played submissive and had some really great contact.
Later, I crawled down to the silverback and sat a short distance
from him. At the same time, a tiny little gorilla, probably a year
old, jumped down beside me. The silverback watched me closely
while the little one put on a great demonstration of leaps and
somersaults. At one point, the little one charged up to me, stood
up to its full height of maybe twenty-five centimetres and beat its
chest. I had a hard time not bursting out laughing.

Of all the things I have done in the military, those moments
rate up in the top few. I loved those apes. I went back every time
I could. I could easily see why Dian Fossey had become obsessed
with these creatures. They were magnificent.

————————

During the middle of September, thirty medics were sent home.
There was not enough work for the whole unit. The clinic in
Ruhengari was seeing more patients than our hospital on some
days. On 15 September, the co had a meeting with his staff. The
reason? The doctors wanted to go home. Their private practices
were suffering.

All of the doctors had their own clinics back in Canada and these were losing money while they were away. Since nothing was going on here in Rwanda, they wanted to get back to some more lucrative work. When it was occasionally mentioned that we might be ordered to move around the country or stay longer than the three months originally intended, there were howls of protest from the doctors.

In the security platoon, we couldn't believe it. Not only had these people had their schooling paid for by the military, they were also allowed to run their own private practices while serving in the Forces. Now, it seemed to us that, probably for the first time in their careers, the military needed their skills and they felt it was an imposition. If one of us tried to get out of a tour because our home business was suffering, we would be laughed out of the Forces. After the tour, of course.

We accepted this situation like everything else. We shrugged and carried on. In our line of work you become a fatalist pretty quick. What happens, happens. If you can't change things, accept them. Otherwise, all the sick and dying kids we saw in the camps would drive us crazy.

We lost a lot of respect for the doctors as a result. I lost even more respect after an incident in Ruhengari. It had started to rain pretty heavily and everyone, the locals included, sought shelter wherever they could. Across the street from the clinic, a dozen people were squeezed in under a bus shelter. Suddenly, an older man slipped on the muddy ground and fell down into the ditch beside the road. We could see he was hurt because he began shaking uncontrollably and throwing his arms about. The other Rwandans in the shelter began waving to us to come and help the man.

I grabbed Fafard and we ran across the road to have a look. The guy was in the ditch and lying very still now. His breathing was coming in gasps and his colour was fading to an ashen grey. I knew he was dying and sent Fafard to get a doctor quick. I was trying to assess his situation when Fafard returned carrying a stretcher. The doctors wouldn't come out in the rain. They wanted us to carry the guy back to them, Fafard reported. Typical!

We laid the stretcher out on the road and climbed down into the ditch to get the guy. Fafard slipped in the mud and fell into the water at the bottom of the ditch. On contacting the water, he howled and leapt back up the bank.

"It's electrified!" he shouted.

I looked over at the nearby telephone pole and could now see an electrical cable running down into the water. It had been hidden from view until we had climbed down into the ditch. The cable was live.

This didn't impress me much, because I was now straddling the ditch and my feet were only centimetres from the water. I could see a metal signpost touching the man's leg and knew immediately he had grounded on it. Fafard had been saved because the charge was dispersed in the water. I reached up and Fafard grabbed my outstretched hand and hauled me out of danger.

Once again my luck and instincts had saved me. While Fafard had gone for the doctors, I should have been getting the guy's vital signs. I had no reason to suspect electrocution in a country as damaged as Rwanda. I thought it was a head wound or a broken hip. Yet, I had held back. All of our training dictated I get in there and try to stabilize the guy, but I had hesitated. Good thing, because if I had so much as laid a hand on the guy, I would be beside him drawing my last breath. As we watched, the poor soul shuddered and died. Still no sign of the doctors. Bastards.

Later that day, a kid found a old grenade. The pin was missing and it was in poor condition. In this state, it was highly dangerous. We gently relieved the kid of the grenade and placed it under some sandbags. We couldn't leave it there, so we built a sandbag mound in the back of the Five-Quarter and placed the grenade in it. We were going to take it back to the engineers and have them blow it with C–4. Now we only needed a volunteer to drive the truck. I figured that it wasn't my day to die and drove the truck back to Mareru.

We had a couple of other close calls during the last few weeks of our stay in Mareru. The first occurred when a local worker approached one of the doctors and offered to sell him some cocaine. The doctor agreed and they arranged to meet in a dark corner of the compound at midnight. After the worker left, the doctor went to our two Military Policemen attached to the hospital and reported the exchange.

These two MPs had been sent to keep an eye on the Airborne troops. So far, all they had done was guard the hospital entrance gate. Now, finally, they had a job. The MPs informed Captain Simkin, the CO and the RSM. A trap was set. When the worker arrived at the rendezvous, the MPs grabbed him. He was discovered to be carrying a large quantity of cocaine. The worker was whisked inside the compound and taken to the MP tent for interrogation.

Outside, my section was on duty and we were placed on a high state of alert. The MPs guessed the drugs were worth about fifteen thousand dollars back home. It was a cinch that this kid didn't own it, so sooner or later someone was going to come looking for their delivery boy.

The kid was terrified and didn't need any prompting to explain that the drugs had been brought into the country by a British aid worker. He said he was just supposed to sell the stuff. Eventually, the drugs were burned in front of him and he was led kicking to the front gate. He pleaded not to be released. No doubt he was concerned about the treatment he would receive from his business partners when they discovered what had happened.

We could have cared less and threw him out the gate and locked it behind him. The kid looked at us one last time for any sign of mercy and then sprinted into the darkness. Later that night a large group of men carrying rifles arrived outside our gate. They paced up and down the road, staring into the compound, trying to get some idea what had happened to their man and their property. At one point, one of the men crept down to the wire. As he stood in the darkness, considering his next move, he never knew that, less than five metres away, two paratroopers were watching his every move. I had weapons covering the whole compound.

I was about twenty metres from the men as they looked to be getting ready to cross the wire. Graham and I were crouched behind a stone wall, watching them through night vision goggles. I knew we had them cold if they tried to enter the compound. The problem was, what would we do about it? If they attempted to cross the wire, they were not an immediate threat, so, under our vague Rules of Engagement, we couldn't fire. If one of us yelled at them to halt and they opened up, it would mean a lot of killing if they fired at us. If the shooting started, some of them would likely get into the buildings across the street and we could have a bad situation on our hands. It was all looking pretty grim and something needed to be done. I was in charge, so it was up to me.

I whispered over to Graham to follow my lead. Then I stood

up in plain sight of the men outside the wire. Then Graham stood up. We both casually turned our backs and walked away. In pulling this seemingly idiotic stunt, I hoped to accomplish two things. First, they would see two of us emerge from hiding close by and, I was hoping, would begin to wonder how many others they couldn't see that might be watching them from the darkness. Also, I knew my guys could see what we were doing and, if any of the men raised their weapons to fire, then they would present a threat and could legally be taken out.

Graham and I walked slowly away under a big night light. There was no mistaking us as anything but armed security troops. I cringed a bit, but knew their level of marksmanship was probably horrid and that they figured, if they missed with their first shot, they were dead. Nothing happened and the men slowly wandered away into the night.

The local workers were all told the drugs had been destroyed and we hoped the message got back to the owners. With no drugs and no prisoner, we hoped they wouldn't be encouraged to come back. Since nothing else occurred, we assumed we were successful. No one ever saw the delivery boy again though.

Life was becoming a little boring and we were due to leave in mid-October. The owners of the hotel in Gisenyi had opened up the bar inside to serve the RPA garrison and any UN troops with money to spare. Occasionally, our guys would escort a few medics down for an afternoon of beer and relaxation.

Our time was winding down in Rwanda and the hospital began making preparations to close up. Kenny Nunn had been working on a project with the padre for some time and we were all impressed with his efforts.

The hospital had lost about thirty patients during its time in Mareru. Most were beyond help when they arrived. These people had been buried in separate graves in a new cemetery the padre and Ken had put together. Each grave got a little cross with the name and dates inscribed. Ken and the padre had arranged for some local workers to build a stone wall around the graveyard. Then Ken liberated all of the flowering plants growing around the compound and replanted them around the cemetery.

The final touches were placed just before we left Mareru. A small monument was constructed with a plaque commemorating the souls buried in the cemetery and the Canadians' presence in the country.

When it was done, the relatives of the deceased took great comfort in knowing the burials were conducted with respect and with last rites performed by the padre. This was the least we could do. Ken accomplished something lasting in that place. He did a good thing.

Down the road a way was the home of a quaint little old lady. She was white and English by accent. She had been a close friend of Dian Fossey during her life in Rwanda and would host her on occasion. This charming woman was having trouble with her plumbing, so some of the troops went down and fixed up her place for her. They did a bunch of yard work for her and general repairs. It was another one of those jobs no one would order the troops to do, but there was never any shortage of volunteers.

I loved Rwanda. Behind the compound you could see the volcanoes on the Zaire border. One of them was active off and on while we were there. You could see great pillars of steam rising from it by day, and by night it would turn the night sky red in the glow from its caldera.

The people were great and very friendly. When Tim Barratt fell while mountain climbing on his day off, an old man and boy witnessed the fall and rushed to his aid with a homemade stretcher. They were prepared to carry him to the hospital themselves. Later, in the confusion, Tim's Kevlar helmet and glasses were left on the mountain. Several days later, two boys showed up with them at the front gate. The helmet could have fetched a good price from the RPA, but they were too honest for that. You'd be lucky to find that kind of honesty here in Canada.

I was pretty much enamoured of Africa in general, from the horrendous experience in Cairo to the jungles of Karisimba. I knew I wanted to come back, even before I left. But it was time to go home now.

Fortunately, our trip home was by a Forces Boeing A320 and not Air Atlant.

Chapter 11

AIRBORNE!

OUR GUESTS STOOD *across the room. They were keeping to themselves, drinking their beers and looking at the Special Forces and Special Service Force plaques on the wall of the mess. The Canadians in the room had gathered around tables on the opposite side of the lounge. No one was talking. It was like a teenage dance with the girls on one side and the boys on the other and no one wanting to make the first move.*

I had not expected U.S. Army Rangers to be so shy. After Desert One, Grenada, Panama, Somalia, the Gulf, you would figure they wouldn't be worried about a hell of a lot. Or maybe, they don't want to talk to us. Maybe they are a little stuck up and figure we are just a bunch of northern hicks.

Later, after the ice had been broken and we all got together over jugs of draft, I was listening to one of the Rangers talking. He was saying that a lot of their guys were feeling a little intimidated by us. When the Canadians listening to him couldn't figure out why, the Ranger sergeant explained.

"Well, your guys have been in Croatia, Cambodia, Bosnia, Rwanda, Somalia, the Gulf. Those are some pretty rough spots. We've seen how tough you guys are and, hell, you ought to be Rangers!"

I thought about that for a while. Yeah, we had been in a few rough ones. We just didn't think about it that way. Canada doesn't like military heroes, they just sort of get trivialized in the general rush of daily life.

Beside me, a Ranger platoon sergeant was explaining how he pulled a wounded Ranger out of the aircraft door over Panama, moments before they jumped into battle. To him, we were equals: fellow professionals who have shared the dangers of battle and won the respect of their peers. Well, if that were true, how come none of us ever felt that way?

—————

The Green light came on. The wind was rushing through the aircraft and it was cold. The jumpmaster yelled "GO!" above the howl and the first jumper leapt out the open door. On both sides of the aircraft, paratroopers shuffled toward the rear of the plane. As they reached the doorway, they threw their static lines to the rear and pivoted into the opening. With a stamp of their inboard foot, they launched themselves into the abyss.

I was pushman. As the last jumper in the stick, I shuffled along at the back of the line. In less than twenty seconds, the other twenty-one jumpers ahead of me were out the door and it was my turn. As I reached the door, I glanced at the light to make sure it was still green. It was okay, so I threw my static line towards the rear of the plane and turned to jump. Gripping my rifle sling tightly in my right hand, I jabbed out into space.

Immediately the wind and the prop blast threw me towards the rear of the plane. You start counting in your head as you plummet towards the ground, "One thousand, two thousand. . . ." Before you reach four thousand, a great tug jerks you upright and you look up to see your parachute deployed above you.

Up until now, my heart had been going a mile a minute and adrenaline was surging through my system. Then, when I saw my open canopy fluttering above, a wave of calm swept over me. Everything was peaceful now and my body relaxed. Looking around, I checked to make sure I was not going to collide with any other parachutists. Then I looked to the ground to orient myself.

All too soon, I was nearing the ground. Undoing my waist-strap, which held my rifle to my side, I threw it from my shoulder. The rifle fell to the end of its harness three metres below my feet and, with a flick of the foot, I set it swinging.

Now the ground was rushing up. Watching carefully, I tried to judge what direction I was drifting and, moments before impacting, I turned my feet to meet the ground. As I hit, I went limp and rolled onto my side, spreading the impact out across my whole body. The parachute flittered to the ground nearby and I popped a canopy release buckle immediately to collapse it. Down safe once more, I thanked my personal gods and reached for my rifle.

———————

It was early December. 3 Commando was conducting a raid on a simulated drug cartel safe house. We had received a warning order two days before. After orders and rehearsals yesterday, we boarded the two Air Force C130's well before dawn. The planes took off and flew a long, twisting route barely a hundred metres off the ground. Following the contours, the big plane dipped and climbed and stood on its wing tips to bank through narrow river valleys.

Inside the plane we bounced and sagged as the G-forces pulled at our bodies. It was not a luxury flight by any means. As the sun was just beginning to rise in the eastern sky, the plane pulled up to about 250 metres and the doors in the rear of the fuselage were pulled open. Moments later, paratroopers began tumbling out into the still morning air. Thirty minutes later, the Commando had assembled in the woods nearby and we began our approach march to the target.

Airborne Recce, the Pathfinders, were leading the Commando. They had inserted by freefall the night before and had already scouted the target. While some of them kept an eye on the objective, another team had set up the dropzone a safe distance away and were now leading the assault force to the target.

We moved fast and there was no talking. Everyone knew what was required. Even the lowliest trooper knew everything. If it turned out he was the only man with a radio, he could still call for support or send the codewords. Every man could do everyone else's job. If the commanders had been injured, anyone of us could have rallied the survivors and continued with the mission. It was a commando operation and there were no simple followers.

We reached our attack position after several hours of hard marching. Most of it had been through swamps and thick forest.

Our bodies were covered with sweat and our feet soaked by the thawing bogs. We sat motionless in the snow, shivering, while the OC talked with the pathfinders that had been observing the target. The pathfinders had seen little activity, but smoke was coming from the house, so there was someone home. Several vehicles were parked outside and there had been lights on during the night.

The information was passed around. When we were all ready, the OC nodded and the pathfinders led us forward. A support team with machine guns broke away to the north to set up a fire base. The remainder of the commandos wormed their way forward until they were within eyesight of the house.

With a hand signal from the platoon commanders, the sections fanned out into the swampy scrub to the east of the house. Once everyone was in position, we waited. H-hour was when the operation would commence. For fifteen minutes we sat in the snow, watching and waiting. We were dressed in white nylon camouflage and blended in with the frozen ground perfectly.

At H-hour, the first section of paratroopers broke from cover and sprinted to the small barns outside the house. Silently, they entered the barns and swept through them. As each section disappeared inside a barn, another would sprint forward. After a couple of minutes, a paratrooper appeared in a barn window and gave the thumbs up. Buildings clear. Now it was time to assault the main house.

As my section rose from the swamp to move into position, the still morning air was rent by the staccato of a machine gun! Compromised! With nothing for it now, I leapt forward and raced for the barns. I didn't have to look behind me; my section was there. As we reached the shelter of the barn, we met the OC. The plans had changed, he said. There was no time to lose now and the lead platoon would assault the main house. He grabbed his radio headset and issued his instructions. Suddenly, the fire base opened up from the treeline to the north. They raked the northern side of the house while the lead platoon gathered in the nearest barn to make the assault.

After precisely two minutes, the fire base stopped and the assaulters rushed the house. The lead teams ignored the doors and headed for the many windows. They knocked open the shutters and threw in clearing charges. As soon as the explosives went off, the teams went through the windows with weapons blazing. More teams followed and, in less than two minutes, the house was cleared.

Or so we thought. Suddenly, someone spotted a rifle barrel sticking through a vent in the attic. The hostiles were in the attic. My section was called forward to clear it. I grabbed my guys and we sprinted for the house. Once inside, we raced up the stairs to the second floor. There we found the lead teams with their backs into the corners covering the ceiling. They could have started blasting, but the hostiles might have had a bunker built up there. It had to be taken out by entering the attic itself.

Over the stairwell was a hatch to the attic. I signalled my guys to bring over a chair. Silently, they placed it on the landing and I climbed up onto it. I signalled and mouthed the words to my guys. I would toss the charge through the hatch and then jump down. I pointed at one of the smaller guys in the section. As soon as it went off, we would boost him through the hatch. Then I would follow.

When everyone was ready, I tried the hatch. I didn't think it was booby-trapped because someone was up there in the confined space with it. If they expected me to stick my head through, they were going to get a surprise. I smashed the hatch upwards with one hand and threw the charge with the other. Then I leapt clear. There was a momentary burst of firing above me and then the charge went off. The first man was pushed through the hatch firing. As he got through, I followed. The hostile was down and I signalled the all-clear.

Fifteen minutes later the building had been swept for documents and evidence. The commando gathered outside and prepared to leave. We had to move quickly. The cartel had its own private army and we couldn't hope to fight it. This raid was too much of a political hot potato already and we had to get out without being compromised. We intended to split up and make a number of hit and run attacks throughout the day to confuse the reaction forces and then head for a land zone during the night.

Without much talking, the separate elements split up and headed out into the swamps again. Over the next few hours we ambushed vehicles, sniped at cartel buildings, cleared road checkpoints and then melted away into the forests. We caused a great deal of confusion as to our numbers and purpose. Then, after dark, the commando linked up again and headed for the border. We had a twenty-kilometre march to reach our helicopter pick-up at dawn. If we met any resistance now, we would just have to fight through.

During the night, we dodged a few enemy patrols, but on two occasions the cartel had blocked our route and we had to skirmish forward. These actions were short, sharp affairs counting on shock and surprise to succeed.

Carrying our wounded now, we were further slowed by the cold and by sheer exhaustion. The temperature had dropped to minus thirty degrees Celsius and our soaking clothing had frozen stiff. Unable to retain body heat, I had long ago stopped shivering. My troops were in no better shape. Some knew they had worsening frostbite in the feet, but there was no choice but to push on.

None of us had slept in more than twenty-four hours and the constant action and effort had worn down our reserves in the dark of the night. Still we bashed forward. We had to make the pick-up or it was going to be a long walk back to the border.

––––––––––

At 0900 hours the next morning, the exercise ended. We were frozen and exhausted, but happy. There was hot soup and coffee waiting for us back in camp and, for nearly an hour, everyone just relaxed and got some warmth back into their bodies. Then it was the hot wash-up.

Everyone critiqued the exercise. This had gone right, but we have to work on that. No one ever reached the standard; it was always just a little out of reach. We would put our experience away until the next time when we would try to improve even more in that neverending pursuit of perfection. We cleaned our weapons and wiped down our kit. Everyone was home by noon. This was the Canadian Airborne Regiment.

After returning from Rwanda, we all had a couple of weeks off and then as soon as we got back to work, all of the FNGs began their indoctrination course. 2 Commando was running it and there were about forty of us divided into two platoons. We began with the Airborne PT test.

The first event was a six-kilometre run that had to be done in under thirty minutes. Unfortunately, there was twelve centimetres of snow on the ground and a forty-kilometre-an-hour wind in our faces. No matter, weather was an excuse and excuses weren't excepted. I made it, in twenty-eight minutes. For each test there were three grades: gold, silver and bronze. In this event, twenty-four to twenty-six minutes was gold, twenty-six to twenty-eight was silver and anything up to thirty was bronze. Anything after that was a failure.

Next it was chin-ups. Fifteen for gold, ten for silver and seven to pass. After that, push-ups, sit-ups, leg presses, military presses with barbells and finally elbow dips. I finished with a bronze. I wasn't impressed. At least I hadn't failed. A lot of us back from Rwanda were in the same boat. No excuse though.

The next couple of days were spent doing jump refreshers and learning to pack toboggans for parachuting. Finally, we headed out into the field for a week of patrolling, ambushes and raids. We slithered across rope bridges over raging, icy rivers and plowed through deep snow and freezing rain. We lay for hours in the slushy snow waiting to ambush a passing truck. It was a miserable test.

The moment that stands out in my memory, though, was a candidate patrol. Five of us had settled down on the side of a hill, surrounded by thick forests. We were conducting an observation post, watching a far ridgeline for signs of enemy force activity, in this case, played by volunteers from 1 Commando. Just over the crest of the hill, we had established an OP to watch to the north. Our chances of being discovered were slim.

Those of us back in the administration area, on the side of the hill, were relaxing and cooking up a ration. A French candidate was up at the OP. All of a sudden, I got a bad feeling, a really strong sense of impending doom. Immediately, I packed up my kit and got down behind my rucksack. I didn't know why, nor did my fellow candidates. Sure enough, about two minutes later, a clearing patrol was spotted sweeping toward our position. I swung my rucksack on my back and made ready to go. The others were scrambling to get their kit packed up. We barely made it out in time.

Later, I was still trying to figure out how I had anticipated the trouble. I chalked it up to my good luck and forgot about it.

At the end of the week, we were presented with our Airborne coins. Each is serialized and is the only true way to identify a paratrooper other then official records. Like the American army, where everyone who retires claims to have served in Special Forces, no doubt future retirees in Canada will claim the same about the Airborne. If anyone is going around boasting about being in the Regiment, ask to see his coin. If he doesn't have it, he is a liar.

The coin also serves as a recognition symbol between soldiers. If you spot another paratrooper somewhere, you can pull out your coin and "coin" him. By doing this, he must either present his coin or buy the rounds. If there is no beer available, it is owed at a future date. The downside is, if you coin someone and he does have his coin, you buy.

Coins are widespread in the community and Rangers, Special Forces and Army Airborne each have them. You can be coined by a member of the 82nd Airborne from the States as well as your fellow Canadians. The coin is a symbol of the brotherhood you have joined.

As I relaxed with my family during Christmas of 1994 I was content. I had figured my career was on the downside after Sarajevo, that nothing I could do would ever compare with that experience. Now, all that had changed. I was on the upswing again. My career had risen from the ashes and I was looking forward to getting back to work.

Ken, Warren and I had become close friends after Rwanda and often spent a few hours in the mess after work. I had some really good friends again, I was challenged—life was looking pretty good. I was getting that same feeling I had with Recce back in Europe.

When we returned to work in early January 1995, there was some exciting news waiting for us. NDHQ had decided to send the Airborne to Bosnia in March to allow them to clear their name.

Another tour! I was stunned. This was starting off to be a great year. The Regiment came alive. Courses were planned, training activities prepared. Everyone was striding around with a sense of purpose. It felt like the old days back in Germany before my first tour. I felt alive again.

Then the first video hit the press. *Esprit de Corps* magazine had got ahold of someone's home videotapes from Somalia. Because the Somalia court martials were in full swing, the video was topical. The only problem was, *Esprit de Corps* editor Scott

Taylor's plan to show the Canadian public the horrendous conditions the paratroops had endured and the good work that they had done had backfired. The television media picked out a ten-second sound bite from a two-hour video showing a couple of guys from 2 Commando clowning around and saying they were going to kill "niggers."

Immediately, we were all branded as racists. This was news to the blacks, Asians and Native Canadians serving in the Regiment. Everyone knew 2 Commando were rednecks; they were all recruited from the Patricias. Racists though? No way!

Admittedly, there had been some bad characters around in the late 1980s and early 1990s. These were just a couple of double-y-chromosome types and were exclusive to 2 Commando. Certainly, when Lt Colonel Kenward took over command after Somalia, these clowns had disappeared. Most had been kicked out altogether.

While we were still listening to the media misreport the first video, some loser who had washed out of 1 Commando presented his hazing video to the media. We were sitting around in 3 Commando shacks when the video first came on the news and when we saw the content we were disgusted. They were Van Doos though, and those guys were still incomprehensible to me.

I had a hard time with it because the only hazing that went on in 3 Commando involved the new guys running down to the village and buying a case of beer. Then everyone had a party in the shacks before heading downtown. I was an FNG and I certainly hadn't been hazed.

Amongst the troops, we talked pretty freely about the stupid things soldiers do. Telling war stories really. We all looked at each other. No one had heard of this one. The next clip came from an interview with the "whistleblower." Him, the guys recognized. They were all laughing as they related to the rest of us that, in their opinion, this guy had been a chronic failure and didn't measure up, a Walter Mitty type. Apparently, he decided the Forces weren't for him and quit. Still, we could all see the public relations damage this could do. It seemed to us this guy was getting revenge against people he couldn't compete with in the light of day.

The phone rang out in the hallway. Somebody answered it and took a message. We had been ordered to stay in the 3 Commando lines until told otherwise. The OC was in O Group with the CO and would be down to see us shortly. As we waited, we wondered what was going on now in the halls of power at the headshed. When Major Horn arrived, we could see he could barely hold back his emotions. He appeared ready to cry. I got a sinking feeling in my gut.

In a voice wracked by emotion, he explained that we were in deep trouble with the release of the new video. The future of the Regiment hung in the balance. We had been instructed to keep quiet and were not to speak to the media. I immediately assumed that in the halls of power there was a PR campaign being put together to defend the Airborne. A good friend of mine, who is black, wanted to get all the black soldiers in the Regiment together to go to the media and shoot down the notion of racism. The gag order effectively stopped that.

After the speech by Major Horn, we were all sent home for the day. Warren, Ken and I went to the mess for a few beers. As we sat there sipping our mugs of draft, we just couldn't believe it. What the hell was going on?

Over the next few days, we were visited by a variety of senior officers. They wanted to address the troops and show them some support. General Vernon and General Jeffries spoke to us, saying they would resign before the Airborne was allowed to be broken up.

A few days later the mission to Bosnia was cancelled.

Finally, on 23 January, it happened.

We all knew the Minister of National Defense was going to give a news conference and the entire Regiment was gathered in their respective common areas to watch. I sat on the weight bench at the back of the 3 Commando TV room. The rest of the Commando was packed onto the ratty furniture spread through the room and along the walls.

David Collenette came on and spoke about problems with the Regiment and the poor opinions we were generating in the media. Since it had only been a couple of days since the release of the last video, we knew he hadn't had time to look into the present state of the Regiment. We were worried that he didn't realize the Regiment was not the same unit now that it had been in Somalia and before. We all expected, or hoped, he would announce that he would see to it that the problems were straightened out and he would restore public confidence in the Forces. Unfortunately, we overestimated the courage of the politicians in charge.

"Due to the systemic problems within the Airborne Regiment, it has been decided that the only possible solution to restore public confidence in our military is to disband the Canadian Airborne Regiment," Collenette announced.

There was silence in the room. No one moved. We were stunned. I looked at Warren, beside me. His look said it all. We all got up and headed out onto the parade square. Lt Colonel Kenward wanted to talk to us.

He could barely speak. It was all he could do to choke back the tears. For a long time he stood with his back to us, summoning his composure. Around him, many of the officers were openly crying. So were no small number of the troops and NCOs. Not sobbing or wailing, but just little tears running down cheeks as emotions welled up within us.

I cannot quote the CO's speech. My memory is mostly of the content and message, not his precise words. In those moments my head was swirling. I was in shock. Everything I had worked towards, all of us had worked towards and believed in, had been taken away in an instant of political manoeuvring.

The CO told us that day that what the minister said was wrong. We were the best soldiers he had ever worked with and the regiment, Canada's finest. After many long pauses, he told us that the media and the government were now waiting for all the rebels and anarchists we were accused of harbouring to go on a rampage and destroy the base. If we did that, he explained, then they will have won. For the sake of the regiment, for ourselves and for the memory of a great unit, we must become the epitome of perfect soldiers. We would follow their orders to the letter and shove it back in their faces. We were the best and we would show it. He thanked us all for our service and professionalism.

As I walked off the parade square that day, I remember saying to myself, "That's it. I'm out of here." One of the guys heard me and asked me to repeat my statement. "I'm through," I said clearly. "It may take a year or so, but I'm leaving."

———

Over the next six weeks, there was a flurry of activity around us. Movements to save the Airborne and angry letters to the media over the whole issue. In front of a popular bar down in the village of Petawawa, a sign proclaimed, "I'd rather eat shit with the Airborne than steak with Collenette."

The minister didn't realize the extent of what he had done to the soldiers, their families and the community. Or maybe he did. Unlike political parties or lobby groups, an army regiment is a living, breathing thing. Because he never apologized to the members of the unit that were untainted by scandal, about ninety-nine percent of us, for the pain this would cause, he branded all of us as dishonourable murderers and rebels. His failure to separate the bad from the much larger good left us all painted by the same brush.

In the schools, children whose fathers were in the Regiment were teased and taunted. They had to go home and ask their fathers if they really did those things. Relatives across Canada were assaulted by calls about their "shit-eating sons in the criminal regiment."

The wives, who loved the regiment as much as their men, were even more deeply hurt. The men were soldiers and had ways to share their pain in the group. The wives were now isolated and unable to fight back against the pain and disgrace forced on their husbands. It was a very hard time for everyone. The minister hurt us deeply, not only by targeting us, the soldiers, but by hitting us where it hurt most: at home.

During this time, I had an opportunity to speak with General Vernon when he visited the senior NCO's mess for a luncheon. I cornered him and asked the question that was bothering me most. Why, if we had been muzzled and not allowed to come to our own defence, had the Forces Public Affairs branch not come to our aid?

"General, where were the Public Affairs officers before the disbandment? Why weren't they out there flooding the media with good PR in our defence?"

The general looked at me, and I could see I had struck a sore point.

"Sergeant, I have often asked myself the same question. The fact is, our Public Affairs branch was never created to put out good PR for anybody. It was designed from the start to do damage control for the senior brass," he replied.

I walked away from the general. In my mind that confirmed it. We had been set up and betrayed by our military masters. They had cooperated fully with the government's plan to get rid of the regiment, even before the minister had made his decision.

In the days between the release of the second video and the disbandment, every member of the regiment had been placed under a gag order so that we couldn't represent ourselves in the national press. Because this entire crisis was media-driven, the only place to defend ourselves was in the press. NDHQ and the people in charge realized this and gagged us. With the regiment silenced and no defence of our unit coming from our senior leadership, the tide of embarrassing media coverage forced the government into a corner.

We were sacrificed as a political expedient to take the heat off the Forces as a whole. No organization can withstand the media's obsession with scandal for long. In an organization as large as the Forces, there are going to be skeletons in quite a few closets. It's my guess that the chief of defence staff, the deputy minister and the minister decided to hand our heads to the press to sate their thirst for news.

If, in those two weeks, all of us had called every media outlet in the country and offered interviews, called every radio phone-in show, written letters to every member of Parliament and made public displays of protest, the verdict might have been different. The regiment never would have been damaged in the first place if it weren't for the media, and it was that battle that we lost—on the orders of NDHQ.

I had only been a member of the regiment for seven months. I think the reason that it bothered me so much as an FNG was that now I would never get the chance to finish my service with the unit and achieve my goals. Some of the senior veterans of the regiment did not feel the shock as much as the new guys. They had served in the regiment for years and were ready to return to their parent regiments. For us and future generations, there would never be a chance to earn maroon berets and Airborne hat badges. To be Commandos. I felt I had been cheated.

On the weekend of 4–5 March 1996, the Airborne Regiment was disbanded. Visitors came to Petawawa from around the world to say their farewells. Brigadier Hill, the British officer who commanded Canadian Paratroopers in World War Two, was there. Members of the U.S. 82 Airborne sent a guard and two Starlifter aircraft. Retired members of the original Devil's Brigade, the regiment's ancestor, came to bid their farewells. Letters of sympathy flooded in from paratroop units around the world.

In one particularly underhanded blow, the regiment's Honourary Colonel and Chief, Prince Andrew, had never been officially informed of the disbandment of his regiment. He had just visited the unit the previous year and had a fond place in his heart for his paratroopers. A phone call was made from certain people to certain people to prepare his regimental uniform. There was quite a buzz around the regiment when we thought he would come. His surprise arrival at our disbandment would certainly have embarrassed the government. No doubt someone in power heard about it and somehow prevented his arrival.

The ceremonies started off with a regimental parachute drop on Saturday morning. Before an assembled crowd of hundreds, the sky filled with paratroopers from the regiment and other countries all yelling "Airborne!" into the crisp morning air.

Later that day, there was a regimental parade on the Nicklin parade square. As the audience waited for the arrival of the regiment, they got quite a shock when a half a dozen machine guns opened up across the parade square. Suddenly, two helicopters swooped in and troops began rappeling down from thirty metres in the air. Smoke grenades popped around the area while the machine guns kept up a steady roar. Artillery guns let go of several salvoes. Then, five hundred paratroopers poured out of the buildings and sprinted into position on the square.

The parade was impressive and there were many speeches. It was a great parade, despite the rotten occasion. That night there was a huge party in IRCR's drill hall. My parents attended with me and we bumped into none other then General Lewis MacKenzie (Ret'd). I introduced my mother to him and they chatted for quite a while. The party went on well into the night.

The next morning, Sunday, brought the hard duties. First was a Church parade at IRCR's building. It was a rainy, grey day which matched our mood exactly. General de Chastelain showed up and took the salute of the regiment. I had a hard time with that. I wasn't sure I could salute him. I was quite prepared to just lower my weapon and walk off the parade square when he arrived. Up until the moment we presented arms, I didn't know what I would do. In the end, I remembered Lt Colonel Kenward's words. Any sign of disrespect or disloyalty would prove the government justified in our disbandment. So, I presented arms with everyone else.

At least he had the courage to face us. Our executioner, Minister of Defence David Collenette, never showed, nor did he express any regret for his decision to today's members of the regiment. After a very sad service by the padre, the regiment marched through the base and stopped in front of the regimental museum.

This was the moment we had all dreaded. Our Colours, the soul of every regiment, were to be laid up. The Colours were marched past every man as we stood rigidly at attention in the street outside the museum. Tears mixed with the rain as they passed. Even the spectators were crying.

Finally the CO, accompanied by our youngest member, Trooper Fraser, entered the museum with the Colours. The bagpiper began to play "Amazing Grace" and its haunting melody drifted across the soldiers and crowd. The most moving music I know, it was too much for me. Tears streamed down my face as well. No one in the crowd or on parade that day, other than the media wolves, were untouched by that moment.

When the CO emerged without the Colours, it was like the coffin had been lowered. It was over. A cameraman tried to get in front of him for a shot of the CO's tears but he fell back before the CO's glare. In a choking voice, he ordered us to march over to our parade square for a final parade.

Here the CO bid us farewell and uttered our epitaph in a choked voice:

"Obedient to Orders unto the End."

On the order to dismiss, the traditional cry of "Airborne!" echoed out one last time. It was over. The regiment had ceased to exist, except in our memories.

––––––––––

Once the media had their bone to chew on, the controversy died down. Quietly, the Van Doos from 1 Commando all went back to the Van Doos battalions. 2 Commando disappeared back out west, to their parent regiment, and the service tradesmen went on to new postings. Soon, the only vestige of the old Regiment was 3 Commando.

Now called "3 Commando Group," we carried on with the traditions established by our deceased parent. Our existence was a secret to most. Even the minister would deny our continued presence under the maroon beret if challenged. But he didn't care; the media weren't hounding him. As far as the politicians were concerned, the Airborne died with its disbandment.

During the hazing, the Somalia incidents, the acts of hooliganism in the late 1980s, 3 Commando had been uninvolved. During the disbandment process, the other Commandos teased us about when we were releasing our own video. Through it all, the name of 3 Commando had not been associated with any wrongdoings.

With this clean record in mind, we were selected to continue providing a parachute capability until a new unit or units could be formed. Eventually, it was decided to form three parachute companies. One in Valcartier, Quebec, staffed by Van Doos. Another in Edmonton manned by Patricias and finally, our group in Petawawa, manned by RCRs. Sounds a lot like the Airborne Regiment, doesn't it? Well, it isn't.

The parachute companies are now integral parts of regular battalions. The ethos, the relentless pursuit of operational perfection that epitomized the Regiment was gone. It was replaced by the routine, garrison-based, outlook typical of "Leg units."

For the first few months after disbandment, 3 Commando Group was as busy as ever. We were trying to rebuild the morale of a unit driven into the dirt by the military leadership. There was a popular picture posted on the bulletin board outside the company office. It depicted a group of soldiers running from a distance towards an officer pointing at the ground. Beside the officer, a soldier was digging in the soil. The caption read, "Over here lads, I think we've found some morale."

I didn't have too much time to sit and stew about the events of the last few months. I was off to the United States to play rugby for the Forces' national team in early May. When I got back from that it was over to Hereford in the U.K. to work with 22 Special Air Service. I slipped into their selection program to take part in a phase called "Combat Survival." There was another Canadian with me, Sergeant Ambrose Penton, and together we were trained in a wide variety of specialized skills. The course was tough physically and mentally. By the end of it, I was down by twenty-five pounds and thoroughly wiped out. Ambrose was so sick he couldn't keep food down for the next couple of weeks. Despite our debilitated condition, we were left with a distinct admiration for the SAS. They were the ultimate soldiers. From start to finish, it was the most professional organization I had encountered. I had also made some great friends among the guys on selection.

Despite these spells of good work we were doing, life just wasn't the same. Most of us felt like we were just going through the motions. In the modern military world there is no room for a company of airborne infantry. True special forces maybe, but not regular paratroopers. Like tanks, they are only useful when massed. A company was not worth the effort.

Recently, the Forces began building another special forces unit near Ottawa for use in a counter-terrorism role. Many of the troops began trying for selection in the new unit. It was pretty small at that time and the competition was stiff. I thought a lot about it. It was the only place left in the Forces that I wanted to be. The problem for me was that I would still be working for the same political masters who had disbanded the Airborne.

I had vowed at the time of the disbandment that I was going to leave the Forces. My choices were to stay in and go after the new unit or move into the civvy world and try to find some new challenges. At thirty-three, I still had a lot of good years, so I decided to leave. I needed challenges, but I also needed faith. My faith in the Forces' leadership was gone. I still loved the job and my co-workers, but I didn't believe in the program anymore. I decided to resign.

Meanwhile, 3 Commando Group was renamed the "Airborne Holding Unit." Soon that changed to the "RCR Parachute Company." Later, it became "The 2 Canadian Mechanized Brigade Group, Light Infantry Battalion."

Eventually, 3RCR was reformed in Petawawa as a regular battalion. The RCR parachute company would take over Mike company's old position. The Light Infantry Battalion became 3RCR officially in the fall of 1996. In the spring of that year, the old companies were reforming. I was transferred out of the Parachute company after I announced my intention to resign. My new job? Section Commander in November company, 3RCR.

That confirmed it. Eight years earlier, I had been a section 2IC in November company of 3RCR. Often, due to manpower shortages, I was a section commander by default. Now, after all I had been through, I had stepped back eight years in my career to the same job.

I went to see the CO and explained my position. He agreed that it was time for me to move on. He said he would miss me, but he understood. Some men can collect their pay and go home at the end of the day. I couldn't do that. I loved soldiering, but I loved doing it my way. I couldn't go back to garrison life. I have always believed in going forward. To be challenged. Either facing danger or some other career-related obstacle.

The CO suggested, as had many officers before him, that I take a commission. I had worked with a lot of officers. I respected them and am still loyal to a great many. Some I consider close friends. Canada has produced some fine leaders. The occasional bad apple doesn't change that opinion. But I would have to start at the bottom again, with a year of schooling, then junior positions in infantry battalions. I was too old to ever get a company. No, I wanted my life to be productive and never achieving a real command rank would mean I would retire a beat-up old captain living on memories. Combined with my lack of faith in the government, it was not for me.

There must be an unwritten trust between a government and its soldiers. In return for offering to give up their lives to achieve the government's goals at home and abroad, the government must undertake to protect their soldiers and not throw their lives away needlessly. Looking out for their welfare must be a fundamental of building a reliable national army. If the soldiers lose faith in their leadership at a political level, disaster will follow. Historical examples are common. The French in Algiers, the Italians in North africa, the Americans in Vietnam. Once the soldiers no longer believed that their government, from whom they take orders, cared about their lives more than they cared about political aspirations, the armies fell apart.

In disbanding the Airborne Regiment for political necessity, Canada's politicians broke faith with their soldiers. It cannot be argued as a military decision, because all the senior military officers in the Army at that time have stated their opposition to the disbandment. In a complete disregard for the counsel of their senior officers, the government chose to destroy their best fighting unit.

All the problems alluded to in the videos and in the Somalia court-martial testimony had already been taken care of. The rogue element of 2 Commando was broken up, the few racists kicked out, hazing banned, and the unit ruled by the iron fist of a new commanding officer. Disbanding them was irrelevant. The crisis was years behind the Regiment.

No, the politicians broke faith with the soldiers.

So, in October of 1996, I became a civilian.

I have no regrets about my time in the Forces. I had the opportunity to see things and be part of some of the great events of our time. I met famous people and traveled to exotic lands.

Best of all, I got a chance to meet and work with the best people this country will ever produce. The bonds of friendship, the camaraderie, the absolute trust that went with being a member of the Forces was without equal. There is no other place in the world that you will find a closer bunch of individuals than in a country's army. I salute them all and thank God that I had the chance to be a soldier.

AIRBORNE!